Teach

Yourself

C++

Second Edition

Herbert Schildt

Osborne **McGraw-Hill**

Berkeley New York St. Louis San Francisco Auckland Bogotá Hamburg London Madrid Mexico City
Milan Montreal New Delhi Panama City Paris São Paulo Singapore Sydney Tokyo Toronto

PUBLISHER
Lawrence Levitsky

ACQUISITIONS EDITOR
Jeff Pepper

PROJECT EDITOR
Nancy McLaughlin

PROOFREADER
Audrey Baer Johnson

INDEXER
Sheryl Schildt

COMPUTER DESIGNER
Jani Beckwith

SERIES DESIGN
Seventeenth Street Studios

COVER DESIGN
Compass Marketing

Osborne **McGraw-Hill**
2600 Tenth Street
Berkeley, California 94710
U.S.A.

For information on software, translations, or book distributors outside of the
U.S.A., please write to Osborne **McGraw-Hill** at the above address.

Teach Yourself C++, Second Edition

0 DOC 9987

ISBN 0-07-882025-1

Contents

About the Author

Herbert Schildt is the world's leading C/C++ author. His programming books have sold over one million copies and have been translated into all major foreign languages. He is the author of the earlier best-selling edition of **Teach Yourself C++** as well as two editions of the acclaimed **Teach Yourself C**. He has also written **The Annotated ANSI C Standard; C: The Complete Reference, Second Edition; C++: The Complete Reference;** and numerous other C/C++ books. Schildt is the president of Universal Computing laboratories, a software consulting firm in Mahomet, Illinois. He holds a master's degree in computer science from the University of Illinois.

Introduction

C++ is the C programmer's answer to Object-Oriented Programming (OOP). Built upon the solid foundation of C, C++ adds support for OOP (and many other new features) without sacrificing any of C's power, elegance, or flexibility. In fact, many programmers view C++ as a "better C," independent of its support for object-oriented programming. Whether you will be writing object-oriented programs or you simply want to make the writing of structured programs easier, C++ will simplify your programming efforts.

Since C++ is based on C, virtually everything you know about C is applicable to C++. This, beyond any other reason, is why C++ has become the dominant object-oriented programming language of the 90's. There is no need for the accomplished C programmer to learn an entirely new language. Instead, you only need to learn the few extensions added by C++. You will be surprised at how rapidly you progress.

C++ was invented in 1980 by Bjarne Stroustrup at Bell Laboratories in Murray Hill, New Jersey. Initially it was called "C with classes." The name was changed to C++ in 1983. Since 1980, C++ has undergone two major revisions, one in 1985 and another in 1990. Currently, work is in progress to create an ANSI (American National Standards Institute) standard for C++. The first draft of the proposed standard was created on January 25, 1994. The ANSI C++ committee (of which I am a member) has kept virtually all of the features defined by Stroustrup and has added several new ones as well.

The standardization process is typically a slow one, and it will probably be years before the C++ standard is finally adopted. Therefore, keep in mind that C++ is still a "work in progress" and that some features are still being developed and added. However, the material presented in this book is stable. It is applicable to all contemporary C++ compilers and is in compliance with the currently proposed ANSI standard for C++. Therefore, using this book, you can learn with confidence.

What Is New in the Second Edition

This book is the second edition of *Teach Yourself C++*. It includes all of the material contained in the first edition. All of the previous material has been brought up-to-date, rechecked, and retested. This book also includes a new section (in Chapter 5) devoted to copy constructors, and a new chapter (Chapter 11) that discusses templates and exception handling. Templates and exceptions are new features to C++; they did not exist when the first edition was written. However, they are now supported by several compilers, and are part of the proposed ANSI C++ standard.

If You're Using Windows

If your computer uses Windows and your goal is to write Windows-based programs, then you have chosen to learn the right language. C++ is completely at home with Windows programming. However, none of the programs in this book are Windows programs. Instead, they are console-based programs. The reason for this is easy to understand: Windows programs are, by their nature, large and complex. The overhead required to create even a minimal Windows skeletal program is 50 to 70 lines of code. To write Windows programs that demonstrate the features of C++ would require hundreds of lines of code each. Put simply, Windows is not an appropriate environment in which to learn programming. However, you can still use a Windows-based compiler to compile the programs in this book. It is just that you will need to use the command-prompt (console) interface.

Once you have mastered C++, you will be able to apply your knowledge to Windows programming. In fact, Windows programming using C++ allows the use of class libraries that can greatly simplify the development of a Windows program (in comparison to its corresponding C version). Also, many of the Windows programs being created today are coded in C++, rather than in C.

How This Book Is Organized

This book is unique because it teaches you the C++ language by applying mastery learning. It presents one idea at a time, followed by numerous examples and exercises to help you master each topic. This approach ensures that you fully understand each topic before moving on.

The material is presented sequentially. Therefore, be sure to work carefully through the chapters. Each one assumes that you know the material presented in all preceding chapters. At the start of every chapter (except Chapter 1) there is a *Review Skills Check* that tests your knowledge of the preceding chapter. At the end of each chapter you will find a *Mastery Skills Check* that checks your knowledge of the material present in the chapter. Finally, each chapter concludes with a

Cumulative Skills Check which tests how well you are integrating new material with that presented in earlier chapters. The answers to the book's many exercises are found in Appendix B.

This book assumes that you are already an accomplished C programmer. Put simply, you can't learn to program in C++ until you can program in C. If you can't program in C, take some time to learn it before attempting to use this book.

Diskette Offer

There are many useful and interesting functions, classes, and programs contained in this book. If you're like me, you probably would like to use them, but hate typing code into the computer. When I key in routines from a book it always seems that I type something wrong and spend hours trying to get the program to work. For this reason, I am offering the source code on diskette for all the functions and programs contained in this book for $24.95. Just fill in the order blank on the following page and mail it, along with your payment, to the address shown. Or, if you're in a hurry, just call (217) 586-4021 (the number of my consulting office) and place your order by telephone. (Visa and MasterCard accepted.) You can also order by FAX at (217) 586-4997.

Please send me _____ copies, at $24.95 each, of the programs in *Teach Yourself C++, Second Edition* on an IBM compatible diskette.

Foreign orders only: Checks must be drawn on a U.S. bank. Please add $5.00 shipping and handling.

_____

Name

_____

Address

_____   _____   _____

City   State   Zip

_____

Telephone

Diskette size (check one): 5.25"_____   3.5"_____

Method of payment: Check_____ Visa_____ MC_____

Credit card number: _____

Expiration date: _____

Signature: _____

Send to:

Herbert Schildt
398 County Rd 2500 N
Mahomet, IL 61853

Phone: (217) 586-4021
FAX: (217) 586-4997

1

An Overview of C++

C++ is an enhanced version of the C language. C++ includes everything that is part of C and adds support for object-oriented programming (OOP for short). In addition, C++ also contains many improvements and features that simply make it a "better C," independent of object-oriented programming. With very few, very minor exceptions, C++ is a superset of C. While everything that you know about the C language is fully applicable to C++, understanding its enhanced features will still require a significant investment of time and effort on your part. However, the rewards of programming in C++ will more than justify the effort you put forth.

The purpose of this chapter is to introduce you to several of the most important features of C++. As you know, the elements of a computer language do not exist in a void, separate from one another. Instead, they work together to form the complete language. This interrelatedness is especially pronounced in C++. In fact, it is difficult to discuss one aspect of C++ in isolation because the features of C++ are highly integrated. To help overcome this problem, this chapter provides a brief overview of several C++ features. This overview will enable you to understand the examples discussed later in this book. Keep in mind that most topics discussed here will be more thoroughly explored in later chapters.

In addition to introducing several important C++ features, this chapter also discusses some differences between C and C++ programming styles. There are several features of C++ that allow greater flexibility in the way that you write programs. While some of these features have little or nothing to do with object-oriented programming, they are found in most C++ programs, so it is appropriate to discuss them early in this book.

Since C++ was invented to support object-oriented programming, this chapter begins with a description of OOP. As you will see, many features of C++ are related to OOP in one way or another. In fact, the theory of OOP permeates several aspects of C++. However, it is important to understand that C++ can be used to write programs that are and are _not_ object oriented. How you use C++ is completely up to you.

 NOTE _This book assumes that you know how to compile and execute a program using your C++ compiler. If you don't, you will need to refer to your compiler's user manual. (Because of the differences between compilers, it is impossible to give compilation instructions for each in this book.) Because programming is best learned by doing, you are strongly urged to enter, compile, and run the examples in the book in the order in which they are presented._

Before you begin, a few general comments about the nature and form of C++ are in order. First, for the most part, C++ programs physically look like C programs. Like C, a C++ program begins execution at **main( )**. To include command-line arguments, C++ uses the same **argc, argv** convention that C uses. C++ has the same standard library functions as C. Although C++ defines a few header files that are specific to it, it also contains all the header files found with a C compiler. C++ uses the same control structures as C. C++ has the same built-in data types as C.

Remember, this book assumes that you already know the C programming language. Simply put, you must be able to program in C before you can learn to program in C++. If you don't know C, a good starting place is my book *Teach Yourself C, 2nd Edition* (Berkeley: Osborne/McGraw-Hill, 1994). It applies the same systematic approach used in this book and thoroughly covers the entire C language.

1.1   *WHAT IS OBJECT-ORIENTED PROGRAMMING?*

Object-oriented programming is a new way to approach the task of programming. Since its early beginnings, programming has been governed by various methodologies. At each critical point in the evolution of programming, a new approach was created to help the programmer handle increasingly complex programs. The first progams were created by a process of toggling switches on the front panel of the computer. Obviously, this approach is suitable for only the smallest programs. Next, assembly language was invented, which allowed longer programs to be written. The next advance happened in the 1950s when the first high-level language (FORTRAN) was invented.

By using a high-level language, a programmer was able to write programs that were several thousands of lines long. However, the method of programming used early on was an ad hoc, anything-goes approach. While this is fine for relatively short programs, it yields unreadable (and unmanageable) "spaghetti code" when applied to larger programs. The elimination of spaghetti code became feasible with the invention of *structured programming languages* in the 1960s. These languages include Algol and Pascal. In loose terms, C is a structured language, and most likely the type of programming you have been doing would be called structured programming. Structured programming relies on well-defined control structures, code blocks, the absence (or at least minimal use) of the GOTO, and stand-alone subroutines that support recursion and local variables. The essence of structured programming is the reduction of a program into its constituent elements. Using structured programming, the average programmer can create and maintain programs that are up to 50,000 lines long.

Although structured programming has yielded excellent results when applied to moderately complex programs, even it fails at some point, after a program reaches a certain size. To allow more complex programs to be written, a new approach to the job of programming was needed. Towards this end, object-oriented programming was invented. OOP takes the best of the ideas embodied in structured programming and combines them with powerful new concepts that allow you to organize your programs more effectively. Object-oriented programming encourages you to decompose a problem into related subgroups. Each subgroup becomes a self-contained object that contains its own instructions and data that relate to that object. In this way, complexity is reduced and the programmer can manage larger programs.

All OOP languages, including C++, share three common defining traits: encapsulation, polymorphism, and inheritance. Let's look at these concepts now.

ENCAPSULATION

Encapsulation is the mechanism that binds together code and the data it manipulates, and keeps both safe from outside interference and misuse. In an object-oriented language, code and data may be bound together in such a way that a self-contained "black box" is created. Within the box are all necessary data and code. When code and data are linked together in this fashion, an *object* is created. In other words, an object is the device that supports encapsulation.

Within an object, code, data, or both may be *private* to that object or *public*. Private code or data is known to and accessible only by another part of the object. That is, private code or data may not be accessed by a piece of the program that exists outside the object. When code or data is public, other parts of your program may access it even though it is defined within an object. Typically, the public parts of an object are used to provide a controlled interface to the private parts of the object.

For all intents and purposes, an object is a variable of a user-defined type. It may seen strange that an object that links both code and data can be thought of as a variable. However, in object-oriented programming, this is precisely the case. Each time you define a new object, you are creating a new data type. Each specific instance of this data type is a compound variable.

POLYMORPHISM

Polymorphism (from the Greek, meaning "many forms") is the quality that allows one name to be used for two or more related but technically different purposes. The purpose of polymorphism as it is applied to OOP is to allow one name to be used to specify a general class of actions. Within a general class of actions, the specific action to be applied is determined by the type of data. For example, in C, which does not significantly support polymorphism, the absolute value action requires three distinct functions: **abs( )**, **labs( )**, and **fabs( )**. These functions compute and return the absolute value of an integer, a long integer, and a floating-point value, respectively. However, in C++, which supports polymorphism, each function can be called **abs( )**. (One way this can be accomplished is shown later in this chapter.) The type of data used to call the function determines which specific version of the function is actually used. As you will see, in C++, it is possible to use one function name for many different purposes. This is called *function overloading*.

More generally, the concept of polymorphism is the idea of "one interface, multiple methods." This means that it is possible to design a generic interface to a group of related activities. However, the specific action executed depends upon the data. The advantage of polymorphism is that it helps to reduce complexity by allowing the same interface to be used to specify a *general class of action*. It is the compiler's job to select the *specific action* as it applies to each situation. You, the programmer, don't need to do this selection manually. You need only remember and utilize the general interface. As the example in the preceding paragraph illustrates, having three names for the absolute value function instead of just one makes the general activity of obtaining the absolute value of a number more complex than it actually is.

Polymorphism can be applied to both functions and operators. Virtually all programming languages contain a limited application of polymorphism as it relates to the arithmetic operators. For example, in C, the + sign is used to add integers, long integers, characters, and floating-point values. In these cases, the compiler automatically knows which type of arithmetic to apply. In C++, you can extend this concept to other types of data that you define. This type of polymorphism is called *operator overloading*.

The key point to remember about polymorphism is that it allows you to handle greater complexity by allowing the creation of standard interfaces to related activities.

INHERITANCE

Inheritance is the process by which one object can acquire the properties of another. More specifically, an object can inherit a general set of properties to which it can add those features that are specific only to itself. Inheritance is important because it allows an object to support the concept of *hierarchical classification.* Most information is made manageable by hierarchical classification. For example, think about the description of a house. A house is part of the general class called **building**. In turn, **building** is part of the more general class **structure**, which is part of the even more general class of objects that we call **man-made**. In each case, the child class inherits all those qualities associated with the parent and adds to them its own defining characteristics. Without the use of ordered classifications, each object would have to define all characteristics that relate to it explicitly. However, by using inheritance, it is possible to describe an object by stating what general class (or classes) it belongs to along with those specific traits that make it unique. As you will see, inheritance plays a very important role in OOP.

EXAMPLES

1. Encapsulation is not entirely new to OOP. To a degree, encapsulation can be achieved when using the C language. For example, when you use a library function, you are, in effect, using a black-box routine, the internals of which you cannot alter or affect (except, perhaps, through malicious actions).

   Consider the **fopen( )** function. When it is used to open a file, several internal variables are created and initialized. As far as your program is concerned, these variables are hidden and not accessible. However, C++ provides a much more secure approach to encapsulation.

2. In the real world, examples of polymorphism are quite common. For example, consider the steering wheel on your car. It works the same whether your car uses power steering, rack-and-pinion steering, or standard, manual steering. The point is that the interface (the steering wheel) is the same no matter what type of actual steering mechanism (method) is used.

3. As stated, inheritance of properties and the more general concept of classification are fundamental to the way knowledge is organized. For example, celery is a member of the **vegetable** class, which is part of the **plant** class. In turn, plants are living organisms, and so forth. Without hierarchical classification, systems of knowledge would not be possible.

EXERCISE

---

1. Think about the way that classification and polymorphism play an important role in our day-to-day lives.

1.2   *C++ CONSOLE I/O*

Since C++ is a superset of C, all elements of the C language are also contained in the C++ language. This implies that all C programs are also C++ programs by default. (Actually, there are some very minor exceptions to this rule, which are discussed later in this book.) Therefore, it is possible to write C++ programs that look just like C programs. While there is nothing wrong with this per se, it does mean that you will not be taking full advantage of C++.

Most C++ programmers write programs that use a style and features that are unique to C++. One reason for this is that it helps you to begin thinking in terms of C++ instead of C. Also, by using C++ features, you immediately let anyone reading your program know that it is a C++, not a C, program.

Perhaps the most common C++-specific feature used by C++ programmers is its approach to console I/O. While you may still use functions like **printf( )** and **scanf( )**, C++ provides a new, and better, way to perform these types of I/O operations. In C++, I/O is performed using *I/O operators* instead of I/O functions. The output operator is << and the input operator is >>. As you know, in C, these are the left and right shift operators, respectively. In C++, they still retain their original meanings (left and right shift) but they also take on the expanded role of performing input and output. Consider this C++ statement:

```
cout << "This string is output to the screen.\n";
```

This statement causes the string to be displayed on the computer's screen. **cout** is a predefined stream that is automatically linked to the console when a C++ program begins execution. It is similar to C's **stdout**. As in C, C++ console I/O may be redirected, but for the rest of this discussion, it is assumed that the console is being used.

By using the << output operator, it is possible to output any of C++'s basic types. For example, this statement outputs the value 100.99:

```
cout << 100.99;
```

In general, to output to the console, use this general form of the << operator:

> cout << *expression*;

Here, *expression* may be any valid C++ expression—including another output expression.

To input a value from the keyboard, use the >> input operator. For example, this fragment inputs an integer value into **num**:

```
int num;
cin >> num;
```

Notice that **num** is *not* preceded by an **&**. As you know, when you input values by using C's **scanf( )** function, variables must have their addresses passed to the function so they can receive the values entered by the user. This is not the case when using C++'s input operator. (The reason for this will become clear as you learn more about C++.)

In general, to input values from the keyboard, use this form of >>:

> cin >> *variable*;

 NOTE *The expanded roles of* << *and* >> *are examples of operator overloading.*

In order to use the C++ I/O operators, you must include the header file **iostream.h** in your program. This is one of C++'s standard header files and is supplied by your C++ compiler.

EXAMPLES

1. This program outputs a string, two integer values, and a double floating-point value:

```
#include <iostream.h>

main()
{
   int i, j;
   double d;

   i = 10;
   j = 20;
   d = 99.101;
```

```
cout << "Here are some values: ";
cout << i;
cout << ' ';
cout << j;
cout << ' ';
cout << d;

return 0;
}
```

NOTE *As this example shows, the value 0 is returned from* **main()**. *While not technically necessary, it is a good idea for a program to return a known value to the calling process (usually the operating system) when it terminates. (All programs in this book follow this convention.) Without the* **return** *statement, an undefined value would be returned.*

2. It is possible to output more than one value in a single I/O expression. For example, this version of the program described in Example 1 shows a more efficient way to code the I/O statements:

```
#include <iostream.h>

main()
{
  int i, j;
  double d;

  i = 10;
  j = 20;
  d = 99.101;

  cout << "Here are some values: ";
  cout << i << ' '<< j << ' ' << d;

  return 0;
}
```

Here, the line

```
cout << i << ' '<< j << ' ' << d;
```

outputs several items in one expression. In general, you can use a single statement to output as many items as you like. If this seems confusing, simply remember that the << output operator behaves like any other C++ operator, and can be part of an arbitrarily long expression.

Notice that you must explicitly include spaces between items when needed. If the spaces are left out, the data will run together when displayed on the screen.

3. This program prompts the user for an integer value:

```
#include <iostream.h>

main()
{
  int i;

  cout << "Enter a value: ";
  cin >> i;
  cout << "Here's your number: " << i << "\n";

  return 0;
}
```

4. The next program prompts the user for an integer value, a floating-point value, and a string. It then uses one input statement to read all three.

```
#include <iostream.h>

main()
{
  int i;
  float f;
  char s[80];

  cout << "Enter an integer, float, and string: ";
  cin >> i >> f >> s;
  cout << "Here's your data: ";
  cout << i << ' ' << f << ' ' << s;

  return 0;
}
```

As this example illustrates, you can input as many items as you like in one input statement. As in C, individual data items must be separated by whitespace (spaces, tabs, and newlines).

When a string is read, input will stop when the first whitespace character is read. For example, if you enter this input to the preceding program:

```
10 100.12 This is a test
```

the program will display this:

```
10 100.12 This
```

The string is incomplete because the reading of the string stopped with the space after **This.** The remainder of the string is left in the input buffer, awaiting a subsequent input operation. (This is similar to inputting a string by using **scanf( )** with the **%s** format.)

5. By default, when you use **>>**, all input is line buffered. This means that no information is passed to your C++ program until you press (Enter). Most C compilers also use line-buffered input when working with scanf( ), so line-buffered input should not be new to you.) To see the effect of line-buffered input, try this program:

```cpp
#include <iostream.h>

main()
{
  char ch;

  cout << "Enter keys, x to stop.\n";

  do {
    cout << ": ";
    cin >> ch;
  } while (ch != 'x');

  return 0;
}
```

As you try this program, you will have to press (Enter) after each key you type in order for the corresponding character to be sent to the program.

EXERCISES

1. Write a program that inputs the number of hours that an employee works and the employee's wage. Then display the employee's gross pay. (Be sure to prompt for input.)

2. Write a program that converts feet to inches. Prompt the user for feet and display the equivalent number of inches. Repeat this process until the user enters 0 for the number of feet.

3. Here is a C program. Rewrite it so it uses C++-style I/O statements.

```
/* Convert this C program into C++ style.
   This program computes the lowest common
   denominator.
*/
#include <stdio.h>
main()
{
  int a, b, d, min;

  printf("Enter two numbers: ");
  scanf("%d%d", &a, &b);
  min = a > b ? b : a;
  for(d = 2; d<min; d++)
    if(((a%d)==0) && ((b%d)==0)) break;
  if(d==min) {
    printf("No common denominators\n");
    return 0;
  }
  printf("The lowest common denominator is %d\n", d);
  return 0;
}
```

1.3   *C*++ COMMENTS

In C++, you may include comments in your program two different ways. First, you may use the standard, C-like comment mechanism. That is, begin a comment with /* and end it with */. As with C, this type of comment may not be nested in C++.

The second way that you can add a comment to your C++ program is to use the *single-line comment*. A single-line comment begins with a // and stops at the end of the line. Other than the physical end of the line (that is, a carriage-return/linefeed combination), a single-line comment uses no comment terminator symbol.

Typically, C++ programmers use C-like comments for multiline comments and reserve C++-style single-line comments for short commentaries.

EXAMPLES

1. Here is a program that contains both C and C++-style comments:

```
/*
    This is a C-like comment.
    This program determines whether an integer
    is odd or even.
*/

#include <iostream.h>

main()
{
  int num;   // this is a C++, single-line comment

  // read the number
  cout << "Enter number to be tested: ";
  cin >> num;

  // see if even or odd
  if((num%2)==0) cout << "Number is even\n";
  else cout << "Number is odd\n";

  return 0;
}
```

2. While C-like comments cannot be nested, it is possible to nest a single-line C++ comment within a C-like multiline comment. For example, this is perfectly valid:

```
/* This is a multiline comment
   inside of which // is nested a single-line comment.
   Here is the end of the multiline comment.
*/
```

The fact that single-line comments can be nested within multiline comments makes it easier for you to "comment out" several lines of code for debugging purposes.

EXERCISES

1. As an experiment, determine if this comment (which nests a C-like comment within a C++-style, single-line comment) is valid:

```
// This is a strange /* way to do a comment */
```

2. On your own, add comments to the answers to the exercises in Section 1.1.

CLASSES: A FIRST LOOK

Perhaps the single most important feature of C++ is the class. The class is the mechanism that is used to create objects. As such, the class is at the heart of many C++ features. Although the subject of classes is covered in great detail throughout this book, they are so fundamental to C++ programming that a brief overview is necessary here.

The syntax of a class declaration is similar to that of a structure. Its general form is shown here:

```
class class-name {
    private functions and variables of the class
public:
    public functions and variables of the class
} object-list;
```

In a class declaration, the *object-list* is optional. As with a structure, you can declare class objects later, as needed. While the *class-name* is also technically optional, from a practical point of view, it is virtually always needed. The reason for this is that the *class-name* becomes a new type name that is used to declare objects of the class.

Functions and variables declared inside a class declaration are said to be *members* of that class. By default, all functions and variables declared inside a class are private to that class. This means that they are accessible only by other members of that class. To declare public class members, the **public** keyword is used, followed by a colon. All functions and variables declared after the **public** specifier are accessible both by other members of the class and by any other part of the program that contains the class.

Here is a simple class declaration:

```
class myclass {
  // private to myclass
  int a;
public:
  void set_a(int num);
  int get_a();
};
```

This class has one private variable, called **a**, and two public functions, **set_a( )** and **get_a( )**. Notice that functions are declared within a class using their prototype forms. Functions that are declared to be part of a class are called *member functions*.

Since **a** is private, it is not accessible by any code outside **myclass**. However, since **set_a( )** and **get_a( )** are members of **myclass**, they can access **a**. Further, **get_a( )** and **set_a( )** are declared as public members of **myclass**, and can be called by any other part of the program that contains **myclass**.

Although the functions **get_a( )** and **set_a( )** are declared by **myclass**, they are not yet defined. To define a member function, you must link the type name of the class of which the member function is part with the name of the function. You do this by preceding the function name with the class name followed by two colons. The two colons are called the *scope resolution operator*. For example, here is the way the member functions **set_a( )** and **get_a( )** are defined:

```
void myclass::set_a(int num)
{
  a = num;
}
int myclass::get_a()
{
  return a;
}
```

Notice that both **set_a( )** and **get_a( )** have access to **a**, which is private to **myclass**. Because **set_a( )** and **get_a( )** are members of **myclass**, they can directly access its private data.

When you define a member function, use this general form:

type class-name::func-name(parameter-list)
{
    ... // body of function
}

The declaration of **myclass** did not define any objects of type **myclass**—it only defines the type of object that will be created when one is actually declared. To create an object, use the class name as a type specifier. For example, this line declares two objects of type **myclass**:

```
myclass ob1, ob2; // these are objects of type myclass
```

REMEMBER *A class declaration is a logical abstraction that defines a new type that determines what an object of that type will look like. An object declaration creates a physical entity of that type. (That is, an object occupies memory space, but a type definition does not.)*

Once an object of a class has been created, your program may reference its public members by using the dot (period) operator in much the same way that structure members are accessed. Assuming the preceding object declaration, this statement calls **set_a( )** for objects **ob1** and **ob2**:

```
ob1.set_a(10); // sets ob1's version of a to 10
ob2.set_a(99); // sets ob2's version of a to 99
```

As the comments indicate, these statements set **ob1**'s copy of **a** to 10 and **ob2**'s copy to 99. Each object contains its own copy of all data declared in the class. This means that **ob1**'s **a** is distinct and different from the **a** linked to **ob2**.

 REMEMBER *Each object of a class has its own copy of every variable declared within the class.*

EXAMPLES

1. As a simple first example, this program uses **myclass**, described in the text, to set the value of **a** for **ob1** and **ob2** and to display **a**'s value for each object:

```cpp
#include <iostream.h>

class myclass {
   // private to myclass
   int a;
public:
   void set_a(int num);
   int get_a();
};

void myclass::set_a(int num)
{
   a = num;
}

int myclass::get_a()
{
   return a;
}

main()
```

```
{
  myclass ob1, ob2;

  ob1.set_a(10);
  ob2.set_a(99);

  cout << ob1.get_a() << "\n";
  cout << ob2.get_a() << "\n";
  return 0;
}
```

As you should expect, this program displays the values 10 and 99 on the screen.

2. In **myclass** from the preceding example, **a** is private. This means that only member functions of **myclass** can access it directly. (This is one reason why the public function **get_a( )** is required.) If you try to access a private member of a class from some part of your program that is not a member of that class, a compile-time error will result. For example, assuming that **myclass** is defined as shown in the preceding example, the following **main( )** function will cause an error:

```
// This fragment contains an error.
#include <iostream.h>

main()
{
  myclass ob1, ob2;

  ob1.a = 10; // ERROR! cannot access private member
  ob2.a = 99; // by non-member functions.

  cout << ob1.get_a() << "\n";
  cout << ob2.get_a() << "\n";

  return 0;
}
```

3. Just as there can be public member functions, there can be public member variables as well. For example, if **a** were declared in the public section of **myclass**, then **a** could be referenced by any part of the program, as shown here:

```
#include <iostream.h>

class myclass {
public:
  // now a is public
```

```
      int a;
      // and there is no need for set_a() or get_a()
};
main()
{
  myclass ob1, ob2;

  // here, a is accessed directly
  ob1.a = 10;
  ob2.a = 99;

  cout << ob1.a << "\n";
  cout << ob2.a << "\n";

  return 0;
}
```

In this example, since **a** is declared as a public member of **myclass**, it is directly accessible from **main( )**. Notice how the dot operator is used to access **a**. In general, whether you are calling a member function or accessing a member variable, the object's name followed by the dot operator followed by the member's name is required to fully specify which object's member you are referring to.

4. To get a taste of the power of objects, let's look at a more practical example. This program creates a class called **stack** that implements a stack that can be used to store characters:

```
#include <iostream.h>

#define SIZE 10

// Declare a stack class for characters
class stack {
  char stck[SIZE]; // holds the stack
  int tos; // index of top-of-stack

public:
  void init(); // initialize stack
  void push(char ch); // push character on stack
  char pop(); // pop character from stack
};

// Initialize the stack
void stack::init()
{
  tos = 0;
}
```

```
// Push a character.
void stack::push(char ch)
{
  if(tos==SIZE) {
    cout << "Stack is full";
    return;
  }
  stck[tos] = ch;
  tos++;
}

// Pop a character.
char stack::pop()
{
  if(tos==0) {
    cout << "Stack is empty";
    return 0; // return null on empty stack
  }
  tos--;
  return stck[tos];
}
main()
{
  stack s1, s2;  // create two stacks
  int i;
  // initialize the stacks
  s1.init();
  s2.init();

  s1.push('a');
  s2.push('x');
  s1.push('b');
  s2.push('y');
  s1.push('c');
  s2.push('z');

  for(i=0; i<3; i++) cout << "Pop s1: " << s1.pop() << "\n";
  for(i=0; i<3; i++) cout << "Pop s2: " << s2.pop() << "\n";

  return 0;
}
```

This program displays the following output:

```
Pop s1: c
Pop s1: b
Pop s1: a
Pop s2: z
Pop s2: y
Pop s2: x
```

Let's take a close look at this program now. The class **stack** contains two private variables: **stck** and **tos**. The array **stck** actually holds the characters pushed onto the stack, and **tos** contains the index to the top of the stack. The public stack functions are **init( )**, **push( )**, and **pop( )**, which initialize the stack, push a value, and pop a value, respectively.

Inside **main( )**, two stacks, **s1** and **s2**, are created, and three characters are pushed onto each stack. It is important to understand that each stack object is separate from the other. That is, the characters pushed onto **s1** *in no way* affect the characters pushed onto **s2**. Each object contains its own copy of **stck** and **tos**. This concept is fundamental to understanding objects. Although all objects of a class share their member functions, each object creates and maintains *its own data.*

EXERCISES

1. If you have not done so, enter and run the programs shown in the examples for this section.

2. Create a class called **card** that maintains a library card catalog entry. Have the class store a book's title, author, and number of copies on hand. Store the title and author as strings and the number on hand as an integer. Use a public member function called **store( )** to store a book's information and a public member function called **show( )** to display the information. Include a short **main( )** to demonstrate the class.

3. Create a queue class that maintains a circular queue of integers. Make the queue size 100 integers long. Include a short **main( )** function that demonstrates its operation.

1.5 SOME DIFFERENCES BETWEEN C AND C++

Although C++ is a superset of C, there are some slight differences between the two that will almost certainly affect you when you begin to write your own C++ programs. Although each of these differences is minor, they tend to permeate C++

programs. Therefore, before proceeding, take some time to review these differences, which are discussed here.

First, in C, when a function takes no parameters, its prototype has the word **void** inside its function parameter list. For example, in C, if a function called **f1( )** takes no parameters (and returns a **char**), then its prototype will look like this:

```
char f1(void);
```

However, in C++, the **void** is optional. Therefore, in C++, the prototype for **f1( )** is usually written like this:

```
char f1();
```

C++ differs from C in the way that an empty parameter list is specified. If the preceding prototype had occurred in a C program, it would simply mean that *nothing* is said about the parameters to the function. In C++, it means that the function has *no* parameters. This is the reason that several of the preceding examples did not explicitly use **void** to declare an empty parameters list. (The use of **void** to declare an empty parameter list is not illegal; it is just redundant. Since most C++ programmers pursue efficiency with a nearly religious zeal, you will almost never see **void** used in this way.) Remember, in C++, these two declarations are equivalent:

```
int f1();
int f1(void);
```

Another subtle difference between C and C++ is that in a C++ program, all functions must be prototyped. Remember, in C, prototypes are recommended but technically optional. In C++, they are required. As the examples from the previous section show, a member function's prototype contained in a class also serves as its general prototype, and no other separate prototype is required.

A third difference between C and C++ is that in C++, if a function is declared as returning a value, then it must return a value. That is, if a function has a return type other than **void** then any **return** statement within that function must contain a value. In C, a non-**void** function is not required to actually return a value. If it doesn't, a garbage value is "returned."

One other difference between C and C++ that you will commonly encounter in C++ programs has to do with where local variables may be declared. In C, local variables may be declared only at the start of a block, prior to any "action" statements. In C++, local variables can be declared anywhere. One advantage of this approach is that local variables can be declared close to where they are first used, thus helping to prevent unwanted side effects.

---

1. In a C program, it is common practice to declare **main( )** as shown here if it takes no command-line arguments:

   ```
   main(void)
   ```

   However, in C++, the use of **void** is redundant and unnecessary.

2. This short C++ program will not compile because the function **sum( )** is not prototyped:

   ```
   // This program will not compile.
   #include <iostream.h>

   main()
   {
     int a, b, c;
     cout << "Enter two numbers: ";
     cin >> a >> b;
     c = sum(a, b);
     cout << "Sum is: " << c;

     return 0;
   }

   // This function needs a prototype.
   sum(int a, int b)
   {
     return a+b;
   }
   ```

3. Here is a short program that illustrates how local variables can be declared anywhere within a block:

   ```
   #include <iostream.h>

   main()
   {
     int i; // local vars declared at start of block

     cout << "Enter number: ";
     cin >> i;

     // compute factorial
     int j, fact=1; // vars declared after action statements

     for(j=i; j>=1; j--) fact = fact * j;
   ```

```
  cout << "Factorial is " << fact;

  return 0;
}
```

The declaration of **j** and **fact** near the point of first use is of little value in this short example; however, in large functions, the ability to declare variables close to the point of their first use can help clarify your code and prevent unintentional side effects. This feature of C++ is commonly used in C++ programs when large functions are involved.

EXERCISES

1. The following program will not compile as a C++ program. Why not?

```
#include <iostream.h>

main()
{
  char s[80];

  cout << "Enter a string: ";
  cin >> s;

  cout << "Length is: ";
  cout << strlen(s);

  return 0;
}
```

2. On your own, try declaring local variables at various points in a C++ program. Try the same in a C program, paying attention to which declarations generate errors.

1.6 ***INTRODUCING FUNCTION***
OVERLOADING

After classes, perhaps the next most important and pervasive C++ feature is *function overloading*. Not only does function overloading provide the mechanism by which C++ achieves one type of polymorphism, it also forms the basis by which the C++ programming environment can be dynamically extended. Because of the importance of overloading, a brief introduction is given here.

In C++, two or more functions can share the same name as long as either the type of their arguments differs or the number of their arguments differs—or both. When two or more functions share the same name, they are said to be *overloaded*. Overloaded functions can help reduce the complexity of a program by allowing related operations to be referred to by the same name.

It is very easy to overload a function: simply declare and define all required versions. The compiler will automatically select the correct version to call based upon the number and/or type of the arguments used to call the function.

 NOTE *It is also possible in C++ to overload operators. However, before you can fully understand operator overloading, you will need to know more about C++.*

EXAMPLES

1. One of the main uses for function overloading is to achieve compile-time polymorphism, which embodies the philosophy of one interface, many methods. As you know, in C programming, it is common to have a number of related functions that differ only by the type of data on which they operate. The classic example of this situation is found in the C standard library. As mentioned earlier in this chapter, the library contains the functions **abs( )**, **labs( )**, and **fabs( )**, which return the absolute value of an integer, a long integer, and a floating-point value, respectively.

   However, because three different names are needed due to the three different data types, the situation is more complicated than it needs to be. In all three cases, the absolute value is being returned; only the data types are different. In C++, you can correct this situation by overloading one name for the three types of data, as this example illustrates:

   ```
   #include <iostream.h>

   // Overload abs() three ways
   int abs(int n);
   long abs(long n);
   double abs(double n);
   ```

```
main()
{
  cout << "Absolute value of -10: " << abs(-10) << "\n";
  cout << "Absolute value of -10L: " << abs(-10L) << "\n";
  cout << "Absolute value of -10.01: " << abs(-10.01) << "\n";

  return 0;
}

// abs() for ints
int abs(int n)
{
  cout << "In integer abs()\n";
  return n<0 ? -n : n;
}

// abs() for longs
long abs(long n)
{
  cout << "In long abs()\n";
  return n<0 ? -n : n;
}

// abs() for doubles
double abs(double n)
{
  cout << "In double abs()\n";
  return n<0 ? -n : n;
}
```

As you can see, this program defines three functions called **abs( )**—one for each data type. Inside **main( )**, **abs( )** is called using three different types of arguments. The compiler automatically calls the correct version of **abs( )** based upon the type of data used as an argument.

Although this example is quite simple, it still illustrates the value of function overloading. Because a single name can be used to describe a general class of action, the artificial complexity caused by three slightly different names—in this case, **abs( )**, **fabs( )**, and **labs( )**—is eliminated. You now must remember only one name—the one that describes the *general* action. It is left to the compiler to choose the appropriate *specific* version of the function (that is, the method) to call. This has the net effect of reducing complexity. Thus, through the use of polymorphism, three names have been reduced to one.

While the use of polymorphism in this example is fairly trivial, you should be able to see how in a very large program, the "one interface, multiple methods" approach can be quite effective.

2. Here is another example of function overloading. In this case, the function **date( )** is overloaded to accept the date either as a string or as three integers. In both cases, the function displays the date passed to it.

```cpp
#include <iostream.h>

void date(char *date); // date as a string
void date(int month, int day, int year); // date as numbers

main()
{
  date("8/23/95");
  date(8, 23, 95);

  return 0;
}
// Date as string.
void date(char *date)
{
  cout << "Date: " << date << "\n";
}

// Date as integers.
void date(int month, int day, int year)
{
  cout << "Date: " << month << "/";
  cout << day << "/" << year << "\n";
}
```

This example illustrates how function overloading can provide the most natural interface to a function. Since it is very common for the date to be represented as either a string or as three integers containing the month, day, and year, you are free to select the most convenient form relative to the situation at hand.

3. So far, you have seen overloaded functions that differ in the data types of their arguments. However, overloaded functions may also differ in the number of arguments, as this example illustrates:

```cpp
#include <iostream.h>

void f1(int a);
void f1(int a, int b);

main()
{
  f1(10);
  f1(10, 20);
```

```
  return 0;
}

void f1(int a)
{
  cout << "In f1(int a)\n";
}

void f1(int a, int b)
{
  cout << "In f1(int a, int b)\n";
}
```

4. It is important to understand that the return type alone is not a sufficient difference to allow function overloading. If two functions differ only in the type of data they return, the compiler will not always be able to select the proper one to call. For example, this fragment is incorrect because it is inherently ambiguous:

```
// This is incorrect and will not compile
int f1(int a);
double f1(int a);
  .
  .
  .
f1(10); // which function does the compiler call???
```

As the comment indicates, the compiler has no way of knowing which version of **f1( )** to call.

1. Create a function called **sroot( )** that returns the square root of its argument. Overload **sroot( )** three ways: have it return the square root of an integer, a long integer, and a **double**. (To actually compute the square root, you may use the standard library function **sqrt( )**.)

2. The C++ standard library contains these three functions:

```
double atof(const char *s);
int atoi(const char *s);
long atol(const char *s);
```

which return the numeric value contained in the string pointed to by **s**. Specifically, **atof( )** returns a **double**, **atoi( )** returns an integer, and **atol( )** returns a **long**. Why is it not possible to overload these functions?

3. Create a function called **min( )** that returns the smaller of the two numeric arguments used to call the function. Overload **min( )** so it accepts characters, integers, and **double**s as arguments.

4. Create a function called **sleep( )** that pauses the computer for the number of seconds specified by its single argument. Overload **sleep( )** so it can be called with either an integer or a string representation of an integer. For example, both of these calls to **sleep( )** will cause the computer to pause for 10 seconds:

```
sleep(10);
sleep("10");
```

Demonstrate that your functions work by including them in a short program. (Feel free to use a delay loop to pause the computer.)

1.7 **C++ KEYWORDS**

In addition to the 32 keywords that form the C language, the proposed ANSI standard for C++ adds 29 more. These keywords are shown in Table 1-1. However, at the time of this writing, the keywords **bool**, **const_cast**, **dynamic_cast**, **false**, **mutable**, **namespace**, **reinterpret_cast**, **static_cast**, **true**, **typeid**, **using** and **wchar_t** are in the process of being defined by the ANSI C++ standards committee, and are not implemented by any commonly available

asm	friend	protected	try
bool	inline	public	typeid
catch	mutable	reinterpret_cast	using
class	namespace	static_cast	virtual
const_cast	new	template	wchar_t
delete	operator	this	
dynamic_cast	overload	throw	
false	private	true	

TABLE 1-1 *The C++ Keywords* ▼

compiler. These keywords were not part of the original specification for C++ created by Bjarne Stroustrup. They are being added primarily to allow C++ to accommodate some special case situations, and are subject to change or deletion. (These keywords are briefly discussed in Appendix A.) Also, the **overload** keyword is obsolete, but is included for compatibility with older C++ programs. You will want to check your compiler user's manual to determine precisely what C++ keywords are supported by your compiler.

**mastery
skills check**

1. Give brief descriptions of polymorphism, encapsulation, and inheritance.

2. How may comments be included in a C++ program?

3. Write a program that uses C++-style I/O to input two integers from the keyboard and then displays the result of raising the first to the power of the second. (For example, if the user enters 2 and 4, then the result is 2^4, or 16.)

4. Create a function called **rev_str( )** that reverses a string. Overload **rev_str( )** so it can be called with either one character array or two. When it is called with one string, have that one string contain the reversal. When it is called with two strings, return the reversed string in the second argument. For example:

```
char s1[80], s2[80];
strcpy(s1, "hello");
rev_str(s1, s2); // reversed string goes in s2, s1 untouched
rev_str(s1); // reversed string is returned in s1
```

2

Introducing Classes

chapter objectives

2.1 Constructor and destructor functions

2.2 Constructors taking parameters

2.3 Introducing inheritance

2.4 Object pointers

2.5 Classes, structures, and unions are related

2.6 In-line functions

2.7 Automatic in-lining

TH I S chapter introduces classes and objects. Several important topics are covered that relate to virtually all aspects of C++ programming, so a careful reading is advised.

review

skills check

Before proceeding, you should be able to correctly answer the following questions and do the exercises.

1. Write a program that uses C++-style I/O to prompt the user for a string and then display its length.

2. Create a class that holds name and address information. Store all the information in character strings in the private part of the class. Include a public function that stores the name and address. Also include a public function that displays the name and address. (Call these functions **store( )** and **display( )**.)

3. Create an overloaded **rotate( )** function that left-rotates the bits in its argument and returns the result. Overload it so it accepts integers and **longs**. (A rotate is similar to a shift except that the bit shifted off one end is shifted onto the other end.)

4. What is wrong with the following fragment?

```cpp
#include <iostream.h>

class myclass {
    int i;
public:
.

.

.
};

main()
{
    myclass ob;
```

```
     ob.i = 10;
       .
       .
       .
     }
```

2.1 CONSTRUCTOR AND DESTRUCTOR FUNCTIONS

If you have been writing programs for very long, you know that it is common for parts of your program to require initialization. The need for initialization is even more common when you are working with objects. In fact, when applied to real problems, virtually every object you create will require some sort of initialization. To address this situation, C++ allows a *constructor function* to be included in a class declaration. A class's constructor is called each time an object of that class is created. Thus, any initializations that need to be performed on an object can be done automatically by the constructor function.

A constructor function has the same name as the class it is a part of, and has no return type. For example, here is a short class that contains a constructor function:

```cpp
#include <iostream.h>

class myclass {
   int a;
public:
   myclass(); // constructor
   void show();
};

myclass::myclass()
{
   cout << "In constructor\n";
   a = 10;
}

void myclass::show()
{
   cout << a;
}

main()
{
   myclass ob;
```

```
ob.show();

return 0;
}
```

In this simple example, the value of **a** is initialized by the constructor **myclass( )**. The constructor is called when the object **ob** is created. An object is created when that object's declaration statement is executed. It is important to understand that in C++, a variable declaration statement is an "action statement." When programming in C, it is easy to think of declaration statements as simply establishing variables. However, in C++, because an object may have a constructor, a variable declaration statement may, in fact, cause considerable actions to occur.

Notice how **myclass( )** is defined. As stated, it has no return type. According to the C++ formal syntax rules, it is illegal for a constructor to have a return type.

For global objects, an object's constructor is called once, when the program first begins execution. For local objects, the constructor is called each time the declaration statement is executed.

The complement of a constructor is the *destructor*. This function is called when an object is destroyed. When working with objects, it is very common to have to perform some actions when an object is destroyed. For example, an object that allocates memory when it is created will want to free that memory when it is destroyed. The name of a destructor is the name of the class that it is part of, preceded by a ~. For example, this class contains a destructor function:

```
#include <iostream.h>

class myclass {
  int a;
public:
  myclass(); // constructor
  ~myclass(); // destructor
  void show();
};

myclass::myclass()
{
  cout << "In constructor\n";
  a = 10;
}
myclass::~myclass()
{
  cout << "Destructing...\n";
```

```
}

void myclass::show()
{
  cout << a << "\n";
}

main()
{
  myclass ob;

  ob.show();

  return 0;
}
```

A class's destructor is called when an object is destroyed. Local objects are destroyed when they go out of scope. Global objects are destroyed when the program ends.

It is not possible to take the address of either a constructor or a destructor.

 NOTE *Technically, a constructor or a destructor can perform any type of operation. The code that occurs within these functions does not have to initialize or reset anything related to the class for which they are defined. For example, a constructor for the preceding examples could have computed pi to 100 places. However, having a constructor or destructor perform actions not directly related to the initialization or orderly destruction of an object makes for very poor programming style and should be avoided.*

EXAMPLES

1. You should recall that the **stack** class created in Chapter 1 required an initialization function to set the stack index variable. This is precisely the sort of operation that a constructor function was designed to perform. Here is an improved version of the **stack** class that uses a constructor to automatically initialize a stack object when it is created:

```
#include <iostream.h>
```

```
#define SIZE 10

// Declare a stack class for characters
class stack {
  char stck[SIZE]; // holds the stack
  int tos; // index of top-of-stack
public:
  stack(); // constructor
  void push(char ch); // push character on stack
  char pop(); // pop character from stack
};

// Initialize the stack
stack::stack()
{
  cout << "Constructing a stack\n";
  tos = 0;
}

// Push a character.
void stack::push(char ch)
{
  if(tos==SIZE) {
    cout << "Stack is full\n";
    return;
  }
  stck[tos] = ch;
  tos++;
}

// Pop a character.
char stack::pop()
{
  if(tos==0) {
    cout << "Stack is empty";
    return 0; // return null on empty stack
  }
  tos--;
  return stck[tos];
}

main()
{
  // create two stacks that are automatically initialized
  stack s1, s2;
  int i;

  s1.push('a');
  s2.push('x');
  s1.push('b');
```

```
  s2.push('y');
  s1.push('c');
  s2.push('z');

  for(i=0; i<3; i++) cout << "Pop s1: " << s1.pop() << "\n";
  for(i=0; i<3; i++) cout << "Pop s2: " << s2.pop() << "\n";

  return 0;
}
```

As you can see, now the initialization task is performed automatically by the constructor function rather than by a separate function that must be explicitly called by the program. This is an important point. When an initialization is performed automatically when an object is created, it eliminates any prospect that, by error, the initialization will not be performed. This is another way that objects help reduce program complexity. You, as the programmer, don't need to worry about initialization—it is performed automatically when the object is brought into existence.

2. Here is an example that shows the need for both a constructor and destructor function. It creates a simple string class, called **strtype**, that contains a string and its length. When a **strtype** object is created, memory is allocated to hold the string and its initial length is set to zero. When a **strtype** object is destroyed, that memory is released.

```
#include <iostream.h>
#include <malloc.h>
#include <string.h>
#include <stdlib.h>

#define SIZE 255

class strtype {
  char *p;
  int len;
public:
  strtype(); // constructor
  ~strtype(); //destructor
  void set(char *ptr);
  void show();
};

// Initialize a string object.
strtype::strtype()
{
  p = (char *) malloc(SIZE);
  if(!p) {
```

```
        cout << "Allocation error\n";
        exit(1);
      }
      *p = '\0';
      len = 0;
    }

    // Free memory when destroying string object.
    strtype::~strtype()
    {
      cout << "Freeing p\n";
      free(p);
    }

    void strtype::set(char *ptr)
    {     (strlen(ptr)
      if(strlen(p) > SIZE) {
        cout << "String too big\n";
        return;
      }
      strcpy(p, ptr);
      len = strlen(p);
    }

    void strtype::show()
    {
      cout << p << " - length: " << len;
      cout << "\n";
    }

    main()
    {
      strtype s1, s2;

      s1.set("This is a test");
      s2.set("I like C++");

      s1.show();
      s2.show();

      return 0;
    }
```

NOTE *This program uses* **malloc( )** *and* **free( )** *to allocate and free memory. While this is perfectly valid, C++ does provide another way to dynamically manage memory, as you will see later in this book.*

3. Here is an interesting way to use an object's constructor and destructor. This program uses an object of the **timer** class to time the interval

between when an object of type **timer** is created and when it is destroyed. When the object's destructor is called, the elapsed time is displayed. You could use an object like this to time the duration of a program or the length of time a function spends within a block. Just make sure that the object goes out of scope at the point at which you want the timing interval to end.

```cpp
#include <iostream.h>
#include <time.h>

class timer {
  clock_t start;
public:
  timer(); // constructor
  ~timer(); // destructor
};

timer::timer()
{
  start = clock();
}

timer::~timer()
{
  clock_t end;

  end = clock();
  cout << "Elapsed time: " << (end-start) / CLK_TCK << "\n";
}

main()
{
  timer ob;
  char c;

  // delay ...
  cout << "Press a key followed by ENTER: ";
  cin >> c;

  return 0;
}
```

This program uses the standard library function **clock( )**, which returns the number of clock cycles that have taken place since the program started running. Dividing this value by **CLK_TCK** converts the value to seconds.

EXERCISES

1. Rework the **queue** class that you developed as an exercise in Chapter 1 so it replaces its initialization function with a constructor.

2. Create a class called **stopwatch** that emulates a stopwatch that keeps track of elapsed time. Use a constructor to initially set the elapsed time to zero. Provide two member functions called **start( )** and **stop( )** that turn on and off the timer, respectively. Include a member function called **show( )** that displays the elapsed time. Also, have the destructor function automatically display elapsed time when a **stopwatch** object is destroyed. (To simplify, report the time in seconds.)

3. What is wrong with the constructor shown in the following fragment?

```
class sample {
  double a, b, c;
public:
  double sample();  // error, why?
};
```

2.2 _C_ONSTRUCTORS TAKING PARAMETERS

It is possible to pass arguments to a constructor function. To allow this, simply add the appropriate parameters to the constructor function's declaration and definition. Then, when you declare an object, specify the parameters as arguments. To see how this is accomplished, let's begin with the short example shown here:

```
#include <iostream.h>

class myclass {
  int a;
public:
  myclass(int x); // constructor
  void show();
};

myclass::myclass(int x)
{
  cout << "In constructor\n";
  a = x;
}
```

```
void myclass::show()
{
  cout << a << "\n";
}

main()
{
  myclass ob(4);

  ob.show();

  return 0;
}
```

Here, the constructor for **myclass** takes one parameter. The value passed to **myclass( )** is used to initialize **a**. Pay special attention to how **ob** is declared in **main( )**. The value 4, specified in the parentheses following **ob**, is the argument that is passed to **myclass( )**'s parameter **x**, which is used to initialize **a**.

Actually, the syntax for passing an argument to a parameterized constructor is shorthand for this longer form:

```
myclass ob = myclass(4);
```

However, most C++ programmers use the short form, and you should too.

 NOTE *Unlike constructor functions, destructor functions cannot have parameters. The reason for this is simple enough to understand: there exists no mechanism by which to pass arguments to an object that is being destroyed.*

EXAMPLES

1. It is possible—in fact, quite common—to pass a constructor more than one argument. Here, **myclass( )** is passed two arguments:

```
#include <iostream.h>

class myclass {
  int a, b;
public:
  myclass(int x, int y); // constructor
  void show();
```

```
};

myclass::myclass(int x, int y)
{
  cout << "In constructor\n";
  a = x;
  b = y;
}

void myclass::show()
{
  cout << a << ' ' << b << "\n";
}

main()
{
  myclass ob(4, 7);

  ob.show();

  return 0;
}
```

Here, 4 is passed to **x** and 7 is passed to **y**. This same general approach is used to pass any number of arguments you like (up to the limit set by the compiler, of course).

2. Here is another version of the **stack** class that uses a parameterized constructor to pass a "name" to a stack. This single character name is used to identify which stack is being referred to when an error occurs.

```
#include <iostream.h>

#define SIZE 10

// Declare a stack class for characters
class stack {
  char stck[SIZE]; // holds the stack
  int tos; // index of top-of-stack
  char who; // identifies stack
public:
  stack(char c); // constructor
  void push(char ch); // push character on stack
  char pop(); // pop character from stack
};

// Initialize the stack
stack::stack(char c)
{
  tos = 0;
```

```
  who = c;
  cout << "Constructing stack " << who << "\n";
}

// Push a character.
void stack::push(char ch)
{
  if(tos==SIZE) {
    cout << "Stack " << who << " is full\n";
    return;
  }
  stck[tos] = ch;
  tos++;
}

// Pop a character.
char stack::pop()
{
  if(tos==0) {
    cout << "Stack " << who << " is empty\n";
    return 0; // return null on empty stack
  }
  tos--;
  return stck[tos];
}

main()
{
  // create two stacks that are automatically initialized
  stack s1('A'), s2('B');
  int i;

  s1.push('a');
  s2.push('x');
  s1.push('b');
  s2.push('y');
  s1.push('c');
  s2.push('z');

  // This will generate some error messages
  for(i=0; i<5; i++) cout << "Pop s1: " << s1.pop() << "\n";
  for(i=0; i<5; i++) cout << "Pop s2: " << s2.pop() << "\n";

  return 0;
}
```

Giving objects a "name," as shown in this example, is especially useful during debugging, when it is important to know which object generates an error.

3. Here is a different way to implement the **strtype** class (developed earlier) that uses a parameterized constructor function:

```cpp
#include <iostream.h>
#include <malloc.h>
#include <string.h>
#include <stdlib.h>

class strtype {
  char *p;
  int len;
public:
  strtype(char *ptr);
  ~strtype();
  void show();
};

strtype::strtype(char *ptr)
{
  len = strlen(ptr);
  p = (char *) malloc(len+1);
  if(!p) {
    cout << "Allocation error\n";
    exit(1);
  }
  strcpy(p, ptr);
}

strtype::~strtype()
{
  cout << "Freeing p\n";
  free(p);
}

void strtype::show()
{
  cout << p << " - length: " << len;
  cout << "\n";
}

main()
{
  strtype s1("This is a test"), s2("I like C++");

  s1.show();
  s2.show();
  return 0;
}
```

In this version of **strtype**, a string is given an initial value using the constructor function.

4. Although the previous examples have used constants, you can pass an object's constructor any valid expression, including variables. For example, this program uses user input to construct an object:

```cpp
#include <iostream.h>

class myclass {
  int i, j;
public:
  myclass(int a, int b);
  void show();
};

myclass::myclass(int a, int b)
{
  i = a;
  j = b;
}

void myclass::show()
{
  cout << i << ' ' << j << "\n";
}

main()
{
  int x, y;

  cout << "Enter two integers: ";
  cin >> x >> y;

  // use variables to construct ob
  myclass ob(x, y);

  ob.show();

  return 0;
}
```

This program illustrates an important point about objects. They can be constructed as needed to fit the exact situation at the time of their creation. As you learn more about C++, you will see how useful constructing objects "on the fly" is.

1. Change the **stack** class so it dynamically allocates memory for the stack. Have the size of the stack specified by a parameter to the constructor function. (Don't forget to free this memory with a destructor function.)

2. Create a class called **t_and_d** that is passed the current system time and date as a parameter to its constructor when it is created. Have the class include a member function that displays this time and date on the screen. (Hint: Use the standard time and date functions found in the standard library to find and display the date.)

3. Create a class called **box**, whose constructor function is passed three **double** values, which represent the length of the sides of a box. Have the **box** class compute the volume of the cube and store the result in a **double** variable. Include a member function called **vol( )** that displays the volume of each **box** object.

2.3 *I*NTRODUCING INHERITANCE

Although inheritance is discussed more fully in Chapter 7, it needs to be introduced at this time. As it applies to C++, inheritance is the mechanism by which one class can inherit the properties of another. Inheritance allows a hierarchy of classes to be built, moving from the most general to the most specific.

To begin, it is necessary to define two terms commonly used when discussing inheritance. When one class is inherited by another, the class that is inherited is called the *base class*. The inheriting class is called the *derived class*. In general, the process of inheritance begins with the definition of a base class. The base class defines all qualities that will be common to any derived class. In essence, the base class represents the most general description of a set of traits. A derived class inherits those general traits and adds those properties that are specific to that class.

To understand how one class can inherit another, let's first begin with an example that, although simple, illustrates many key features of inheritance.

To start, here is the declaration for the base class:

```
// Define base class.
class B {
  int i;
public:
  void set_i(int n);
  int get_i();
};
```

Using this base class, here is a derived class that inherits it:

```
// Define derived class.
class D : public B {
   int j;
public:
   void set_j(int n);
   int mul();
};
```

Look closely at this declaration. Notice that after the class name **D**, there is a colon followed by the keyword **public** and the class name **B**. This tells the compiler that class **D** will inherit all components of class **B**. The keyword **public** tells the compiler that **B** will be inherited such that all public elements of the base class will also be public elements of the derived class. However, all private elements of the base class remain private to it and are not directly accessible by the derived class.

Here is an entire program that uses the **B** and **D** classes:

```
// A simple example of inheritance.
#include <iostream.h>

// Define base class.
class base {
   int i;
public:
   void set_i(int n);
   int get_i();
};

// Define derived class.
class derived : public base {
   int j;
public:
   void set_j(int n);
   int mul();
};

// Set value i in base.
void base::set_i(int n)
{
   i = n;
}

// Return value of i in base.
int base::get_i()
{
```

```
    return i;
}

// Set value of j in derived.
void derived::set_j(int n)
{
   j = n;
}

// Return value of base's i times derived's j.
int derived::mul()
{
   // derived class can call base class public member functions
   return j * get_i();
}

main()
{
   derived ob;

   ob.set_i(10); // load i in base
   ob.set_j(4);  // load j in derived

   cout << ob.mul();  // displays 40

   return 0;
}
```

Look at the definition of **mul( )**. Notice that it calls **get_i( )**, which is a member of the base class **B**, not of **D**, without linking it to any specific object. This is possible because the public members of **B** become public members of **D**. However, the reason that **mul( )** must call **get_i( )** instead of accessing **i** directly is that the private members of a base class (in this case, **i**) remain private to it and not accessible by any derived class. The reason that private members of a class are not accessible to derived classes is to maintain encapsulation. If the private members of a class could be made public simply by inheriting the class, encapsulation could be easily circumvented.

The general form used to inherit a base class is shown here:

class *derived-class-name* : *access-specifier base-class-name* {

    .

    .

    .

};

Here, *access-specifier* is one of the following three keywords: **public**, **private**, or **protected**. For now, just use **public** when inheriting a class. A complete description of the access specifiers will be given later in this book.

1. Here is a program that defines a generic base class called **fruit** that describes certain characteristics about fruit. This class is inherited by two derived classes called **Apple** and **Orange**. These classes supply specific information to **fruit** that are related to these types of fruit.

```cpp
// An example of class inheritance.
#include <iostream.h>
#include <string.h>

enum yn {no, yes};
enum color {red, yellow, green, orange};

void out(enum yn x);

char *c[] = {
  "red", "yellow", "green", "orange"};

// Generic fruit class.
class fruit {
// in this base, all elements are public
public:
  enum yn annual;
  enum yn perennial;
  enum yn tree;
  enum yn tropical;
  enum color clr;
  char name[40];
};


// Derive Apple class.
class Apple : public fruit {
  enum yn cooking;
  enum yn crunchy;
  enum yn eating;
```

```
    public:
      void seta(char *n, enum color c, enum yn ck, enum yn crchy,
               enum yn e);
      void show();
    };

    // Derive orange class.
    class Orange : public fruit {
      enum yn juice;
      enum yn sour;
      enum yn eating;
    public:
      void seto(char *n, enum color c, enum yn j, enum yn sr,
               enum yn e);
      void show();
    };

    void Apple::seta(char *n, enum color c, enum yn ck,
                     enum yn crchy, enum yn e)
    {
      strcpy(name, n);
      annual = no;
      perennial = yes;
      tree = yes;
      tropical = no;
      clr = c;
      cooking = ck;
      crunchy = crchy;
      eating = e;
    }

    void Orange::seto(char *n, enum color c, enum yn j,
                      enum yn sr, enum yn e)
    {
      strcpy(name, n);
      annual = no;
      perennial = yes;
      tree = yes;
      tropical = yes;
      clr = c;
      juice = j;
      sour = sr;
      eating = e;
    }

    void Apple::show()
    {
      cout << name << " apple is: " << "\n";
      cout << "Annual: ";  out(annual);
```

```
      cout << "Perennial: ";  out(perennial);
      cout << "Tree: "; out(tree);
      cout << "Tropical: "; out(tropical);
      cout << "Color: " << c[clr] << "\n";
      cout << "Good for cooking: "; out(cooking);
      cout << "Crunchy: ";  out(crunchy);
      cout << "Good for eating: ";  out(eating);
      cout << "\n";
}

void Orange::show()
{
   cout << name << " orange is: " << "\n";
   cout << "Annual: ";  out(annual);
   cout << "Perennial: ";  out(perennial);
   cout << "Tree: ";  out(tree);
   cout << "Tropical: ";  out(tropical);
   cout << "Color: " << c[clr] << "\n";
   cout << "Good for juice: ";  out(juice);
   cout << "Sour: ";  out(sour);
   cout << "Good for eating: ";  out(eating);
   cout << "\n";
}

void out(enum yn x)
{
   if(x==no) cout << "no\n";
   else cout << "yes\n";
}

main()
{
   Apple a1, a2;
   Orange o1, o2;

   a1.seta("Red Delicious", red, no, yes, yes);
   a2.seta("Jonathan", red, yes, no, yes);

   o1.seto("Navel", orange, no, no, yes);
   o2.seto("Valencia", orange, yes, yes, no);

   a1.show();
   a2.show();

   o1.show();
   o2.show();

   return 0;
}
```

As you can see, the base class **fruit** defines several characteristics that are common to all types of fruit. (Of course, in order to keep this example short enough to fit conveniently in a book, the **fruit** class is somewhat simplified.) For example, all fruit grows on either annual or perennial plants. All fruit grows either on trees or on other types of plants, such as vines or bushes. All fruit has a color and a name. This base class is then inherited by the **Apple** and **Orange** classes. Each of these classes supplies information specific to its type of fruit.

This example illustrates the basic reason for inheritance. Here, a base class is created that defines the general traits associated with *all* fruit. It is left to the derived classes to supply those traits that are specific to each *individual* case.

This program illustrates another important fact about inheritance: A base class is not exclusively "owned" by a derived class. A base class may be inherited by any number of classes.

EXERCISE

1. Given the following base class:

```
class area_cl {
public:
  double height;
  double width;
};
```

create two derived classes called **box** and **isosceles** that inherit **area_cl**. Have each class include a function called **area( )** that returns the area of a box or isosceles triangle, respectively. Use parameterized constructors to initialize **height** and **width**.

2.4 *OBJECT POINTERS*

So far, you have been accessing members of an object by using the dot operator. This is the correct method when you are working with an object. However, it is also possible to access a member of an object via a pointer to that object. When this is the case, the arrow operator (–>) rather than the dot operator is employed. (This is exactly the same way the arrow operator is used when given a pointer to a structure.)

You declare an object pointer just like you declare a pointer to any other type of variable. Specify its class name, and then precede the variable name with an asterisk. To obtain the address of an object, precede the object with the **&** operator, just as you do when taking the address of any other type of variable.

Just like pointers to other types, when you increment an object pointer, it will point to the next object of its type.

EXAMPLE

1. Here is a simple example that uses an object pointer:

```
#include <iostream.h>

class myclass {
   int a;
public:
   myclass(int x); // constructor
   int get();
};

myclass::myclass(int x)
{
   a = x;
}

int myclass::get()
{
   return a;
}

main()
{
   myclass ob(120);  // create object
   myclass *p;  // create pointer to object

   p = &ob; // put address of ob into p

   cout << "Value using object: " << ob.get();
   cout << "\n";
```

```
    cout << "Value using pointer: " << p->get();

    return 0;
}
```

Notice how the declaration

```
myclass *p;
```

creates a pointer to an object of **myclass**. It is important to understand that creation of an object pointer does *not* create an object—it creates just a pointer to one. The address of **ob** is put into **p** by using this statement:

```
p = &ob;
```

Finally, the program shows how an object can be referenced by use of a pointer to it.

We will come back to the subject of object pointers in Chapter 4, once you know more about C++. There are several special features that relate to them.

2.5 CLASSES, STRUCTURES, AND UNIONS ARE RELATED

As you have seen, the class is syntactically similar to the structure. You might be surprised to learn, however, that the class and the structure have virtually identical capabilities. In C++, the definition of a structure has been expanded so that it can also include member functions, including constructor and destructor functions, in just the same way that a class can. In fact, the only difference between a structure and a class is that, by default, the members of a class are private but the members of a structure are public. The expanded syntax of a structure is shown here:

```
struct tag-name {
    // public function and data members
private:
    // private function and data members
} object-list;
```

In fact, according to the formal C++ syntax, both **struct** and **class** create new class *types*. Notice that a new keyword is introduced. It is **private**, and it tells the compiler that the members that follow are private to that class.

On the surface, there is a seeming redundancy in the fact that structures and classes have virtually identical capabilities. Many newcomers to C++ wonder why this apparent duplication exists. In fact, it is not uncommon to hear the suggestion that the **class** keyword is unnecessary.

The answer to this line of reasoning has both a "strong" and "weak" form. The "strong" (or compelling) reason concerns maintaining upward compatibility from C. As C++ is currently defined, a standard C structure is also perfectly acceptable in a C++ program. Since in C all structure members are public by default, this convention is also maintained in C++. Further, because **class** is a syntactically separate entity from **struct**, the definition of a class is free to evolve in a way that will not be compatible with a C-like structure definition. Since the two are separated, the future direction of C++ is not restricted by compatibility concerns.

The "weak" reason for having two similar constructs is that there is no disadvantage to expanding the definition of a structure in C++ to include member functions.

Although structures have the same capabilities as classes, most programmers restrict their use of structures to adhere to their C-like form and do not use them to include function members. Most programmers use the **class** keyword when defining objects that contain both data and code. However, this is a stylistic matter and is subject to your own preference. (After this section, this book reserves the use of **struct** for objects that have no function members.)

If you find the connection between classes and structures interesting, so will you find this next revelation about C++: unions and classes are also related! In C++, a union also defines a class type which can contain both functions and data as members. A union is like a structure in that, by default, all members are public until the **private** specifier is used. It is just that in a union, all data members share the same memory location (just as in C). Unions can contain constructor and destructor functions. Fortunately, C unions are upwardly compatible with C++ unions.

Although structures and classes seem on the surface to be redundant, this is not the case with unions. In an object-oriented language, it is important to preserve encapsulation. Thus, the union's ability to link code and data allows you to create class types in which all data uses a shared location. This is something that you cannot do using a class.

There are several restrictions that apply to unions as they relate to C++. First, they cannot inherit any other class and they cannot be used as a base class for any other type. Unions must not have any **static** members. They also must not contain any object that has a constructor or destructor. (The union, itself, *can* have a constructor and destructor, though.)

NOTE *Some C++ compilers do not allow unions to have private members, so, for the sake of the greatest compatibility, you may wish to avoid using **private** inside of a union.*

EXAMPLES

1. Here is a short program that uses a **struct** to create a class:

```
#include <iostream.h>
#include <string.h>

// use struct to define a class type
struct st_type {
  st_type(double b, char *n);
  void show();
private:
  double balance;
  char name[40];
} ;

st_type::st_type(double b, char *n)
{
  balance = b;
  strcpy(name, n);
}

void st_type::show()
{
  cout << "Name: " << name;
  cout << ": $" << balance;
  if(balance<0.0) cout << "***";
  cout << "\n";
}

main()
{
  st_type acc1(100.12, "Johnson");
  st_type acc2(-12.34, "Hedricks");

  acc1.show();
  acc2.show();
  return 0;
}
```

Notice that, as stated, the members of a structure are public by default. The **private** keyword must be used to declare private members.

Also, notice one difference between C-like structures and C++-like structures. In C++, the structure tag-name also becomes a complete type name that can be used to declare objects. In C, the tag-name requires that the keyword **struct** precede it before it becomes a complete type.

Here is the same program, rewritten using a class:

```cpp
#include <iostream.h>
#include <string.h>

class cl_type {
  double balance;
  char name[40];
public:
  cl_type(double b, char *n);
  void show();
} ;

cl_type::cl_type(double b, char *n)
{
  balance = b;
  strcpy(name, n);
}

void cl_type::show()
{
  cout << "Name: " << name;
  cout << ": $" << balance;
  if(balance<0.0) cout << "***";
  cout << "\n";
}

main()
{
  cl_type acc1(100.12, "Johnson");
  cl_type acc2(-12.34, "Hedricks");

  acc1.show();
  acc2.show();

  return 0;
}
```

2. Here is an example that uses a union to display the binary bit pattern, byte by byte, contained within a **double** value.

```cpp
#include <iostream.h>
```

```
union bits {
  bits(double n);
  void show_bits();
  double d;
  unsigned char c[sizeof(double)];
};

bits::bits(double n)
{
  d = n;
}

void bits::show_bits()
{
  int i, j;

  for(j = sizeof(double)-1; j>=0; j--) {
    cout << "Bit pattern in byte " << j << ": ";
    for(i = 128; i; i >>= 1)
      if(i & c[j]) cout << "1";
      else cout << "0";
    cout << "\n";
  }
}

main()
{
  bits ob(1991.829);

  ob.show_bits();

  return 0;
}
```

The output of this program is

```
Bit pattern in byte 7: 01000000
Bit pattern in byte 6: 10011111
Bit pattern in byte 5: 00011111
Bit pattern in byte 4: 01010000
Bit pattern in byte 3: 11100101
Bit pattern in byte 2: 01100000
Bit pattern in byte 1: 01000001
Bit pattern in byte 0: 10001001
```

3. Both structures and unions can have constructors and destructors. The following example shows the **strtype** class reworked as a structure. It contains both a constructor and a destructor function.

```cpp
#include <iostream.h>
#include <malloc.h>
#include <string.h>
#include <stdlib.h>

struct strtype {
  strtype(char *ptr);
  ~strtype();
  void show();
private:
  char *p;
  int len;
};

strtype::strtype(char *ptr)
{
  len = strlen(ptr);
  p = (char *) malloc(len+1);
  if(!p) {
    cout << "Allocation error\n";
    exit(1);
  }
  strcpy(p, ptr);
}

strtype::~strtype()
{
  cout << "Freeing p\n";
  free(p);
}

void strtype::show()
{
  cout << p << " - length: " << len;
  cout << "\n";
}

main()
{
  strtype s1("This is a test"), s2("I like C++");

  s1.show();
  s2.show();

  return 0;
}
```

EXERCISES

1. Rewrite the **stack** class presented in Section 2.1 so it uses a structure rather than a class.

2. Use a **union** class to swap the low- and high-order bytes of an integer (assuming 16-bit integers; if your computer uses 32-bit integers, swap the bytes of a **short int**).

2.6 *IN-LINE FUNCTIONS*

Before we continue this examination of classes, a short but related digression is needed. In C++, it is possible to define functions that are not actually called but, rather, are expanded in line, at the point of each call. This is much the same way that a C-like parameterized macro works. The advantage of *in-line* functions is that they have no overhead associated with the function call and return mechanism. This means that in-line functions can be executed much faster than normal functions. (Remember, the machine instructions that generate the function call and return take time each time a function is called. If there are parameters, even more time overhead is generated.)

The disadvantage of in-line functions is that if they are too large and called too often, your program grows larger. For this reason, in general only short functions are declared as in-line functions.

To declare an in-line function, simply precede the function's definition with the **inline** specifier. For example, this short program shows how to declare an in-line function:

```
// Example of an in-line function
#include <iostream.h>

inline int even(int x)
{
  return !(x%2);
}

main()
{
```

```
    if(even(10)) cout << "10 is even\n";
    if(even(11)) cout << "11 is even\n";

    return 0;
}
```

In this example, the function **even( )**, which returns true if its argument is even, is declared as being in-line. This means that the line

```
if(even(10))  cout << "10 is even\n";
```

is functionally equivalent to

```
if(!(10%2)) cout << "10 is even\n";
```

This example also points out another important feature of using **inline:** an in-line function must be defined *before* it is first called. If it isn't, the compiler has no way to know that it is supposed to be expanded in-line. This is why **even( )** was defined before **main( )**.

The advantage of using **inline** rather than parameterized macros is twofold. First, it provides a more structured way to expand short functions in-line. For example, when you are creating a parameterized macro, it is easy to forget that extra parentheses are often needed to ensure proper in-line expansion in every case. Using in-line functions prevents such problems.

Second, an in-line function might be able to be optimized more thoroughly by the compiler than a macro expansion. In any event, C++ programmers virtually never use parameterized macros, instead relying on **inline** to avoid the overhead of a function call associated with a short function.

It is important to understand that the **inline** specifier is a *request,* not a command, to the compiler. If, for various reasons, the compiler is unable to fulfill the request, the function is compiled as a normal function and the **inline** request is ignored.

Depending upon your compiler, several restrictions to in-line functions may apply. For example, some compilers will not in-line a function if it contains a **static** variable, a loop statement, a **switch** or a **goto**, or if the function is recursive. You should check your compiler's user manual for specific restrictions to in-line functions that may affect you.

 REMEMBER *If any in-line restriction is violated, the compiler is free to generate a normal function.*

EXAMPLES

1. Any type of function can be in-lined, including functions that are members of classes. For example, here the member function **divisible( )** is in-lined for fast execution. (The function returns true if its first argument can be evenly divided by its second.)

```
// Demonstrate in-lining a member function.
#include <iostream.h>

class samp {
  int i, j;
public:
  samp(int a, int b);
  int divisible(); // in-lined in its definition
};

samp::samp(int a, int b)
{
  i = a;
  j = b;
}

/* Return 1 if i is evenly divisible by j.
   This member function is expanded in line.
*/
inline int samp::divisible()
{
  return !(i%j);
}

main()
{
  samp ob1(10, 2), ob2(10, 3);

  // this is true
  if(ob1.divisible()) cout << "10 divisible by 2\n";

  // this is false
  if(ob2.divisible()) cout << "10 divisible by 3\n";

  return 0;
}
```

2. It is perfectly permissible to in-line an overloaded function. For example, this program overloads **min( )** three ways. Each way is also declared as **inline**.

```
#include <iostream.h>
```

```
// Overload min() three ways.

// integers
inline int min(int a, int b)
{
  return a<b ? a : b;
}

// longs
inline long min(long a, long b)
{
  return a<b ? a : b;
}

// doubles
inline double min(double a, double b)
{
  return a<b ? a : b;
}

main()
{
  cout << min(-10, 10) << "\n";
  cout << min(-10.01, 100.002) << "\n";
  cout << min(-10L, 12L) << "\n";

  return 0;
}
```

EXERCISES

1. In Chapter 1 you overloaded the **abs**( ) function so that it could find the absolute value of integers, long integers, and **double**s. Modify that program so that those functions are expanded in line.

2. Why might the following function not be in-lined by your compiler?

```
void f1()
{
  int i;

  for(i=0; i<10; i++) cout << i;
}
```

| 2.7 | # A*UTOMATIC IN-LINING* |

If a member function's definition is short enough, its definition may be included inside the class declaration. Doing so causes the function to automatically become an in-line function, if possible. When a function is defined within a class declaration, the **inline** keyword is no longer necessary. (However, it is not an error to use it in this situation.) For example, the **divisible( )** function from the preceding section can be automatically in-lined as shown here:

```
#include <iostream.h>

class samp {
  int i, j;
public:
  samp(int a, int b);

  /* divisible is defined here and automatically
     in-lined. */
  int divisible() { return !(i%j); }
};

samp::samp(int a, int b)
{
  i = a;
  j = b;
}

main()
{
  samp ob1(10, 2), ob2(10, 3);

  // this is true
  if(ob1.divisible()) cout << "10 divisible by 2\n";

  // this is false
  if(ob2.divisible()) cout << "10 divisible by 3\n";

  return 0;
}
```

As you can see, the code associated with **divisible( )** occurs inside the declaration for the class **samp**. Further notice that no other definition of **divisible( )** is needed— or permitted. Defining **divisible( )** inside **samp** causes it to be made into an in-line function automatically.

When a function defined inside a class declaration cannot be made into an in-line function (because a restriction has been violated) it is automatically made into a regular function.

Notice how **divisible( )** is defined within **samp**, particularly the body. It occurs all on one line. This format is very common in C++ programs when a function is declared within a class declaration. It allows the declaration to be more compact. However, the **samp** class could have been written like this:

```
class samp {
  int i, j;
public:
  samp(int a, int b);

  /* divisible is defined here and automatically
     inlined. */
  int divisible()
  {
    return !(i%j);
  }
};
```

In this version, the layout of **divisible( )** uses the more or less standard indentation style. From the compiler's point of view, there is no difference between the compact style and the standard style. However, the compact style is commonly found in C++ programs when short functions are defined inside a class definition.

The same restrictions that apply to "normal" in-line functions apply to automatic in-line functions within a class declaration.

EXAMPLES

1. Perhaps the most common use of in-line functions defined within a class is to define constructor and destructor functions. For example, the **samp** class can more efficiently be defined like this:

```
#include <iostream.h>

class samp {
  int i, j;
public:
  // inline constructor
  samp(int a, int b) { i = a; j = b; }
  int divisible() { return !(i%j); }
};
```

The definition of **samp( )** within the class **samp** is sufficient, and no other definition of **samp( )** is needed or allowed.

2. Sometimes a short function will be included in a class declaration even though the automatic in-lining feature is of little or no value. Consider this class declaration:

```
class myclass {
  int i;
public:
  myclass(int n) { i = n; }
  void show() { cout << i; }
};
```

Here, the function **show( )** is made into an in-line function automatically. However, as you should know, I/O operations are (generally) so slow relative to CPU/memory operations that any effect of eliminating the function call overhead is virtually lost. Even so, in C++ programs, it is still common to see small functions of this type declared within a class simply for the sake of convenience, and because no harm is caused.

EXERCISES

1. Convert the **stack** class from Section 2.1, Example 1, so that it uses automatic in-line functions where appropriate.

2. Convert the **strtype** class from Section 2.2, Example 3, so that it uses automatic in-line functions.

mastery
skills check

At this point you should be able to perform the following exercises and answer the questions.

1. What is a constructor? What is a destructor? When are they executed?

2. Create a class called **line** that draws a line on the screen. Store the line length in a private integer variable called **len**. Have **line**'s constructor take one parameter: the line length. Have the constructor store the length and actually draw the line. If your system does not support graphics, display the line by using *. Optional: Give **line** a destructor that erases the line.

3. What does the following program display?

```
#include <iostream.h>

main()
{
  int i = 10;
  long l = 1000000;
  double d = -0.0009;

  cout << i << ' ' << l << ' ' << d;
  cout << "\n";

  return 0;
}
```

4. Add another derived class that inherits **area_cl** from Section 3, Exercise 1. Call this class **cylinder** and have it compute its surface area. Hint: The surface area of a cylinder is $2 * pi * R^2 + pi * D * height$.

5. What is an in-line function? What are its advantages and disavantages?

6. Modify the following program so that all member functions are automatically in-lined:

```
#include <iostream.h>

class myclass {
  int i, j;
public:
  myclass(int x, int y);
  void show();
};

myclass::myclass(int x, int y)
{
  i = x;
  j = y;
}
void myclass::show()
{
  cout << i << " " << j << "\n";
```

```
      }

  main()
  {
    myclass count(2, 3);

    count.show();

    return 0;
  }
```

7. What is the difference between a class and a structure?

cumulative
skills check

This section checks how well you have integrated material in this chapter with that from the preceding chapter.

1. Create a class called **prompt**. Pass its constructor function a prompting string of your own choosing. Have the constructor display the string and then input an integer. Store this value in a private variable called **count**. When an object of type **prompt** is destroyed, ring the bell on the terminal as many times as the user entered.

2. In Chapter 1 you created a program that converted feet to inches. Now, create a class that does the same thing. Have the class store the number of feet and its equivalent number of inches. Pass to the class's constructor the number of feet and have the constructor display the number of inches.

3. Create a class called **dice** that contains one private integer variable. Create a function called **roll( )** that uses the standard random number generator, **rand( )**, to generate a number between 1 and 6. Then have **roll( )** display that value.

3

A Closer Look at Classes

chapter objectives

3.1 Assigning objects

3.2 Passing objects to functions

3.3 Returning objects from functions

3.4 Introducing friend functions

N this chapter you continue to explore the class. You will learn about assigning objects, passing objects to functions, and returning objects from functions. You will also learn about an important new type of function: the friend.

Before proceeding, you should be able to correctly answer the following questions and do the exercises.

1. Given the following class, what are the names of its constructor and destructor functions?

```
class widgit {
   int x, y;
public:
   // ... fill in constructor and destructor functions
};
```

2. When is a constructor function called? When is a destructor function called?

3. Given the following base class, show how it can be inherited by a derived class called **Mars**.

```
class planet {
   int moons;
   double dist_from_sun;
   double diameter;
   double mass;
public:
 // ...
};
```

4. There are two ways to cause a function to be expanded in-line. What are they?

5. Give two possible restrictions to in-line functions.

6. Given the following class, show how an object called **ob** is declared that passes the value 100 to **a** and **X** to **c**.

```
class sample {
  int a;
  char c;
public:
  sample(int x, char ch) { a = x; c = ch; }
  // ...
};
```

3.1 ASSIGNING OBJECTS

One object may be assigned to another provided that both objects are of the same type. By default, when one object is assigned to another, a bitwise copy of all the data members is performed. For example, when an object called **A** is assigned to another object called **B**, the contents of all of **A**'s data are copied into the equivalent members of **B**. Consider this short example:

```
// An example of object assignment.
#include <iostream.h>

class myclass {
  int a, b;
public:
  void set(int i, int j) { a = i; b = j; }
  void show() { cout << a << ' ' << b << "\n"; }
};

main()
{
  myclass o1, o2;

  o1.set(10, 4);

  // assign o1 to o2
  o2 = o1;

  o1.show();
  o2.show();

  return 0;
}
```

Here, object **o1** has its member variables **a** and **b** set to the values 10 and 4, respectively. Next, **o1** is assigned to **o2**. This causes the current value of **o1.a** to be assigned to **o2.a** and **o1.b** to be assigned to **o2.b**. Thus, when run, this program displays

```
10 4
10 4
```

Keep in mind that an assignment between two objects simply makes the data in those objects identical. The two objects are still completely separate. For example, after the assignment, calling **o1.set( )** to set the value of **o1.a** has no effect on **o2** or its **a** value.

EXAMPLES

1. Only objects of the same type may be used in an assignment statement. If the objects are not of the same type, a compile-time error is reported. Further, it is not sufficient that the types just be physically similar—their type names must be the same. For example, this is not a valid program:

```cpp
// This program has an error.
#include <iostream.h>

class myclass {
  int a, b;
public:
  void set(int i, int j) { a = i; b = j; }
  void show() { cout << a << ' ' << b << "\n"; }
};

/* This class is similar to myclass but uses a
   different class name and thus appears as a different
   type to the compiler.
*/
class yourclass {
  int a, b;
public:
  void set(int i, int j) { a = i; b = j; }
  void show() { cout << a << ' ' << b << "\n"; }
};

main()
{
  myclass o1;
  yourclass o2;
```

```
    o1.set(10, 4);

    o2 = o1; // ERROR, objects not of same type

    o1.show();
    o2.show();

    return 0;
}
```

In this case, even though **myclass** and **yourclass** are physically the same, because they have different type names, they are treated as differing types by the compiler.

2. It is important to understand that all data members of one object are assigned to another when an assignment is performed. This includes complex data such as arrays. For example, in the following version of the **stack** example, only **s1** has any characters actually pushed onto it. However, because of the assignment, **s2**'s **stck** array will also contain the characters **a**, **b**, and **c**.

```
#include <iostream.h>

#define SIZE 10

// Declare a stack class for characters
class stack {
  char stck[SIZE]; // holds the stack
  int tos; // index of top-of-stack
public:
  stack(); // constructor
  void push(char ch); // push character on stack
  char pop(); // pop character from stack
};

// Initialize the stack
stack::stack()
{
  cout << "Constructing a stack\n";
  tos = 0;
}

// Push a character.
void stack::push(char ch)
{
  if(tos==SIZE) {
    cout << "Stack is full";
    return;
  }
```

```
      stck[tos] = ch;
      tos++;
    }

    // Pop a character.
    char stack::pop()
    {
      if(tos==0) {
        cout << "Stack is empty";
        return 0; // return null on empty stack
      }
      tos--;
      return stck[tos];
    }

    main()
    {
      // create two stacks that are automatically initialized
      stack s1, s2;
      int i;

      s1.push('a');
      s1.push('b');
      s1.push('c');

      // clone s1
      s2 = s1;  // now s1 and s2 are identical

      for(i=0; i<3; i++) cout << "Pop s1: " << s1.pop() << "\n";
      for(i=0; i<3; i++) cout << "Pop s2: " << s2.pop() << "\n";

      return 0;
    }
```

3. You must exercise some care when assigning one object to another. For example, here is the **strtype** class developed in Chapter 2, along with a short **main( )**. See if you can find an error in this program.

```
// This program contains an error.

#include <iostream.h>
#include <malloc.h>
#include <string.h>
#include <stdlib.h>

class strtype {
  char *p;
  int len;
public:
  strtype(char *ptr);
```

```
  ~strtype();
  void show();
};

strtype::strtype(char *ptr)
{
  len = strlen(ptr);
  p = (char *) malloc(len+1);
  if(!p) {
    cout << "Allocation error\n";
    exit(1);
  }
  strcpy(p, ptr);
}

strtype::~strtype()
{
  cout << "Freeing p\n";
  free(p);
}

void strtype::show()
{
  cout << p << " - length: " << len;
  cout << "\n";
}

main()
{
  strtype s1("This is a test"), s2("I like C++");

  s1.show();
  s2.show();

  // assign s1 to s2 - - this generates an error
  s2 = s1;

  s1.show();
  s2.show();

  return 0;
}
```

The trouble with this program is quite insidious. When **s1** and **s2** are created, both allocate memory to hold their respective strings. A pointer to each object's allocated memory is stored in **p**. When a **strtype** object is destroyed, this memory is released. However, when **s1** is assigned to **s2**, **s2**'s **p** now points to the same memory as **s1**'s **p**. Thus, when these objects are destroyed, the memory pointed to by **s1**'s

p is freed *twice* and the memory originally pointed to by **s2**'s **p** is not freed *at all*.

While benign in this context, this sort of problem occurring in a real program will cause the dynamic allocation system to fail, and possibly even cause a program crash. As you can see from the preceding example, when assigning one object to another, you must make sure you are not destroying information that may be needed later.

EXERCISES

1. What is wrong with the following fragment?

```
// This program has an error.
#include <iostream.h>

class cl1 {
  int i, j;
public:
  cl1(int a, int b) { i = a; j = b; }
  // ...
};

class cl2 {
  int i, j;
public:
  cl2(int a, int b) { i = a; j = b; }
  // ...
};

main()
{
  cl1 x(10, 20);
  cl2 y(0, 0);
  x = y;

  // ...
}
```

2. Using the **queue** class that you created for Chapter 2, Section 1, Exercise 1, show how one queue may be assigned to another.

3. If the **queue** class from the preceding question dynamically allocates memory to hold the queue, why, in this situation, can one queue not be assigned to another?

3.2 PASSING OBJECTS TO FUNCTIONS

Objects may be passed to functions as arguments in just the same way that other types of data are passed. Simply declare the function's parameter as a class type and then use an object of that class as an argument when calling the function. As with other types of data, by default all objects are passed by value to a function.

EXAMPLES

1. Here is a short example that passes an object to a function:

```cpp
#include <iostream.h>

class samp {
  int i;
public:
  samp(int n) { i = n; }
  int get_i() { return i; }
};

// Return square of o.i.
int sqr_it(samp o)
{
  return o.get_i() * o.get_i();
}

main()
{
  samp a(10), b(2);

  cout << sqr_it(a) << "\n";
  cout << sqr_it(b) << "\n";

  return 0;
}
```

This program creates a class called **samp** that contains one integer variable called **i**. The function **sqr_it( )** takes an argument of type **samp** and returns the square of that object's **i** value. The output from this program is 100 followed by 4.

2. As stated, the default method of parameter passing in C++, including objects, is by value. This means that a bitwise copy of the argument is made and it is this copy that is used by the function. Therefore, changes to the object inside the function do not affect the calling object. This is illustrated by the following example:

```
/*
    Remember, objects, like other parameters, are passed
    by value. Thus changes to the parameter inside a
    function have no effect on the object used in the call.
*/
#include <iostream.h>

class samp {
   int i;
public:
   samp(int n) { i = n; }
   void set_i(int n) { i = n; }
   int get_i() { return i; }
};

/* Set o.i to its square. This has no effect on the
   object used to call sqr_it(), however.
*/
void sqr_it(samp o)
{
   o.set_i(o.get_i() * o.get_i());

   cout << "Copy of a has i value of " << o.get_i();
   cout << "\n";
}

main()
{
   samp a(10);

   sqr_it(a); // a passed by value

   cout << "But, a.i is unchanged in main: ";
   cout << a.get_i();   // displays 10

   return 0;
}
```

The output displayed by this program is

```
Copy of a has i value of 100
But, a.i is unchanged in main: 10
```

3. Like other types of variables, the address of an object may be passed to a function so that the argument used in the call can be modified by the function. For example, the following version of the program in the preceding example does, indeed, modify the value of the object whose address is used in the call to **sqr_it( )**.

```
/*
    Now that the address of an object is passed to sqr_it(),
    the function may modify the value of the argument whose
    address is used in the call.
*/
#include <iostream.h>

class samp {
    int i;
public:
    samp(int n) { i = n; }
    void set_i(int n) { i = n; }
    int get_i() { return i; }
};

/* Set o.i to its square. This affects the calling
    argument.
*/
void sqr_it(samp *o)
{
    o->set_i(o->get_i() * o->get_i());

    cout << "Copy of a has i value of " << o->get_i();
    cout << "\n";
}

main()
{
    samp a(10);

    sqr_it(&a); // pass a's address to sqr_it()

    cout << "Now, a in main() has been changed: ";
    cout << a.get_i();  // displays 100

    return 0;
}
```

This program now displays the following output:

```
Copy of a has i value of 100
Now, a in main() has been changed: 100
```

4. When a copy of an object is made when being passed to a function, it means that a new object comes into existence. Also, when the function that the object was passed to terminates, the copy of the argument is destroyed. This raises two questions. First, is the object's constructor called when the copy is made? Second, is the object's destructor called when the copy is destroyed? The answer may, at first, seem surprising.

When a copy of an object is made to be used in a function call, the constructor function is *not* called. The reason for this is simple to understand if you think about it. Since a constructor function is generally used to initialize some aspect of an object, it must not be called when making a copy of an already existing object passed to a function. Doing so would alter the contents of the object. When passing an object to a function, you want the current state of the object, not its initial state.

However, when the function terminates and the copy is destroyed, the destructor function *is* called. This is because the object might perform some operation that must be undone when it goes out of scope. For example, the copy may allocate memory that must be released.

To summarize, when a copy of an object is created because it is used as an argument to a function, the constructor function is not called. However, when the copy is destroyed (usually by going out of scope when the function returns), the destructor function is called.

The following program illustrates the preceding discussion:

```cpp
#include <iostream.h>

class samp {
  int i;
public:
  samp(int n) {
    i = n;
    cout << "Constructing\n";
  }
  ~samp() { cout << "Destructing\n"; }
  int get_i() { return i; }
};

// Return square of o.i.
int sqr_it(samp o)
{
  return o.get_i() * o.get_i();
```

```
}

main()
{
  samp a(10);

  cout << sqr_it(a) << "\n";

  return 0;
}
```

This function displays the following:

```
Constructing
Destructing
100
Destructing
```

As you can see, only one call to the constructor function is made. This occurs when **a** is created. However, two calls to the destructor are made. One is for the copy created when **a** is passed to **sqr_it( )**. The other is for **a**, itself.

The fact that the destructor for the object that is the copy of the argument used to call a function is executed when the function terminates can be a source of problems. For example, if the object used as the argument allocates dynamic memory and frees that memory when destroyed, then its copy will free the same memory when its destructor is called. This will leave the original object damaged and effectively useless. (See Exercise 2, just ahead in this section, for an example.) It is important to guard against this type of error and to make sure that the destructor function of the copy of an object used an an argument does not cause side effects that alter the original argument.

As you might guess, one way around the problem of a parameter's destructor function destroying data needed by the calling argument is to pass the address of the object and not the object itself. When an address is passed, no new object is created, and therefore, no destructor is called when the function returns. (As you will see in the next chapter, C++ provides a variation on this theme that offers a very elegant alternative.) However, an even better solution exists, which you can use after you have learned about a special type of constructor called a *copy constructor*. A copy constructor lets you define precisely how copies of objects are made. (Copy constructors are discussed in Chapter 5.)

1. Using the **stack** example from Section 3.1, Example 2, add a function called **showstack( )** that is passed an object of type **stack**. Have this function display the contents of a stack.

2. As you know, when an object is passed to a function, a copy of that object is made. Further, when that function returns, the copy's destructor function is called. Keeping this in mind, what is wrong with the following program?

```
// This program contains an error.
#include <iostream.h>
#include <stdlib.h>

class dyna {
  int *p;
public:
  dyna(int i);
  ~dyna() { free(p); cout << "freeing \n"; }
  int get() { return *p; }
};

dyna::dyna(int i)
{
  p = (int *) malloc(sizeof(int));
  if(!p) {
    cout << "Allocation failure\n";
    exit(1);
  }

  *p = i;
}

// Return negative value of *ob.p
int neg(dyna ob)
{
  return -ob.get();
}

main()
{
  dyna o(-10);

  cout << o.get() << "\n";
  cout << neg(o) << "\n";
```

```
    dyna o2(20);
    cout << o2.get() << "\n";
    cout << neg(o2) << "\n";

    cout << o.get() << "\n";
    cout << neg(o) << "\n";

    return 0;
  }
```

3.3 # *R*ETURNING OBJECTS FROM FUNCTIONS

Just as you may pass objects to functions, functions may return objects. To do so, first declare the function as returning a class type. Second, return an object of that type using the normal **return** statement.

There is one important point to understand about returning objects from functions, however: When an object is returned by a function, a temporary object is automatically created which holds the return value. It is this object that is actually returned by the function. After the value has been returned, this object is destroyed. The destruction of this temporary object may cause unexpected side effects in some situations, as is illustrated in Example 2 below.

EXAMPLES

1. Here is an example of a function that returns an object:

```
// Returning an object
#include <iostream.h>
#include <string.h>

class samp {
  char s[80];
public:
  void show() { cout << s << "\n"; }
  void set(char *str) { strcpy(s, str); }
};

// Return an object of type samp
samp input()
{
  char s[80];
```

```
    samp str;

    cout << "Enter a string: ";
    cin >> s;

    str.set(s);

    return str;
  }

main()
{
  samp ob;

  // assign returned object to ob
  ob = input();
  ob.show();

  return 0;
}
```

In this example, **input( )** creates a local object called **str** and then reads a string from the keyboard. This string is copied into **str.s** and then **str** is returned by the function. This object is then assigned to **ob** inside **main( )** when it is returned by the call to **input( )**.

2. You must be careful about returning objects from functions if those objects contain destructor functions because the returned object goes out of scope as soon as the value is returned to the calling routine. For example, if the object returned by the function has a destructor that frees dynamically allocated memory, that memory will be freed even though the object that is assigned the return value is still using it. For example, consider this incorrect version of the preceding program:

```
// An error generated by returning an object.
#include <iostream.h>
#include <string.h>
#include <stdlib.h>

class samp {
  char *s;
public:
  samp() { s = '\0'; }
  ~samp() { if(s) free(s); cout << "Freeing s\n"; }
  void show() { cout << s << "\n"; }
  void set(char *str);
};
```

```
// Load a string.
void samp::set(char *str)
{
  s = (char *) malloc(strlen(str));
  if(!s) {
    cout << "Allocation error\n";
    exit(1);
  }

  strcpy(s, str);
}

// Return an object of type samp.
samp input()
{
  char s[80];
  samp str;

  cout << "Enter a string: ";
  cin >> s;

  str.set(s);
  return str;
}

main()
{
  samp ob;

  // assign returned object to ob
  ob = input();  // This causes an error!!!!
  ob.show();

  return 0;
}
```

The output from this program is shown here:

```
Enter a string: Hello
Freeing s
Freeing s
Hello
Freeing s
Null pointer assignment
```

Notice that **samp**'s destructor function is called three times. First, it is called when the local object **str** goes out of scope when **input( )** returns. The second time ~**samp( )** is called is when the temporary object returned by **input( )** is destroyed.

Remember, when an object is returned from a function, an invisible (to you) temporary object is automatically generated which holds the return value. In this case, this object is simply a copy of **str**, which is the return value of the function. Therefore, after the function has returned, the temporary object's destructor is executed. Finally, the destructor for object **ob**, inside **main( )**, is called when the program terminates.

The trouble is that in this situation, the first time the destructor executes, the memory allocated to hold the string input by **input( )** is freed. Thus, not only do the other two calls to **samp**'s destructor try to free an already released piece of dynamic memory, but they destroy the dynamic allocation system in the process, as evidenced by the run-time message "Null pointer assignment." (Depending upon your compiler, the memory model used for compilation, and the like, you may or may not see this message if you try this program.)

The key point to be understood from this example is that when an object is returned from a function, the temporary object used to effect the return will have its destructor function called. Thus, you should avoid returning objects in which this situation is harmful. (As you will learn in Chapter 5, it is possible to use a copy constructor to manage this situation.)

EXERCISES

1. To illustrate exactly when an object is constructed and destructed when returned from a function, create a class called **who**. Have **who**'s constructor take one character argument that will be used to identify an object. Have the constructor display a message similar to this when constructing an object:

```
Constructing who #x
```

where **x** is the identifying character associated with each object. When an object is destroyed, have a message similar to this displayed:

```
Destroying who #x
```

where, again, **x** is the identifying character. Finally, create a function called **make_who( )** that returns a **who** object. Give each object a unique name. Note the output dislayed by the program.

2. Other than the incorrect freeing of dynamically allocated memory, think of a situation in which it would be improper to return an object from a function.

<hr>

3.4 *INTRODUCING FRIEND FUNCTIONS*

There will be times when you want a function to have access to the private members of a class without that function actually being a member of that class. Towards this end, C++ supports friend functions. A friend is not a member of a class but still has access to its private elements.

Two reasons that friend functions are useful have to do with operator overloading and the creation of certain types of I/O functions. You will have to wait until later to see these uses of a friend in action. However, a third reason for friend functions is that there will be times when you want one function to have access to the private members of *two or more* different classes. It is this use that is examined here.

A friend function is defined as a regular, nonmember function. However, inside the class declaration for which it will be a friend, its prototype is also included, prefaced by the keyword **friend**. To understand how this works, examine this short program:

```
// A example of a friend function.
#include <iostream.h>

class myclass {
  int n, d;
public:
  myclass(int i, int j) { n = i; d = j; }
  // declare a friend of myclass
  friend int isfactor(myclass ob);
};

/* Here is friend function definition. It returns true
   if d is a factor of n. Notice that the keyword
   friend is not used in the definition of isfactor().
*/
int isfactor(myclass ob)
{
  if(!(ob.n % ob.d)) return 1;
```

```
    else return 0;
}

main()
{
  myclass ob1(10, 2), ob2(13, 3);

  if(isfactor(ob1)) cout << "2 is a factor of 10\n";
  else cout << "2 is not a factor of 10\n";

  if(isfactor(ob2)) cout << "3 is a factor of 13\n";
  else cout << "3 is not a factor of 13\n";

  return 0;
}
```

In this example, **myclass** declares its constructor function and the friend **isfactor( )** inside its class declaration. Because **isfactor( )** is a friend of **myclass**, **isfactor( )** has access to the private parts of it. This is why, within **isfactor( )**, it is possible to directly refer to **ob.n** and **ob.d**.

It is important to understand that a friend function is not a member of the class for which it is a friend. Thus, it is not possible to call a friend function by using an object name and a class member access operator (a dot or arrow). For example, given the preceding example, this statement is wrong:

```
ob1.isfactor(); // wrong, isfactor is not a member function
```

Instead, friends are called just like regular functions.

Although a friend function has knowledge of the private elements of the class for which it is a friend, it may only access them through an object of the class. That is, unlike a member function of **myclass**, which can refer to **n** or **d** directly, a friend can access these variables only in conjunction with an object that is declared within or passed to the friend function.

 NOTE *The preceding paragraph brings up an important side issue. When a member function refers to a private element, it does so directly because a member function is executed only in conjunction with an object of that class. Thus, when a member function refers to a private element, the compiler knows which object that private element belongs to by the object that is linked to the function when that member function is called. However, a friend function is not linked to any object. It simply is granted access to the private elements of a class. Thus, inside the friend function, it is meaningless to refer to a private member without reference to a specific object.*

Because friends are not members of a class, they will typically be passed one or more objects of the class for which they are defined to operate upon. This is the case with **isfactor( )**. It is passed an object of **myclass**, called **ob**. However, because **isfactor( )** is a friend of **myclass**, it may access **ob**'s private elements. If **isfactor( )** had not been made a friend of **myclass**, it would not be able to access **ob.d** or **ob.n** since **n** and **d** are private members of **myclass**.

REMEMBER *A friend function is not a member and it may not be qualified by an object name. It must be called just like a normal function.*

A friend function is not inherited. That is, when a base class includes a friend function, that friend function is not a friend of a derived class.

One other important point about friend functions is that a friend function may be friends with more than one class.

EXAMPLES

1. One common (and good) use of a friend function occurs when two different types of classes have some quantity in common that needs to be compared. For example, consider the following program, which creates a class called **car** and a class called **truck**, each containing, as a private variable, the speed of the vehicle it represents:

```cpp
#include <iostream.h>

class truck; // a forward reference

class car {
  int passengers;
  int speed;
public:
  car(int p, int s) { passengers = p; speed = s; }
  friend int sp_greater(car c, truck t);
};

class truck {
  int weight;
  int speed;
public:
  truck(int w, int s) { weight = w, speed = s; }
  friend int sp_greater(car c, truck t);
};
```

```
/* Return positive if car speed faster than truck.
   Return 0 if speeds are the same.
   Return negative if truck speed faster than car.
*/
int sp_greater(car c, truck t)
{
  return c.speed-t.speed;
}

main()
{
  int t;
  car c1(6, 55), c2(2, 120);
  truck t1(10000, 55), t2(20000, 72);

  cout << "Comparing c1 and t1:\n";
  t = sp_greater(c1, t1);
  if(t<0) cout << "Truck is faster.\n";
  else if(t==0) cout << "Car and truck speed is the same.\n";
  else cout << "Car is faster.\n";

  cout << "\nComparing c2 and t2:\n";
  t = sp_greater(c2, t2);
  if(t<0) cout << "Truck is faster.\n";
  else if(t==0) cout << "Car and truck speed is the same.\n";
  else cout << "Car is faster.\n";

  return 0;
}
```

This program contains the function **sp_ greater( )**, which is a friend function of both the **car** and **truck** classes. (As stated, a function may be a friend of two or more classes.) This function returns positive if the **car** object is going faster than the **truck** object, zero if their speeds are the same, and negative if the **truck** is going faster.

This program illustrates one important C++ syntax element: the *forward reference*. Because **sp_ greater( )** takes parameters of both the **car** and the **truck** classes, it is logically impossible to declare both before including **sp_ greater( )** in either. Therefore, there needs to be some way to tell the compiler about a class name without actually declaring it. This is called a forward reference. In C++, to tell the compiler that an identifier is the name of a class, use a line like this before the class name is first used:

class *class-name*;

For example, in the preceding program, the forward reference is

```
class truck;
```

Now, **truck** can be used in the friend declaration of **sp_greater( )** without generating a compile-time error.

2. A function may be a member of one class and a friend of another. For example, here is the preceding example rewritten so that **sp_greater( )** is a member of **car** and a friend of **truck**:

```cpp
#include <iostream.h>

class truck; // a forward reference

class car {
  int passengers;
  int speed;
public:
  car(int p, int s) { passengers = p; speed = s; }
  int sp_greater(truck t);
};

class truck {
  int weight;
  int speed;
public:
  truck(int w, int s) { weight = w, speed = s; }

  // note new use of the scope resolution operator
  friend int car::sp_greater(truck t);
};

/* Return positive if car speed faster than truck.
   Return 0 if speeds are the same.
   Return negative if truck speed faster than car.
*/
int car::sp_greater(truck t)
{
  /* Since sp_greater() is member of car, only a
     truck object must be passed to it. */

  return speed-t.speed;
}

main()
{
  int t;
  car c1(6, 55), c2(2, 120);
  truck t1(10000, 55), t2(20000, 72);

  cout << "Comparing c1 and t1:\n";
  t = c1.sp_greater(t1);  // evoke as member function of car
  if(t<0) cout << "Truck is faster.\n";
```

```
      else if(t==0) cout << "Car and truck speed is the same.\n";
      else cout << "Car is faster.\n";

      cout << "\nComparing c2 and t2:\n";
      t = c2.sp_greater(t2); // evoke as member function of car
      if(t<0) cout << "Truck is faster.\n";
      else if(t==0) cout << "Car and truck speed is the same.\n";
      else cout << "Car is faster.\n";

      return 0;
}
```

Notice the new use of the scope resolution operator as it occurs in the friend declaration within the **truck** class declaration. In this case, it is used to tell the compiler that the function **sp_greater( )** is a member of the **car** class.

One easy way to remember how to use the scope resolution operator is that the class name followed by the scope resolution operator followed by the member name fully specifies a class member.

In fact, when referring to a member of a class, it is never wrong to fully specify its name. However, when an object is used to call a member function or access a member variable, the full name is redundant and seldom used. For example,

```
t = c1.sp_greater(t1);
```

can be written using the (redundant) scope resolution operator and the class name **car** like this:

```
t = c1.car::sp_greater(t1);
```

However, since **c1** is an object of type **car**, the compiler already knows that **sp_greater( )** is a member of the **car** class, making the full class specification unnecessary.

1. Imagine a situation in which two classes, called **pr1** and **pr2**, shown here, share one printer. Further, imagine that other parts of your program need to know when the printer is in use by an object of either of these two classes. Create a function called **inuse( )** that returns true when the printer

is being used by either and false otherwise. Make this function a friend of both **pr1** and **pr2**.

```
class pr1 {
  int printing;
  // ...
public:
  pr1() { printing = 0; }
  void set_print(int status) { printing = status; }
  // ...
};

class pr2 {
  int printing;
  // ...
public:
  pr2() { printing = 0; }
  void set_print(int status) { printing = status; }
  // ...
};
```

mastery
skills check

Before proceeding, you should be able to answer the following questions and perform the exercises:

1. What single prerequisite must be met in order for one object to be assigned to another?

2. Given this class fragment:

```
class samp {
  double *p;
public:
  samp(double d) {
    p = (double *) malloc(sizeof(double));
    if(!p) exit(1);  // allocation error
    *p = d;
```

```
    }
    ~samp() { free(p); }
    // ...
};

// ...
samp ob1(123.09), ob2(0.0);
// ...
ob2 = ob1;
```

what problem is caused by the assignment of **ob1** to **ob2**?

3. Given this class:

```
class planet {
    int moons;
    double dist_from_sun; // in miles
    double diameter;
    double mass;
public:
    //...
    double get_miles() { return dist_from_sun; }
};
```

create a function called **light( )** that takes as an argument an object of type **planet** and returns the number of seconds that it takes light from the sun to reach the planet. (Assume that light travels at 186,000 miles per second and that **dist_from_sun** is specified in miles.)

4. May the address of an object be passed to a function as an argument?

5. Using the **stack** class, write a function called **loadstack( )** that returns a stack that is already loaded with the letters of the alphabet (a-z). Assign this stack to another object in the calling routine and prove that it contains the alphabet. Be sure to change the stack size so it is large enough to hold the alphabet.

6. Explain why you must be careful when passing objects to a function or returning objects from a function.

7. What is a friend function?

This section checks how well you have integrated the material in this chapter with that from earlier chapters.

1. Functions may be overloaded as long as the number or type of their parameters differs. Overload **loadstack( )** from Exercise 5 of the Mastery Skills Check so that it takes an integer, called **upper**, as a parameter. In the overloaded version, if **upper** is 1, load the stack with the uppercase alphabet. Otherwise, load it with the lowercase alphabet.

2. Using the **strtype** class shown in Section 3.1, Example 3, add a friend function that takes as an argument a pointer to an object of type **strtype** and returns a pointer to the string pointed to by that object. (That is, have the function return **p**.) Call this function **get_string( )**.

3. Experiment: When an object of a derived class is assigned to another object of the same derived class, is the data associated with the base class also copied? To find out, use the following two classes and write a program that demonstrates what happens.

```
class base {
  int a;
public:
  void load_a(int n) { a = n; }
  int get_a() { return a; }
};

class derived : public base {
  int b;
public:
  void load_b(int n) { b = n; }
  int get_b() { return b; }
};
```

4

Arrays, Pointers, and References

T H I S chapter examines several important issues involving arrays of objects and pointers to objects. It concludes with a discussion of one of C++'s most important innovations: the reference. The reference is crucial to many C++ features, so a careful reading is advised.

review

skills check

Before proceeding, you should be able to correctly answer the following questions and do the exercises.

1. When one object is assigned to another, what precisely takes place?

2. Can any troubles or side effects occur when assigning one object to another? (Give an example.)

3. When an object is passed as an argument to a function, a copy of that object is made. Is the copy's constructor function called? Is its destructor called?

4. By default, objects are passed to functions by value, which means that what occurs to the copy inside the function is not supposed to affect the argument used in the call. Can there be a violation of this principle? If so, give an example.

5. Given the following class, create a function called **make_sum( )** that returns an object of type **summation**. Have this function prompt the user for a number and then construct an object having this value and return it to the calling procedure. Demonstrate that the function works.

```
class summation {
  int num;
  long sum; // summation of num
public:
  void set_sum(int n);
  void show_sum() {
    cout << num << " summed is " << sum << "\n";
  }
};

void summation::set_sum(int n)
{
  int i;
```

```
    num = n;

    sum = 0;
    for(i=1; i<=n; i++)
      sum += i;
}
```

6. In the preceding question, the function **set_sum( )** was not defined in line within the **summation** class declaration. Give a reason why this might be necessary for some compilers.

7. Given the following class, show how to add a friend function called **isneg( )**, which takes one parameter of type **myclass** and returns true if **num** is negative and false otherwise.

```
class myclass {
  int num;
public:
  myclass(int x) { num = x; }
};
```

8. Can a friend function be friends with more than one class?

4.1   ARRAYS OF OBJECTS

As has been stated several times, objects are variables and have the same capabilities and attributes as any other type of variable. Therefore, it is perfectly acceptable for objects to be arrayed. The syntax for declaring an array of objects is exactly like that used to declare an array of any other type of variable. Further, arrays of objects are accessed just like arrays of other types of variables.

EXAMPLES

1. Here is an example of an array of objects:

```
#include <iostream.h>

class samp {
  int a;
public:
  void set_a(int n) { a = n; }
  int get_a() { return a; }
};
```

```
main()
{
  samp ob[4];
  int i;

  for(i=0; i<4; i++) ob[i].set_a(i);

  for(i=0; i<4; i++) cout << ob[i].get_a( );

  cout << "\n";

  return 0;
}
```

This program creates a four-element array of objects of type **samp** and then loads each element's **a** with a value between 0 and 3. Notice how member functions are called relative to each array element. The array name, in this case **ob**, is indexed; then the member access operator is applied, followed by the name of the member function to be called.

2. If a class type includes a constructor, an array of objects can be initialized. For example, here **ob** is an initialized array:

```
// Initialize an array.
#include <iostream.h>

class samp {
  int a;
public:
  samp(int n) { a = n; }
  int get_a() { return a; }
};

main()
{
  samp ob[4] = { -1, -2, -3, -4 };
  int i;

  for(i=0; i<4; i++) cout << ob[i].get_a() << ' ';

  cout << "\n";

  return 0;
}
```

This program displays "-1 -2 -3 -4" on the screen. In this example, the values -1 through -4 are passed to the **ob** constructor function.

Actually, the syntax shown in the initialization list is shorthand for this longer form (first shown in Chapter 2):

```
samp ob[4] = { samp(-1), samp(- 2),
               samp(-3), samp(- 4) };
```

However, when initializing a single dimension, the form used in the program is more common (although, as you will see, this form will work only with arrays whose constructors take only one argument).

3. You may also have multi-dimensional arrays of objects. For example, here is a program that creates a two-dimensional array of objects and initializes them:

```
// Create a two-dimensional array of objects.
#include <iostream.h>

class samp {
  int a;
public:
  samp(int n) { a = n; }
  int get_a() { return a; }
};

main()
{
  samp ob[4][2] = {
    1, 2,
    3, 4,
    5, 6,
    7, 8
  };
  int i;


  for(i=0; i<4; i++) {
    cout << ob[i][0].get_a() << ' ';
    cout << ob[i][1].get_a() << "\n";
  }

  cout << "\n";

  return 0;
}
```

This program displays

```
1 2
3 4
5 6
7 8
```

4. As you know, a constructor can take more than one argument. When initializing an array of objects whose constructor takes more than one argument, you must use the alternative form of initialization mentioned earlier. Let's begin with an example:

```cpp
#include <iostream.h>

class samp {
  int a, b;
public:
  samp(int n, int m) { a = n; b = m; }
  int get_a() { return a; }
  int get_b() { return b; }
};

main()
{
  samp ob[4][2] = {
    samp(1, 2), samp(3, 4),
    samp(5, 6), samp(7, 8),
    samp(9, 10), samp(11, 12),
    samp(13, 14), samp(15, 16)
  };

  int i;

  for(i=0; i<4; i++) {
    cout << ob[i][0].get_a() << ' ';
    cout << ob[i][0].get_b() << "\n";
    cout << ob[i][1].get_a() << ' ';
    cout << ob[i][1].get_b() << "\n";
  }

  cout << "\n";

  return 0;
}
```

In this example, **samp**'s constructor takes two arguments. Here, the array **ob** is declared and initialized in **main( )** by using direct calls to **samp**'s constructor. This is necessary because the formal C++ syntax allows only one argument at a time in a comma-separated list. There is no way, for example, to specify two (or more) arguments per entry in the list. Therefore, when you initialize arrays of objects that have constructors that take more than one argument, you must use the "long form" initialization syntax rather than the "shorthand form."

NOTE *You can always use the long form of initialization even if the object takes only one argument. It's just that the short form is more convenient in this case.*

The preceding program displays

```
1 2
3 4
5 6
7 8
9 10
11 12
13 14
15 16
```

EXERCISES

1. Using the following class declaration, create a ten-element array and initialize the **ch** element with the values A through J. Demonstrate that the array does, indeed, contain these values.

```
#include <iostream.h>

class letters {
  char ch;
public:
  letters(char c) { ch = c; }
  char get_ch() { return ch; }
};
```

2. Using the following class declaration, create a ten-element array, initialize **num** to the values 1 through 10, and initialize **sqr** to **num**'s square.

```
#include <iostream.h>

class squares {
  int num, sqr;
public:
  squares(int a, int b) { num = a; sqr = b; }
```

```
      void show() {cout << num << ' ' << sqr << "\n"; }
    };
```

3. Change **ob**'s initialization in Exercise 1 so it uses the long form. (That is, invoke **ob**'s constructor explicitly in the initialization list.)

4.2   # *U*SING POINTERS TO OBJECTS

As discussed in Chapter 2, objects may be accessed via pointers. As you know, when using a pointer to an object, the object's members are referenced using the arrow (–>) operator instead of the dot (.) operator.

Pointer arithmetic for an object is the same as it is for any other data type: it is performed relative to the object. For example, when an object pointer is incremented, it points to the next object. When an object pointer is decremented, it points to the previous object.

EXAMPLE

1. Here is an example of object pointer arithmetic:

```
// Pointers to objects.
#include <iostream.h>

class samp {
  int a, b;
public:
  samp(int n, int m) { a = n; b = m; }
  int get_a() { return a; }
  int get_b() { return b; }
};

main()
{
  samp ob[4] = {
    samp(1, 2),
    samp(3, 4),
    samp(5, 6),
    samp(7, 8)
  };
  int i;

  samp *p;
```

```
      p = ob; // get starting address of array

      for(i=0; i<4; i++) {
        cout << p->get_a() << ' ';
        cout << p->get_b() << "\n";
        p++;  // advance to next object
      }

      cout << "\n";

      return 0;
    }
```

This program displays

```
1 2
3 4
5 6
7 8
```

As evidenced by the output, each time **p** is incremented, it points to the next object in the array.

EXERCISES

1. Rewrite Example 1 so it displays the contents of the **ob** array in reverse order.

2. Change Section 4.1, Example 3 so the two-dimensional array is accessed via a pointer. Hint: In C++, as in C, all arrays are stored contiguously, left to right, low to high.

4.3   *T*HE *this* POINTER

C++ contains a special pointer that is called **this**. **this** is a pointer that is automatically passed to any member function when it is called, and it is a pointer to the object that generates the call. For example, given this statement:

```
ob.f1();  // assume that ob is an object
```

the function **f1( )** is automatically passed a pointer to **ob**—which is the object that generates the call. This pointer is referred to as **this**.

It is important to understand that only member functions are passed a **this** pointer. For example, a friend does not have a **this** pointer.

EXAMPLE

1. As you have seen, when a member function references another member of a class, it does so without qualifying the reference with either a class or an object specification. For example, examine this short program, which creates a simple inventory class:

```
// Demonstrate the this pointer.
#include <iostream.h>
#include <string.h>

class inventory {
  char item[20];
  double cost;
  int on_hand;
public:
  inventory(char *i, double c, int o)
  {
     strcpy(item, i);
     cost = c;
     on_hand = o;
   }
   void show();
};

void inventory::show()
{
  cout << item;
  cout << ": $" << cost;
  cout << "  On hand: " << on_hand << "\n";
}

main()
{
  inventory ob("wrench", 4.95, 4);

  ob.show();

  return 0;
}
```

As you can see, within the constructor **inventory( )** and member function **show( )**, the member variables **item, cost,** and **on_hand** are referred to directly. This is because a member function can be called only when linked to an object. Therefore, the compiler knows which object's data is being referred to.

However, there is an even more subtle explanation. When a member function is called, it is automatically passed a **this** pointer to the object that evoked the call. Thus, the preceding program could be rewritten as shown here:

```
// Demonstrate the this pointer.
#include <iostream.h>
#include <string.h>

class inventory {
  char item[20];
  double cost;
  int on_hand;
public:
  inventory(char *i, double c, int o)
  {
    strcpy(this->item, i); // access members
    this->cost = c;   // through the this
    this->on_hand = o; // pointer
  }
  void show();
};

void inventory::show()
{
  cout << this->item; // use this to access members
  cout << ": $" << this->cost;
  cout << "  On hand: " << this->on_hand << "\n";
}

main()
{
  inventory ob("wrench", 4.95, 4);

  ob.show();

  return 0;
}
```

Here, the member variables of **ob** are accessed explicitly through the **this** pointer. Thus, within **show( )**, these two statements are equivalent:

```
cost = 123.23;
this->cost = 123.23;
```

In fact, the first form is, loosely speaking, a shorthand for the second.

While no C++ programmer would use the **this** pointer to access a class member as just shown, because the shorthand form is much easier, it is important to understand what the shorthand implies.

The **this** pointer has several uses, including aiding in overloading operators. This use will be detailed in Chapter 6. For now, the important thing to understand is that by default, all member functions are automatically passed a pointer to the object that evoked the call.

EXERCISE

1. Given the following program, convert all appropriate references to class members to explicit **this** pointer references.

```
#include <iostream.h>

class myclass {
  int a, b;
public:
  myclass(int n, int m) { a = n; b = m; }
  int add() { return a+b; }
  void show();
};

void myclass::show()
{
  int t;

  t = add(); // call member function
  cout << t << "\n";
}

main()
{
  myclass ob(10, 14);

  ob.show();

  return 0;
}
```

4.4 *U*SING *new* AND *delete*

Up to now, when dynamic memory needed to be allocated, you have been using **malloc( )** and you have been freeing allocated memory by using **free( )**. While these standard functions continue to be available in C++, C++ provides a safer and more convenient way to allocate and free memory. In C++, you may allocate memory using **new** and release it using **delete**. These operators take these general forms:

> *p-var* = new *type*;
> delete *p-var*;

Here, *type* is the type specifier of the object that you want to allocate memory for and *p-var* is a pointer to that type. **new** is an operator that returns a pointer to dynamically allocated memory that is large enough to hold an object of type *type*. **delete** releases that memory when it is no longer needed.

Like **malloc( )**, if there is insufficient available memory to fill an allocation request, **new** returns a null pointer. Also, **delete** must be called only with a pointer previously allocated by using **new**. If you call **delete** with an invalid pointer, the allocation system will be destroyed, possibly crashing your program.

Although **new** and **delete** perform functions similar to **malloc( )** and **free( )**, they have several advantages. First, **new** automatically allocates enough memory to hold an object of the specified type. You do not need to use **sizeof**, for example, to compute the number of bytes required. This reduces the possibility for error. Second, **new** automatically returns a pointer of the specified type. You do not need to use an explicit type cast the way you did when you allocated memory by using **malloc( )** (see the following note). Third, both **new** and **delete** may be overloaded, enabling you to easily implement your own custom allocation system. Fourth, it is possible to intialize a dynamically allocated object. Finally, you no longer need to include **malloc.h** (or **stdlib.h**) with your programs.

 NOTE *In C, no type cast is required when assigning the return value of **malloc( )** to a pointer because the **void *** returned by **malloc( )** is automatically converted into a pointer compatible with the type of pointer on the left side of the assignment. However, this is not the case in C++, which requires an explicit type cast when you use **malloc( )**. The reason for this difference is that it allows C++ to enforce more rigorous type checking as applied to function return types. However, the **new** operator performs this cast for you automatically.*

Now that **new** and **delete** have been introduced, they will be used instead of **malloc( )** and **free( )**.

1. As a short first example, this program allocates memory to hold an integer:

```cpp
// A simple example of new and delete.
#include <iostream.h>

main()
{
  int *p;

  p = new int; // allocate room for an integer

  // always make sure that allocation succeeded
  if(!p) {
    cout << "Allocation error\n";
    return 1;
  }

  *p = 1000;

  cout << "Here is integer at p: " << *p << "\n";

  delete p;   // release memory

  return 0;
}
```

Notice that the value returned by **new** is checked before it is used. You must never assume that the pointer returned by **new** is valid.

2. Here is an example that allocates an object dynamically:

```cpp
// Allocating dynamic objects.
#include <iostream.h>

class samp {
  int i, j;
public:
  void set_ij(int a, int b) { i=a; j=b; }
  int get_product() { return i*j; }
};

main()
{
  samp *p;

  p = new samp; // allocate object
  if(!p) {
```

```
            cout << "Allocation error\n";
            return 1;
        }

        p->set_ij(4, 5);

        cout << "Product is: " << p->get_product() << "\n";

        return 0;
    }
```

EXERCISES

1. Write a program that uses **new** to dynamically allocate a **float**, a **long**, and a **char**. Give these dynamic variables values and display their values. Finally, release all dynamically allocated memory by using **delete**.

2. Create a class that contains a person's name and telephone number. Using **new**, dynamically allocate an object of this class and put your name and phone number into these fields within this object.

4.5 *M̲ORE ABOUT new AND delete*

This section discusses two additional features of **new** and **delete**. First, dynamically allocated objects may be given initial values. Second, dynamically allocated arrays can be created.

You may give a dynamically allocated object an initial value by using this form of the **new** statement:

p-var = new *type* (*initial-value*);

To dynamically allocate a one-dimensional array, use this form of **new**:

p-var = new *type* [*size*];

After this statement has executed, *p-var* will point to the start of an array of *size* elements of the type specified. For various technical reasons, it is not possible to intialize an array that is dynamically allocated.

To delete a dynamically allocated array, use this form of **delete**:

delete [ ] _p-var;_

This syntax causes the compiler to call the destructor function for each element in the array. It does _not_ cause _p-var_ to be freed multiple times. _p-var_ is still freed only once.

NOTE _For older compilers, you may need to specify the size of the array that you are deleting between the square brackets of the_ **delete** _statement. This was required by the original definition of C++. However, the size specification is no longer needed._

EXAMPLES

1. This program allocates memory for an integer and initializes that memory:

```cpp
// An example of initializing a dynamic variable.
#include <iostream.h>

main()
{
  int *p;

  p = new int (9); // give initial value of 9

  if(!p) {
    cout << "Allocation error\n";
    return 1;
  }

  cout << "Here is integer at p: " << *p << "\n";

  delete p;  // release memory

  return 0;
}
```

As you should expect, this program displays the value 9, which is the initial value given to the memory pointed to by **p**.

2. The following program passes initial values to a dynamically allocated object:

```
// Allocating dynamic objects.
#include <iostream.h>

class samp {
  int i, j;
public:
  samp(int a, int b) { i=a; j=b; }
  int get_product() { return i*j; }
};

main()
{
  samp *p;

  p = new samp(6, 5); // allocate object with initialization
  if(!p) {
    cout << "Allocation error\n";
    return 1;
  }

  cout << "Product is: " << p->get_product() << "\n";

  delete p;

  return 0;
}
```

When the **samp** object is allocated, its constructor is automatically called and is passed the values 6 and 5.

3. The following program allocates an array of integers:

```
// A simple example of new and delete.
#include <iostream.h>

main()
{
  int *p;

  p = new int [5]; // allocate room for 5 integers

  // always make sure that allocation succeeded
  if(!p) {
    cout << "Allocation error\n";
    return 1;
  }

  int i;

  for(i=0; i<5; i++) p[i] = i;
```

```
    for(i=0; i<5; i++) {
      cout << "Here is integer at p[" << i << "]: ";
      cout << p[i] << "\n";
    }

    delete [] p;   // release memory

    return 0;
}
```

This program displays the following:

```
Here is integer at p[0]: 0
Here is integer at p[1]: 1
Here is integer at p[2]: 2
Here is integer at p[3]: 3
Here is integer at p[4]: 4
```

4. The following program creates a dynamic array of objects:

```
// Allocating dynamic objects.
#include <iostream.h>

class samp {
  int i, j;
public:
  void set_ij(int a, int b) { i=a; j=b; }
  int get_product() { return i*j; }
};

main()
{
  samp *p;
  int i;

  p = new samp [10]; // allocate object array
  if(!p) {
    cout << "Allocation error\n";
    return 1;
  }

  for(i=0; i<10; i++)
    p[i].set_ij(i, i);

  for(i=0; i<10; i++) {
    cout << "Product [" << i << "] is: ";
    cout << p[i].get_product() << "\n";
  }
  delete [] p;
```

```
    return 0;
}
```

This program displays the following:

```
Product [0] is: 0
Product [1] is: 1
Product [2] is: 4
Product [3] is: 9
Product [4] is: 16
Product [5] is: 25
Product [6] is: 36
Product [7] is: 49
Product [8] is: 64
Product [9] is: 81
```

5. The following version of the preceding program gives **samp** a destructor, and now when **p** is freed, each element's destructor is called:

```
// Allocating dynamic objects.
#include <iostream.h>

class samp {
  int i, j;
public:
  void set_ij(int a, int b) { i=a; j=b; }
  ~samp() { cout << "Destroying...\n"; }
  int get_product() { return i*j; }
};

main()
{
  samp *p;
  int i;

  p = new samp [10]; // allocate object array
  if(!p) {
    cout << "Allocation error\n";
    return 1;
  }

  for(i=0; i<10; i++)
    p[i].set_ij(i, i);

  for(i=0; i<10; i++) {
    cout << "Product [" << i << "] is: ";
    cout << p[i].get_product() << "\n";
  }

  delete [] p;
```

```
      return 0;
}
```

This program displays the following:

```
Product [0] is: 0
Product [1] is: 1
Product [2] is: 4
Product [3] is: 9
Product [4] is: 16
Product [5] is: 25
Product [6] is: 36
Product [7] is: 49
Product [8] is: 64
Product [9] is: 81
Destroying...
Destroying...
Destroying...
Destroying...
Destroying...
Destroying...
Destroying...
Destroying...
Destroying...
Destroying...
```

As you can see, **samp**'s destructor is called ten times—once for each element in the array.

EXERCISES

1. Show how to convert the following code into its equivalent that uses **new**.

   ```
   char *p;

   p = (char *) malloc(100);
   // ...
   strcpy(p, "This is a test");
   ```

   Hint: A string is simply an array of characters.

2. Using **new**, show how to allocate a **double** and give it an initial value of −123.0987.

REFERENCES

C++ contains a feature that is related to a pointer, called a *reference*. A reference is an implicit pointer that for all intents and purposes acts like another name for a variable. There are three ways that a reference can be used. First, a reference can be passed to a function. Second, a reference can be returned by a function. Finally, an independent reference can be created. Each of these applications of the reference is examined, beginning with reference parameters.

Without a doubt, the most important use of a reference is as a parameter to a function. To help you understand what a reference parameter is and how it works, let's first start with a program that uses a pointer (not a reference) as a parameter:

```
#include <iostream.h>

void f(int *n);  // use a pointer parameter

main()
{
  int i = 0;

  f(&i);

  cout << "Here is i's new value: " << i << '\n';

  return 0;
}

void f(int *n)
{
  *n = 100; // put 100 into the argument pointed to by n
}
```

Here, f( ) loads the value 100 into the integer pointed to by **n**. In this program, f( ) is called with the address of **i**, in **main**( ). Thus, after f( ) returns, **i** contains the value 100.

This program demonstrates how a pointer is used as a parameter to manually create a call-by-reference parameter-passing mechanism. In a C program, this is the only way to achieve a call-by-reference. However, in C++, you can completely automate this process by using a reference parameter. To see how, let's rework the previous program. Here is a version that uses a reference parameter:

```
#include <iostream.h>

void f(int &n); // declare a reference parameter

main()
{
  int i = 0;

  f(i);

  cout << "Here is i's new value: " << i << '\n';

  return 0;
}

// f() now uses a reference parameter
void f(int &n)
{
  // notice that no * is needed in the following statement
  n = 100; // put 100 into the argument used to call f()
}
```

Examine this program carefully. First, to declare a reference variable or parameter, you precede the variable's name with the **&**. This is how **n** is declared as a parameter to **f( )**. Now that **n** is a reference, it is no longer necessary—or even legal—to apply the * operator. Instead, each time **n** is used within **f( )**, it is automatically treated as a pointer to the argument used to call **f( )**. This means that the statement

```
n = 100;
```

actually puts the value 100 into the variable used to call **f( )**, which, in this case, is **i**. Further, when **f( )** is called, there is no need to precede the argument with the **&**. Instead, because **f( )** is declared as taking a reference parameter, the address to the argument is *automatically* passed to **f( )**.

To review, when you use a reference parameter, the compiler automatically passes the address of the variable used as the argument. There is no need (in fact, it is not allowed) to manually generate the address of the argument by preceding it with an **&**. Further, within the function, the compiler automatically uses the variable pointed to by the reference parameter. There is no need (and again, it is not allowed) to employ the *. Thus, a reference parameter fully automates the call-by-reference parameter-passing mechanism.

It is important to understand that you cannot change what a reference is pointing to. For example, if the statement

```
n++;
```

were put inside **f( )** (in the preceding program), **n** would still be pointing to **i** in **main( )**. Instead of incrementing **n**, this statement increments the value of the variable being referenced (in this case, **i**).

Reference parameters offer several advantages over their (more or less) equivalent pointer alternatives. First, from a practical point of view, you no longer need to remember to pass the address of an argument. When a reference parameter is used, the address is automatically passed. Second, in the opinion of many programmers, reference parameters offer a cleaner, more elegant interface than does the rather clumsy explicit pointer mechanism. Third, as you will see in the next section, when an object is passed to a function as a reference, no copy is made. This is one way to eliminate the troubles associated with the copy of an argument damaging something needed elsewhere in the program when its destructor function is called.

EXAMPLES

1. The classic example of passing arguments by reference is the **swap( )** function, which exchanges the values of the two arguments with which it is called. Here is a version of **swap( )** that uses references to swap its two integer arguments:

```cpp
#include <iostream.h>

void swap(int &x, int &y);

main()
{
  int i, j;

  i = 10;
  j = 19;

  cout << "i: " << i << ", ";
  cout << "j: " << j << "\n";

  swap(i, j);
```

```
  cout << "After swapping: ";
  cout << "i: " << i << ", ";
  cout << "j: " << j << "\n";

  return 0;
}

void swap(int &x, int &y)
{
  int t;

  t = x;
  x = y;
  y = t;
}
```

If **swap( )** had been written using pointers instead of references, it would have looked like this:

```
void swap(int *x, int *y)
{
  int t;

  t = *x;
  *x = *y;
  *y = t;
}
```

As you can see, by using the reference version of **swap( )**, the need for the * operator is eliminated.

2. Here is a program that uses the **round( )** function to round a **double** value. The value to be rounded is passed by reference.

```
#include <iostream.h>
#include <math.h>

void round(double &num);

main()
{
  double i = 100.4;

  cout << i << " rounded is ";
  round(i);
  cout << i << "\n";

  i = 10.9;
  cout << i << " rounded is ";
  round(i);
```

```
    cout << i << "\n";

    return 0;
}
void round(double &num)
{
  double frac;
  double val;

  // decompose num into whole and fractional parts
  frac =  modf(num, &val);

  if(frac < 0.5) num = val;
  else num = val+1.0;
}
```

round( ) uses a relatively obscure standard library function called **modf( )** to decompose a number into its whole number and fractional parts. The fractional part is returned; the whole number is put into the variable pointed to by its second parameter.

EXERCISES

1. Write a function called **neg( )** that reverses the sign of its integer parameter. Write the function two ways—first by using a pointer parameter and then by using a reference parameter. Include a short program to demonstrate their operation.

2. What is wrong with the following program?

```
// This program has an error.
#include <iostream.h>

void triple(double &num);

main()
{
  double d = 7.0;

  triple(&d);

  cout << d;
```

```
      return 0;
    }

    // Triple num's value.
    void triple(double &num)
    {
      num = 3 * num;
    }
```

3. Give some advantages of reference parameters.

PASSING REFERENCES TO OBJECTS

As you learned in Chapter 2, when an object is passed to a function by use of the default call-by-value parameter-passing mechanism, a copy of that object is made. Although the parameter's constructor function is not called, its destructor function is called when the function returns. As you should recall, this can cause serious problems in some instances—when the destructor frees dynamic memory, for example.

One solution to this problem is to pass an object by reference. (The other solution involves the use of copy constructors, which are discussed in Chapter 5.) When you pass the object by reference, no copy is made, and therefore its destructor function is not called when the function returns. Remember, however, that changes made to the object inside the function affect the object used as the argument.

 NOTE *It is critical to understand that a reference is not a pointer. Therefore, when an object is passed by reference, the member access operator remains the dot (.), not the arrow (–>).*

EXAMPLE

1. The following is an example that demonstrates the usefulness of passing an object by reference. First, here is a version of a program that passes an object of **myclass** by value to a function called **f( )**:

```
#include <iostream.h>

class myclass {
```

```
    int who;
public:
  myclass(int n) {
    who = n;
    cout << "Constructing " << who << "\n";
  }
  ~myclass() { cout << "Destructing " << who << "\n"; }
  int id() { return who; }
};

// o is passed by value.
void f(myclass o)
{
  cout << "Received " << o.id() << "\n";
}

main()
{
  myclass  x(1);

  f(x);

  return 0;
}
```

This function displays the following:

```
Constructing 1
Received 1
Destructing 1
Destructing 1
```

As you can see, the destructor function is called twice—first when the copy of object 1 is destroyed when f( ) terminates, and again when the program finishes.

However, if the program is changed so that f( ) uses a reference parameter, no copy is made and, therefore, no destructor is called when f( ) returns:

```
#include <iostream.h>

class myclass {
  int who;
public:
  myclass(int n) {
    who = n;
    cout << "Constructing " << who << "\n";
  }
  ~myclass() { cout << "Destructing " << who << "\n"; }
```

```
   int id() { return who; }
};

// Now, o is passed by reference.
void f(myclass &o)
{
  // note that . operator is still used!!!
  cout << "Received " << o.id() << "\n";
}

main()
{
  myclass  x(1);

  f(x);

  return 0;
}
```

This version displays the following output:

```
Constructing 1
Received 1
Destructing 1
```

REMEMBER _When accessing members of an object by using a reference, use the dot operator, not the arrow._

EXERCISE

1. What is wrong with the following program? Show how it can be fixed by using a reference parameter.

```
// This program has an error.
#include <iostream.h>
#include <string.h>
#include <stdlib.h>

class strtype {
  char *p;
public:
  strtype(char *s);
  ~strtype() { delete p; }
```

```
        char *get() { return p; }
};

strtype::strtype(char *s)
{
  int l;

  l = strlen(s);

  p = new char [l];
  if(!p) {
    cout << "Allocation error\n";
    exit(1);
  }

  strcpy(p, s);
}

void show(strtype x)
{
  char *s;

  s = x.get();
  cout << s << "\n";
}

main()
{
  strtype a("Hello"), b("There");

  show(a);
  show(b);

  return 0;
}
```

4.8   *R*ETURNING REFERENCES

A function may return a reference. As you will see in Chapter 6, returning a reference can be very useful when you are overloading certain types of operators. However, it also can be used to allow a function to be used on the left side of an assignment statement. The effect of this is both powerful and startling.

1. To begin, here is a very simple program that contains a function that returns a reference:

```
// A simple example of a function returning a reference.
#include <iostream.h>

int &f();
int x;

main()
{
   f() = 100;

   cout << x << "\n";

   return 0;
}

// Return an int reference.
int &f()
{
   return x;   // returns a reference to x
}
```

Here, function **f( )** is declared as returning a reference to an integer.
Inside the body of the function, the statement

```
return x;
```

does *not* return the value of the global variable **x**, but rather, it automatically returns **x**'s address (in the form of a reference). Thus, inside **main( )**, the statement

```
f() = 100;
```

puts the value 100 into **x** because **f( )** has returned a reference to it.
To review, function **f( )** returns a reference. Thus, when **f( )** is used on the left side of the assignment statement, it is this reference, returned by **f( )**, that is being assigned to. Since **f( )** returns a reference to **x** (in this example), it is **x** that receives the value 100.

2. You must be careful when returning a reference that the object you refer to does not go out of scope. For example, consider this slight reworking of function **f( )**:

```
// Return an int reference.
int &f()
{
  int x; // x is now a local variable
  return x;  // returns a reference to x
}
```

In this case, **x** is now local to f( ) and will go out of scope when f( )
returns. This effectively means that the reference returned by f( ) is useless.

 NOTE *Some C++ compilers will not allow you to return a reference
to a local variable. However, this type of problem can manifest itself in
other ways, such as when objects are allocated dynamically.*

3. One very good use of returning a reference is found when a bounded
array type is created. As you know, in C and C++, no array boundary
checking occurs. It is therefore possible to overflow or underflow an array.
However, in C++, you can create an array **class** that performs automatic
bounds checking.

The array **class** contains two core functions—one that stores information
into the array and one that retrieves information. These functions can check,
at run time, that the array boundaries are not overrun.

The following program implements a bounds-checking array for characters:

```
// A bounded array example.
#include <iostream.h>
#include <stdlib.h>

class array {
  int size;
  char *p;
public:
  array(int num);
  char &put(int i);
  char get(int i);
};

array::array(int num)
{
  p = new char [num];
  if(!p) {
    cout << "Allocation error\n";
    exit(1);
  }
  size = num;
}
```

```
// Put something into the array.
char &array::put(int i)
{
  if(i<0 || i>=size) {
    cout << "Bounds error!!!\n";
    exit(1);
  }
  return p[i];  // return reference to p[i]
}

// Get something from the array.
char array::get(int i)
{
  if(i<0 || i>=size) {
    cout << "Bounds error!!!\n";
    exit(1);
  }
  return p[i]; // return character
}

main()
{
  array a(10);

  a.put(3) = 'X';
  a.put(2) = 'R';

  cout << a.get(3) << a.get(2);
  cout << "\n";

  // now generate run-time boundary error
  a.put(11) = '!';

  return 0;
}
```

This example is a practical use of functions returning references, and you should examine it closely. Notice that the **put( )** function returns a reference to the array element specified by parameter **i**. This reference can then be used on the left side of an assignment statement to store something in the array—if the index specified by **i** is not out of bounds. The reverse is **get( )**, which returns the value stored at the specified index if that index is within range. This approach to maintaining an array is sometimes referred to as a *safe array*.

One other thing to notice about the preceding program is that the array is allocated dynamically by the use of **new**. This allows arrays of differing lengths to be declared.

As mentioned, the way that bounds checking is performed in this program is a practical application of C++. If you need to have array boundaries verified at run time, this is one way to do it. However, remember that bounds checking slows access to the array. Therefore, it is best to include bounds checking only when there is a real likelihood that an array boundary will be violated.

EXERCISES

1. Write a program that creates a two-by-three two-dimensional safe array of integers. Demonstrate that it works.

2. Is the following fragment valid? If not, why not?

```
int &f();
.
.
.
int *x;

x = f();
```

4.9   *INDEPENDENT REFERENCES AND RESTRICTIONS*

Although not commonly used, you can create an *independent reference*. An independent reference is a reference variable that in all effects is simply another name for another variable. Because references cannot be assigned new values, an independent reference must be initialized when it is declared.

 NOTE *Because independent references are sometimes used, it is important that you know about them. However, most programmers feel that there is no need for them and that they can add confusion to a program. Further, independent references exist in C++ largely because there was no compelling reason to disallow them. But for the most part, their use should be avoided.*

There are a number of restrictions that apply to all types of references. You cannot reference another reference. You cannot obtain the address of a reference. You cannot create arrays of references, and you cannot reference a bit-field. References must be initialized unless they are members of a class, are return values, or are function parameters.

 REMEMBER *References are similar to pointers, but they are not pointers.*

EXAMPLES

1. Here is a program that contains an independent reference:

   ```
   #include <iostream.h>

   main()
   {
     int x;
     int &ref = x; // create an independent reference

     x = 10;  // these two statements
     ref = 10;  // are functionally equivalent

     ref = 100;
     // this prints the number 100 twice
     cout << x << ' ' << ref << "\n";

     return 0;
   }
   ```

   In this program, the independent reference **ref** serves as a different name for **x**. From a practical point of view, **x** and **ref** are equivalent.

2. An independent reference can refer to a constant. For example, this is valid:

   ```
   const int &ref = 10;
   ```

   Again, there is little benefit in this type of reference, but you may see it from time to time in other programs.

EXERCISE

1. On your own, try to think of a good use for an independent reference.

mastery
skills check

At this point, you should be able to perform the following exercises and answer the questions.

1. Given the following class, create a two-by-five two-dimensional array and give each object in the array an initial value of your own choosing.

```
class a_type {
  double a, b;
public:
  a_type(double x, double y) {
    a = x;
    b = y;
  }
  void show() { cout << a << ' ' << b << "\n"; }
};
```

2. Modify your solution to the preceding problem so it accesses the array by using a pointer.

3. What is the **this** pointer?

4. Show the general forms for **new** and **delete**. What are some advantages of using them instead of **malloc( )** and **free( )**?

5. What is a reference? What is one advantage of using a reference parameter?

6. Create a function called **recip( )** that takes one **double** reference parameter. Have the function change the value of that parameter into its reciprocal. Write a program to demonstrate that it works.

This section checks how well you have integrated material in this chapter with that from the preceding chapters.

1. Given a pointer to an object, what operator is used to access a member of that object?

2. In Chapter 2, a **strtype** class was created that dynamically allocated space for a string. Rework the **strtype** class (shown here for your convenience) so it uses **new** and **delete**.

```cpp
#include <iostream.h>
#include <malloc.h>
#include <string.h>
#include <stdlib.h>

class strtype {
  char *p;
  int len;
public:
  strtype(char *ptr);
  ~strtype();
  void show();
};

strtype::strtype(char *ptr)
{
  len = strlen(ptr);
  p = (char *) malloc(len+1);
  if(!p) {
    cout << "Allocation error\n";
    exit(1);
  }
  strcpy(p, ptr);
}

strtype::~strtype()
{
  cout << "Freeing p\n";
  free(p);
}
```

```
void strtype::show()
{
  cout << p << " - length: " << len;
  cout << "\n";
}

main()
{
  strtype s1("This is a test"), s2("I like C++");

  s1.show();
  s2.show();

  return 0;
}
```

3. On your own, rework any program from the preceding chapter so that it uses a reference.

5

Function Overloading

chapter objectives

5.1 Overloading constructor functions

5.2 Creating and using a copy constructor

5.3 The **overload** anachronism

5.4 Using default arguments

5.5 Overloading and ambiguity

5.6 Finding the address of an overloaded function

I N this chapter you will learn more about overloading functions. Although this topic was introduced early in this book, there are several further aspects of it that need to be covered. Among the topics included are how to overload constructor functions, how to create a copy constructor, how to give functions default arguments, and how ambiguity can be avoided when overloading.

review

skills check

Before proceeding, you should be able to correctly answer the following questions and do the exercises.

1. What is a reference? Give two important uses.

2. Show how to allocate a **float** and an **int** by using **new**. Also, show how to free them by using **delete**.

3. What is the general form of **new** that is used to intialize a dynamic variable? Give a concrete example.

4. Given the following class, show how to initialize a ten-element array so that **x** has the values 1 through 10.

```
class samp {
  int x;
public:
  samp(int n) { x = n; }
  int getx() { return x; }
};
```

5. Give one advantage of reference parameters. Give one disadvantage.

6. Can dynamically allocated arrays be initialized?

7. Create a function called **mag( )** using the following prototype that raises **num** to the order of magnitude specified by **order**:

void mag(long &num, long order);

For example, if **num** is 4 and order is 2, then when **mag( )** returns, **num** will be 400. Demonstrate in a program that the function works.

5.1 OVERLOADING CONSTRUCTOR FUNCTIONS

It is possible—indeed, common—to overload a class's constructor function. (It is not possible to overload a destructor, however.) There are three main reasons why you will want to overload a constructor function: to gain flexibility, to support arrays, and to create copy constructors. The first two of these are discussed in this section. Copy constructors are discussed in the next section.

One thing to keep in mind as you study the examples is that a class's constructor function must provide a match for each way that an object of that class is declared. If no match is found, a compile-time error occurs. This is why overloaded constructor functions are so common to C++ programs.

EXAMPLES

1. Perhaps the most frequent use of overloaded constructor functions is to provide the option of either giving an object an initialization or not giving it one. For example, in the following program, **o1** is given an initial value, but **o2** is not. If you remove the constructor that has the empty argument list, the program will not compile because there is no constructor that matches a noninitialized object of type **samp**. The reverse is also true: If you remove the parameterized constructor, the program will not compile because there is no match for an initialized object. Both are needed for this program to compile correctly.

```
#include <iostream.h>

class myclass {
  int x;
public:
  // overload constructor two ways
  myclass() { x = 0; } // no initializer
  myclass(int n) { x = n; } // initializer
  int getx() { return x; }
};

main()
{
  myclass o1(10); // declare with initial value
  myclass o2; // declare without initializer
```

```
    cout << "o1: " << o1.getx() << '\n';
    cout << "o2: " << o2.getx() << '\n';

  return 0;
}
```

2. Another common reason constructor functions are overloaded is to allow both individual objects and arrays of objects to occur within a program. As you probably know from your own programming experience, it is fairly common to initialize a single variable, but it is not as common to initialize an array. (Quite often array values are assigned using information known only when the program is executing.) Thus, to allow uninitialized arrays of objects along with inititialized objects, you must include a constructor that supports initialization and one that does not.

   For example, assuming the class **myclass** from Example 1, both of these declarations are valid:

```
myclass ob(10);
myclass ob[5];
```

By providing constructors for both initialization and no initialization, variables can be initialized or not as needed. For example, this program declares two arrays of type **myclass**; one is initialized the other is not:

```
#include <iostream.h>

class myclass {
  int x;
public:
  // overload constructor two ways
  myclass() { x = 0; } // no initializer
  myclass(int n) { x = n; } // initializer
  int getx() { return x; }
};

main()
{
  myclass o1[10]; // declare array without initializers

  // declare with initializers
  myclass o2[10] = {1, 2, 3, 4, 5, 6, 7, 8, 9, 10};

  int i;

  for(i=0; i<10; i++) {
    cout << "o1[" << i << "]: " << o1[i].getx();
    cout << '\n';
    cout << "o2[" << i << "]: " << o2[i].getx();
```

```
    cout << '\n';
  }

  return 0;
}
```

In this example, all elements of **o1** are set to zero by the constructor function. The elements of **o2** are initialized as shown in the program.

3. Another reason for overloading constructor functions is to allow the programmer to select the most convenient method of initializing an object. To see how, first examine the next example, which creates a class that holds a calendar date. It overloads the **date( )** constructor two ways. One way, it accepts the date as a character string. The other way, the date is passed as three integers.

```
#include <iostream.h>
#include <stdio.h> // included for sscanf()

class date {
  int day, month, year;
public:
  date(char *str);
  date (int m, int d, int y) {
    day = d;
    month = m;
    year = y;
  }
  void show() {
    cout << month << '/' << day << '/';
    cout << year << '\n';
  }
};

date::date(char *str)
{
  sscanf(str, "%d%*c%d%*c%d", &month, &day, &year);
}

main()
{
  // construct date object using string
  date sdate("11/1/95");

  // construct date object using integers
  date idate(11, 1, 95);

  sdate.show();
  idate.show();
```

```
    return 0;
}
```

The advantage of overloading the **date( )** constructor, as shown in this program, is that you are free to use whichever version most conveniently fits the situation in which it is being used. For example, if a **date** object is being created from user input, then the string version is the easiest to use. However, if the **date** object is being constructed through some sort of internal computation, then the three-integer parameter version probably makes more sense.

Although it is possible to overload a constructor as many times as you want, doing so excessively has a destructuring effect on the class. From a stylistic point of view, it is best to overload a constructor to accommodate only those situations that are likely to occur frequently. For example, overloading **date( )** a third time so the date can be entered as three octal integers makes little sense. However, overloading it to accept an object of type **time_t** (a type that stores the system date and time) could be very valuable. (See the Mastery Skills Check exercises at the end of this chapter for an example that does just this.)

4. There is one other situation in which you will need to overload a class's constructor function: when a dynamic array of that class will be allocated. As you should recall from the preceding chapter, a dynamic array cannot be initialized. Thus, if the class contains a constructor that takes an initializer, you must include an overloaded version that takes no initializer. For example, here is a program that allocates an object array dynamically:

```
#include <iostream.h>

class myclass {
  int x;
public:
  // overload constructor two ways
  myclass() { x = 0; } // no initializer
  myclass(int n) { x = n; } // initializer
  int getx() { return x; }
  void setx(int n) { x = n; }
};

main()
{
  myclass *p;
  myclass ob(10);  // initialize single variable

  p = new myclass[10]; // can't use initializers here
  if(!p) {
```

```
        cout << "Allocation error\n";
        return 1;
      }

      int i;

      // initialize all elements to ob
      for(i=0; i<10; i++) p[i] = ob;

      for(i=0; i<10; i++) {
        cout << "p[" << i << "]: " << p[i].getx();
        cout << '\n';
      }

      return 0;
    }
```

Without the overloaded version of **myclass( )** that has no initializer, the **new** statement would have generated a compile-time error and the program would not have been compiled.

EXERCISES

1. Given this partially defined class

```
class strtype {
  char *p;
  int len;
public:
  char *getstring() { return p; }
  int getlength() { return len; }
};
```

add two constructor functions. Have the first one take no parameters. Have this one allocate 255 bytes of memory (using **new**), initialize that memory as a null string, and give **len** a value of 255. Have the other constructor take two parameters. The first is the string to use for initialization and the other is the number of bytes to allocate. Have this version allocate the specified amount of memory and copy the string to that memory. Perform all necessary boundary checks and demonstrate that your constructors work by including a short program.

2. In Exercise 2 of Chapter 2, Section 1, you created a stopwatch emulation. Expand your solution so that the **stopwatch** class provides both a parameterless constructor (as it does already) and an overloaded version that accepts the system time in the form returned by the standard function **clock( )**. Demonstrate that your improvement works.

3. On your own, think about ways in which an overloaded constructor function can be benefical to your own programming tasks.

CREATING AND USING A COPY CONSTRUCTOR

One of the more important forms of an overloaded constructor is the *copy constructor*. As numerous examples from the preceding chapters have shown, problems can occur when an object is passed to or returned from a function. As you will learn in this section, one way to avoid these problems is to define a copy constructor, which is a special type of overloaded constructor function.

To begin, let's restate the problem that a copy constructor is designed to solve. When an object is passed to a function, a bitwise (i.e., exact) copy of that object is made and given to the function parameter that recieves the object. However, there are cases in which this identical copy is not desirable. For example, if the object contains a pointer to allocated memory, then the copy will point to the *same* memory as does the original object. Therefore, if the copy makes a change to the contents of this memory, it will be changed for the original object too! Also, when the function terminates, the copy will be destroyed, causing its destructor to be called. This may lead to undesired side effects that further affect the original object.

A similar situation occurs when an object is returned by a function. Commonly, the compiler will generate a temporary object that holds a copy of the value returned by the function. (This is done automatically and is beyond your control.) This temporary object goes out of scope once the value is returned to the calling routine, causing the temporary's destructor to be called. However, if the destructor destroys something needed by the calling routine (for example, if it frees dynamically allocated memory), then trouble will follow.

At the core of these problems is the fact that a bitwise copy of the object is being made. To prevent these problems, you, the programmer, need to define precisely what occurs when a copy of an object is made so that you can avoid undesired side effects. The way you accomplish this is by creating a copy constructor. By defining a copy constructor, you can fully specify exactly what occurs when a copy of an object is made.

It is important for you to understand that C++ defines two distinct types of situations in which the value of one object is given to another. The first situation is assignment. The second situation is initialization, which can occur three ways:

▼ when an object is used to initialize another in a declaration statement,

▼ when an object is passed as a parameter to a function, and

▼ when a temporary object is created for use as a return value by a function.

The copy constructor only applies to initializations. It does not apply to assignments.

By default, when an initialization occurs, the compiler will automatically provide a bitwise copy. (That is, C++ automatically provides a default copy constructor that simply duplicates the object.) However, it is possible to specify precisely how one object will initialize another by defining a copy constructor. Once defined, the copy constructor is called whenever an object is used to initialize another.

 REMEMBER *Copy constructors do not affect assignment operations.*

All copy constructors have this general form:

classname (const *classname &obj*) {
   // body of constructor
}

Here, *obj* is a reference to an object that is being used to initialize another object. For example, assuming a class called **myclass**, and that **y** is an object of type **myclass**, then the following statements would invoke the **myclass** copy constructor:

```
myclass x = y; // y explicitly initializing x
func1(y); // y passed as a parameter
y = func2(); // y receiving a returned object
```

In the first two cases, a reference to **y** would be passed to the copy constructor. In the third, a reference to the object returned by **func2( )** is passed to the copy constructor.

1. Here is an example that illustrates why an explicit copy constructor function is needed. This program creates a very limited "safe" integer array type which prevents array boundaries from being overrun. Storage for each array is allocated using **new**, and a pointer to the memory is maintained within each array object.

```
/* This program creates a "safe" array class. Since space
   for the array is dynamically allocated, a copy constructor
   is provided to allocate memory when one array object is
   used to initialize another.
*/
#include "iostream.h"
#include "stdlib.h"

class array {
  int *p;
  int size;
public:
  array(int sz) { // constructor
    p = new int[sz];
    if(!p) exit(1);
    size = sz;
    cout << "Using 'normal' constructor\n";
  }
  ~array() {delete [] p;}

  // copy constructor
  array(const array &a);

  void put(int i, int j) {
    if(i>=0 && i<size) p[i] = j;
  }
  int get(int i) {
    return p[i];
  }
};

/* Copy constructor.

In the following case, memory is allocated specifically
for the copy, and the address of this memory is assigned
to p. Therefore, p is not pointing to the same dynamically
allocated memory as the original object:

*/
array::array(const array &a) {
```

```
    int i;

    p = new int[a.size];  // allocate memory for copy
    if(!p) exit(1);
    for(i=0; i<a.size; i++) p[i] = a.p[i]; // copy contents
    cout << "Using copy constructor\n";
}

main()
{
  array num(10);  // this calls "normal" constructor
  int i;

  // put some values into the array
  for(i=0; i<10; i++) num.put(i, i);

  // display num
  for(i=9; i>=0; i--) cout << num.get(i);
  cout << "\n";

  // create another array and initialize with num
  array x = num;  // this invokes copy constructor

  // display x
  for(i=0; i<10; i++) cout << x.get(i);

  return 0;
}
```

When **num** is used to initialize **x**, the copy constructor is called, memory
for the new array is allocated and stored in **x.p**, and the contents of **num**
are copied to **x**'s array. In this way, **x** and **num** have arrays that have the
same values, but each array is separate and distinct. (That is, **num.p** and
x.p do not point to the same piece of memory.) If the copy constructor
had not been created, then the bitwise initialization **array x = num** would
have resulted in **x** and **num** sharing the same memory for their arrays!
(That is, **num.p** and **x.p** would have, indeed, pointed to the same
location.)

The copy constructor is called only for initializations. For example,
the following sequence does not call the copy constructor defined in the
preceding program:

```
array a(10);
array b(10);

b = a; // does not call copy constructor
```

In this case, **b** = **a** performs the assignment operation.

2. To see how the copy constructor helps prevent some of the problems associated with passing certain types of objects to functions, consider this (incorrect) program:

```cpp
// This program has an error.
#include <iostream.h>
#include <string.h>
#include <stdlib.h>

class strtype {
  char *p;
public:
  strtype(char *s);
  ~strtype() { delete [] p; }
  char *get() { return p; }
};

strtype::strtype(char *s)
{
  int l;

  l = strlen(s);

  p = new char [l];
  if(!p) {
    cout << "Allocation error\n";
    exit(1);
  }

  strcpy(p, s);
}

void show(strtype x)
{
  char *s;

  s = x.get();
  cout << s << "\n";
}

main()
{
  strtype a("Hello"), b("There");

  show(a);
  show(b);

  return 0;
}
```

In this program, when a **strtype** object is passed to **show( )**, a bitwise copy is made (since no copy constructor has been defined) and put into parameter **x**. Thus, when the function returns, **x** goes out of scope and is destroyed. This, of course, causes **x**'s destructor to be called, which frees **x.p**. However, the memory being freed is the same memory that is still being used by the object used to call the function. This results in an error.

The solution to the preceding problem is to define a copy constructor for the **strtype** class that allocates memory for the copy when the copy is created. This approach is used by the following, corrected, program:

```
/* This program uses a copy constructor to allow strtype objects
   to be passed to functions. */
#include <iostream.h>
#include <string.h>
#include <stdlib.h>

class strtype {
  char *p;
public:
  strtype(char *s); // constructor
  strtype(const strtype &o); // copy constructor
  ~strtype() { delete [] p; } // destructor
  char *get() { return p; }
};

// "Normal" constructor
strtype::strtype(char *s)
{
  int l;

  l = strlen(s);

  p = new char [l];
  if(!p) {
    cout << "Allocation error\n";
    exit(1);
  }

  strcpy(p, s);
}

// Copy constructor
strtype::strtype(const strtype &o)
{
  int l;

  l = strlen(o.p);
```

```
        p = new char [1]; // allocate memory for new copy
        if(!p) {
          cout << "Allocation error\n";
          exit(1);
        }
        strcpy(p, o.p); // copy string into copy
    }

void show(strtype x)
{
    char *s;

    s = x.get();
    cout << s << "\n";
}

main()
{
    strtype a("Hello"), b("There");

    show(a);
    show(b);

    return 0;
}
```

Now, when **show( )** terminates and **x** goes out of scope, the memory
pointed to by **x.p** (which will be freed) is not the same as the memory still
in use by the object passed to the function.

1. The copy constructor is also invoked when a function generates the temporary
   object that is is used as the function's return value (for those functions that
   return objects). With this in mind, consider the following output:

```
Constructing normally
Constructing normally
Constructing copy
```

   This output was created by the following program. Explain why, and
   describe precisely what is occurring.

```
#include <iostream.h>

class myclass {
public:
  myclass();
  myclass(const myclass &o);
  myclass f();
};

// Normal constructor
myclass::myclass()
{
  cout << "Constructing normally\n";
}

// Copy constructor
myclass::myclass(const myclass &o)
{
  cout << "Constructing copy\n";
}

// Return an object.
myclass myclass::f()
{
  myclass temp;

  return temp;
}

main()
{
  myclass obj;

  obj = obj.f();

  return 0;
}
```

2. Explain what is wrong with the following program, and then fix it.

```
// This program contains an error.
#include <iostream.h>
#include <stdlib.h>

class myclass {
  int *p;
public:
  myclass(int i);
  ~myclass() { delete p; }
  friend int getval(myclass o);
```

```
    };

    myclass::myclass(int i)
    {
      p = new int;

      if(!p) {
        cout << "Allocation error\n";
        exit(1);
      }
      *p = i;
    }

    int getval(myclass o)
    {
      return *o.p; // get value
    }

    main()
    {
      myclass a(1), b(2);

      cout << getval(a) << " " << getval(b);
      cout << "\n";
      cout << getval(a) << " " << getval(b);

      return 0;
    }
```

3. In your own words, explain the purpose of a copy constructor and how it differs from a normal constructor.

5.3 *T*HE overload ANACHRONISM

When C++ was first invented, the keyword **overload** was required to create an overloaded function. Although **overload** is no longer needed, to maintain compatibility with older C++ programs, it is still one of C++'s keywords, and the old-style overloading syntax is still accepted by all C++ compilers. While you should avoid its use, you may still see **overload** used in existing programs, so it is a good idea to understand how it was applied.

The general form of **overload** is shown here:

overload *func-name*;

where *func-name* is the name of the function to be overloaded. This statement must precede the overloaded function declarations. For example, this tells the compiler that you will be overloading a function called **timer( )**:

```
overload timer;
```

 REMEMBER *Because* **overload** *is an anachronism in current C++ programs, its use should be avoided.*

5.4 USING DEFAULT ARGUMENTS

There is a feature of C++ that is related to function overloading. This feature is called a *default argument,* and it allows you to give a parameter a default value when no corresponding argument is specified when the function is called. As you will see, using default arguments is essentially a shorthand form of function overloading.

To give a parameter a default argument, simply follow that parameter with an equal sign and the value you want it to default to if no corresponding argument is present when the function is called. For example, this function gives its two parameters default values of 0:

```
void f(int a=0, int b=0);
```

Notice that this syntax is similar to giving a variable an initialization.

This function can now be called three different ways. First, it can be called with both arguments specified. Second, it can be called with only the first argument specified. In this case, **b** will default to zero. Finally, **f( )** can be called with no arguments, causing both **a** and **b** to default to zero. That is, the following invocations of **f( )** are all valid:

```
f();  // a and b default to 0
f(10);  // a is 10, b defaults to 0
f(10, 99)  // a is 10, b is 99
```

In this example, it should be clear that there is no way to default **a** and specify **b**.

When you create a function that has one or more default arguments, those arguments must be specified only once: either in the definition of the function or in its prototype, but not both. This rule applies even if you simply duplicate the same defaults. (This restriction is really just a quirk in C++'s formal syntax.)

As you can probably guess, all default parameters must be to the right of any parameters that don't have defaults. Further, once you begin to define default parameters, you may not specify any parameters that have no defaults.

One other point about default arguments: they must be constants or global variables. They cannot be local variables or other parameters.

EXAMPLES

1. Here is a program that illustrates the example described in the preceding discussion:

```
// A simple first example of default arguments.
#include <iostream.h>

void f(int a=0, int b=0)
{
  cout << "a: " << a << ", b: " << b;
  cout << '\n';
}
main()
{
  f();
  f(10);
  f(10, 99);

  return 0;
}
```

As you should expect, this program displays the following output:

```
a: 0, b: 0
a: 10, b: 0
a: 10, b: 99
```

Remember that once the first default argument is specified, all following parameters must have defaults as well. For example, this slightly different version of f( ) causes a compile-time error:

```
void f(int a=0, int b) // wrong! b must have default, too
{
  cout << "a: " << a << ", b: " << b;
  cout << '\n';
}
```

2. To understand how default arguments are related to function overloading, first consider the next program, which overloads the function called **box_area( )**. This function returns the area of a rectangle.

```
// Compute area of a box using overloaded functions.
#include <iostream.h>

// Return area of a non-square box.
double box_area(double length, double width)
{
  return length * width;
}

// Return area of a square box.
double box_area(double length)
{
  return length * length;
}

main()
{
  cout  << "10 x 5.8 box has area: ";
  cout << box_area(10.0, 5.8) << '\n';

  cout  << "10 x 10 square box has area: ";
  cout << box_area(10.0) << '\n';
  return 0;
}
```

In this program, **box_area( )** is overloaded two ways. In the first way, both dimensions of a rectangle are passed to the function. This version is used when the rectangle is not a square. However, when the rectangle is a square, only one argument need be specified, and the second version of **box_area( )** is called.

If you think about it, it is clear that in this situation there is really no need to have two different functions. Instead, the second parameter can be defaulted to some value that acts as a flag to **box_area( )**. When this value is seen by the function, it uses the **length** parameter twice. Here is an example of this approach:

```
// Compute area of a box using default arguments.
#include <iostream.h>

// Return area of a box.
double box_area(double length, double width = 0)
{
  if(!width) width = length;
  return length * width;
}

main()
{
```

```
cout  << "10 x 5.8 box has area: ";
cout << box_area(10.0, 5.8) << '\n';

cout  << "10 x 10 square box has area: ";
cout << box_area(10.0) << '\n';

return 0;
}
```

Here, zero is the default value of **width**. This value was chosen because no box will have a width of zero. (Actually, a rectangle with a width of 0 is a line.) Thus, if this default value is seen, **box_area( )** automatically uses the value in **length** for the value of **width**.

As this example shows, default arguments often provide a simple alternative to function overloading. (Of course, there are many situations in which function overloading is still required.)

3. It is not only legal to give constructor functions default arguments, it is also common. As you saw earlier in this chapter, many times a constructor is overloaded simply to allow both intialized and uninitialized objects to be created. In many cases, you can avoid overloading a constructor by giving it one or more default arguments. For example, examine this program:

```
#include <iostream.h>

class myclass {
  int x;
public:
/* Use default argument instead of overloading
   myclass's constructor. */
  myclass(int n = 0) { x = n; }
  int getx() { return x; }
};

main()
{
  myclass o1(10); // declare with initial value
  myclass o2; // declare without initializer

  cout << "o1: " << o1.getx() << '\n';
  cout << "o2: " << o2.getx() << '\n';

  return 0;
}
```

As this example shows, by giving **n** the default value of zero, it is possible to create objects that have explicit initial values and those for which the default value is sufficient.

4. Another good application for a default argument is found when a parameter is used to select an option. It is possible to give that parameter a default value that is used as a flag that tells the function to continue to use the previously selected option. For example, in the following program, the function **print( )** displays a string on the screen. If its **how** parameter is set to **ignore**, the text is displayed as is. If **how** is **upper**, the text is displayed in uppercase. If **how** is **lower**, the text is displayed in lowercase. When **how** is not specified, it defaults to –1, which tells the function to reuse the last **how** value.

```cpp
#include <iostream.h>
#include <ctype.h>

const int ignore = 0;
const int upper = 1;
const int lower = 2;

void print(char *s, int how = -1);

main()
{
  print("Hello There\n", ignore);
  print("Hello There\n", upper);
  print("Hello There\n"); // continue in upper
  print("Hello there\n", lower);
  print("That's all\n");   // continue in lower

  return 0;
}

/* Print a string in the specified case. Use
   last case specified if none is given.
*/
void print(char *s, int how)
{
  static int oldcase = ignore;

  // reuse old case if none specified
  if(how<0) how = oldcase;
  while(*s) {
    switch(how) {
      case upper: cout << (char) toupper(*s);
        break;
```

```
      case lower: cout << (char) tolower(*s);
        break;
      default: cout << *s;
    }
    s++;
  }
  oldcase = how;
}
```

This function displays the following output:

```
Hello There
HELLO THERE
HELLO THERE
hello there
that's all
```

5. Earlier in this chapter you saw the general form of a copy constructor. This general form was shown with only one parameter. However, it is possible to create copy constructors that take additional arguments, as long as the additional arguments have default values. For example, the following is also an acceptable form of a copy constructor:

```
myclass(const myclass &obj, int x=0) {
  // body of constructor
}
```

As long as the first argument is a reference to the object being copied, and all other arguments default, then the function qualifies as a copy constructor. This flexibility allows you to create copy constructors that have other uses.

6. Although default arguments are powerful and convenient, they can be misused. There is no question that, when used correctly, default arguments allow a function to perform its job in an efficient and easy-to-use manner. However, this is only the case when the default value given to a parameter makes sense. For example, if the argument is the value wanted nine times out ten, giving a function a default argument to this effect is obviously a good idea. However, in cases where no one value is more likely to be used than another, or when there is no benefit to using a default argument as a flag value, it makes little sense to provide a default value. Actually, providing a default argument when one is not called for destructures your program and tends to mislead anyone else who has to use that function.

   As with function overloading, part of becoming an excellent C++ programmer is knowing when to use a default argument and when not to.

1. In the C++ standard library is the function **strtol( )**, which has this prototype:

   long strtol(const char *start, const **end, int base);

   The function converts the numeric string pointed to by *start* into a long integer. The number base of the numeric string is specified by *base*. Upon return, *end* points to the character in the string immediately following the end of the number. The long integer equivalent of the numeric string is returned. *base* must be in the range 2 to 38. However, most commonly, base 10 is used.

      Create a function called **mystrtol( )** that works the same as **strtol( )** except that *base* is given the default argument of 10. (Feel free to use **strtol()** to actually perform the conversion. It requires the header **stdlib.h**.) Demonstrate that your version works correctly.

2. What is wrong with the following function protoype?

   char *f(char *p, int x = 0, char *q);

3. Most C++ compilers supply nonstandard functions that allow cursor positioning and the like. If your compiler supplies such functions, create a function called **myclreol( )** that clears the line from the current cursor position to the end of the line. However, give this function a parameter that specifies the number of character positions to clear. If the parameter is not specified, automatically clear the entire line. Otherwise, clear only the number of character positions specified by the parameter.

4. What is wrong with the following prototype, which uses a default argument?

   int f(int count, int max = count);

5.5 *OVERLOADING AND AMBIGUITY*

When overloading functions, it is possible to introduce ambiguity into your program. Overloading-caused ambiguity can be introduced through type conversions, reference parameters, and default arguments. Further, some types of ambiguity are caused by the overloaded functions themselves. Other types occur in the manner in which an overloaded function is called. Ambiguity must be removed before your program will compile without error.

1. One of the most common types of ambiguity is caused by C++'s automatic type conversion rules. As you know, when a function is called with an argument that is of a compatible (but not the same) type as the parameter it is being passed to, the type of the argument is automatically converted to the target type. This is sometimes referred to as *type promotion,* and is perfectly valid. In fact, it is this sort of type conversion that allows a function like **putchar( )** to be called with a character even though its argument is specified as an **int**. However, in some cases, this automatic type conversion will cause an ambiguous situation when a function is overloaded. To see how, examine this program:

```
// This program contains an ambiguity error.
#include <iostream.h>

float f(float i)
{
  return i / 2.0;
}

double f(double i)
{
  return i / 3.0;
}

main()
{
  float x = 10.09;
  double y = 10.09;

  cout << f(x); // unambiguous - use f(float)
  cout << f(y); // unambiguous - use f(double)

  cout << f(10); // ambiguous, convert 10 to double or float??

  return 0;
}
```

As the comments in **main( )** indicate, the compiler is able to select the correct version of **f( )** when it is called with either a **float** or a **double** variable. However, what happens when it is called with an integer? Does the compiler call **f(float)** or **f(double)**? (Both are valid conversions!) In either case, it is valid to promote an integer into either a **float** or a **double**. Thus, the ambiguous situation is created.

This example also points out that ambiguity can be introduced by the way an overloaded function is called. The fact is that there is no inherent ambiguity in the overloaded versions of **f( )** as long as each is called with an unambiguous argument.

2. Here is another example of function overloading that is not ambiguous in and of itself. However, when called with the wrong type of argument, C++'s automatic conversion rules cause an ambiguous situation.

```
// This program is ambiguous.
#include <iostream.h>

void f(unsigned char c)
{
  cout << c;
}

void f(char c)
{
  cout << c;
}

main()
{
  f('c');
  f(86); // which f() is called???

  return 0;
}
```

Here, when **f( )** is called with the numeric constant 86, the compiler cannot know whether to call **f(unsigned char)** or **f(char)**. Either conversion is equally valid, thus leading to ambiguity.

3. One type of ambiguity is caused when you try to overload functions in which the only difference is the fact that one uses a reference parameter and the other uses the default call-by-value parameter. Given C++'s formal syntax, there is no way for the compiler to know which function to call. Remember, there is no syntactical difference between calling a function that takes a value parameter and calling a function that takes a reference parameter. For example:

```
// An ambiguous program.

int f(int a, int b)
{
  return a+b;
}

// this is inherently ambiguous
int f(int a, int &b)
{
  return a-b;
}

main()
{
  int x=1, y=2;

  cout << f(x, y); // which version of f() is called???

  return 0;
}
```

Here, f(x, y) is ambiguous because it could be calling either version of the function. In fact, the compiler will flag an error before this statement is even specified because the overloading of the two functions is inherently ambiguous and no reference to them could be resolved.

4. Another type of ambiguity is caused when overloading a function in which one or more overloaded functions use a default argument. Consider this program:

```
// Ambiguity based on default arguments plus overloading.
#include <iostream.h>

int f(int a)
{
  return a*a;
}

int f(int a, int b = 0)
{
  return a*b;
}

main()
{
  cout << f(10, 2); // calls f(int, int)
  cout << f(10); // ambiguous - call f(int) or f(int, int)???
```

```
      return 0;
    }
```

Again, the overloading of the function is *not* inherently ambiguous. The call **f(10, 2)** is perfectly acceptable and unambiguous. However, the compiler has no way of knowing whether the call **f(10)** is calling the first version of **f( )** or the second version with **b** defaulting.

EXERCISE

1. Try to compile each of the preceding ambiguous programs. Make a mental note of the types of error messages they generate. This will help you recognize ambiguity errors when they creep into your own programs.

5.6 *F*INDING THE ADDRESS OF AN OVERLOADED FUNCTION

To conclude this chapter, you will learn how to find the address of an overloaded function. Just as in C, you can assign the address of a function (that is, its entry point) to a pointer and access that function via that pointer. A function's address is obtained by putting its name on the right side of an assignment statement without any parentheses or arguments. For example, if **zap( )** is a function, assuming proper declarations, this is a valid way to assign **p** the address of **zap( )**:

```
p = zap;
```

In C, any type of pointer may be used to point to a function because there is only one function that it may point to. However, in C++ the situation is a bit more complex because a function may be overloaded. Thus, there must be some mechanism that determines which function's address is obtained.

The solution is both elegant and effective. When obtaining the address of an overloaded function, it is *the way the pointer is declared* that determines which overloaded function's address will be obtained. In essence, the pointer's declaration is matched against those of the overloaded functions. The function whose declaration matches is the one whose address is used.

1. Here is a program that contains two versions of a function called **space( )**. The first version outputs **count** number of spaces to the screen. The second version outputs **count** number of whatever type of character is passed to **ch**. In **main( )**, two function pointers are declared. The first one is specified as a pointer to a function having only one integer parameter. The second is declared as a pointer to a function taking two parameters.

```
/* Illustrate assigning function pointers to
   overloaded functions. */
#include <iostream.h>

// Output count number of spaces.
void space(int count)
{
  for( ; count; count--) cout << ' ';
}


// Output count number of chs.
void space(int count, char ch)
{
  for( ; count; count--) cout << ch;
}

main()
{
  /* Create a pointer to void function with
     one int parameter. */
  void (*fp1)(int);

  /* Create a pointer to void function with
     one int parameter and one character parameter. */
  void (*fp2)(int, char);

  fp1 = space; // gets address of space(int)

  fp2 = space; // gets address of space(int, char)

  fp1(22);  // output 22 spaces
  cout << "|\n";

  fp2(30, 'x'); // output 30 xs
  cout << "|\n";

  return 0;
}
```

As the comments illustrate, the compiler is able to determine which overloaded function to obtain the address of based upon how **fp1** and **fp2** are declared.

To review: When you assign the address of an overloaded function to a function pointer, it is the declaration of the pointer that determines which function's address is assigned. Further, the declaration of the function pointer must exactly match one and only one of the overloaded functions. If it does not, ambiguity will be introduced, causing a compile-time error.

1. Following are two overloaded functions. Show how to obtain the address of each.

   ```
   int dif(int a, int b)
   {
     return a-b;
   }

   float dif(float a, float b)
   {
     return a-b;
   }
   ```

mastery
skills check

At this point you should be able to perform the following exercises and answer the questions.

1. Overload the **date( )** constructor from Section 5.1, Example 3, so that it accepts a parameter of type **time_t**. (Remember, **time_t** is a type

defined by the standard time and date functions found in your C++ compiler's library.)

2. What is wrong with the following fragment?

```
class samp {
   int a;
public:
   samp(int i) { a = i; }
   // ...
}:

// ...

main()
{
   samp x, y(10);

   // ...
}
```

3. Give two reasons why you may want (or need) to overload a class's constructor.

4. What is the general form of a copy constructor?

5. What type of operations will cause the copy constructor to be invoked?

6. Briefly, explain what the **overload** keyword does and why it is no longer needed.

7. Briefly, what is a default argument?

8. Create a function called **reverse( )** that takes two parameters. The first parameter, called **str**, is a pointer to a string that will be reversed upon return from the function. The second parameter is called **count** and it specifies how many characters of **str** to reverse. Give **count** a default value that, when present, tells **reverse( )** to reverse the entire string.

9. What is wrong with the following prototype?

   char *wordwrap(char *str, int size=0, char ch);

10. Explain some ways that ambiguity can be introduced when overloading functions.

11. What is wrong with the following fragment?

```
void compute(double *num, int divisor=1);
void compute(double *num);
// ...
compute(&x);
```

12. When assigning the address of an overloaded function to a pointer, what is it that determines which version of the function is used?

**cumulative
skills check**

This section checks how well you have integrated material in this chapter with that from the preceding chapters.

1. Create a function called **order( )** that takes two integer reference parameters. If the first argument is greater than the second argument, reverse the two arguments. Otherwise, take no action. That is, order the two arguments used to call **order( )** so that, upon return, the first argument will be less than the second. For example, given

```
int x=1, y=0;
order(x, y);
```

   x will be 0 and **y** will be 1.

2. Why are the following two overloaded functions inherently ambiguous?

```
int f(int a);
int f(int &a);
```

3. Explain why using a default argument is related to function overloading.

4. Given the following partial class, add the necessary constructor functions so that both declarations within **main( )** are valid. (Hint: You need to overload **samp( )** twice.)

```
class samp {
  int a;
public:
```

```
     // add constructor functions
     int get_a() { return a; }
};

main()
{
   samp ob(88); // init ob's a to 88
   samp obarray[10]; // noninitialized 10-element array

   // ...
}
```

5. Briefly explain why copy constructors are needed.

6

Introducing
Operator
Overloading

chapter objectives

6.1 The basics of operator overloading

6.2 Overloading binary operators

6.3 Overloading the relational and logical operators

6.4 Overloading a unary operator

6.5 Using friend operator functions

6.6 A closer look at the assignment operator

H I S chapter introduces another important C++ feature: operator overloading. This feature allows you to define the meaning of the C++ operators relative to classes that you define. By overloading operators relative to a class, you can seamlessly add new data types to your program.

review

skills check

Before proceeding, you should be able to correctly answer the following questions and do the exercises.

1. Show how to overload the constructor for the following class so that uninitialized objects can also be created. (When creating uninitialized objects, give **x** and **y** the value 0.)

```
class myclass {
  int x, y;
public:
  myclass(int i, int j) { x=i; y=j; }
  // ...
};
```

2. Using the class from Question 1, show how you can avoid overloading **myclass( )** by using default arguments.

3. What is wrong with the following declaration?

```
int f(int a=0, double balance);
```

4. What is wrong with these two overloaded functions?

```
void f(int a);
void f(int &a);
```

5. When is it appropriate to use default arguments? When is it probably a bad idea?

6. Given the following class definition, is it possible to dynamically allocate an array of these objects?

```
class test {
  char *p;
  int *q;
  int count;
public:
  test(char *x, int *y, int c) {
    p = x;
    q = y;
    count = c;
  }
  // ...
};
```

7. What is a copy constructor and under what circumstances is it called?

6.1   **THE BASICS OF OPERATOR OVERLOADING**

Operator overloading resembles function overloading. In fact, operator overloading is really just a type of function overloading. However, some additional rules apply. For example, an operator is always overloaded relative to a class. Other differences will be discussed as needed.

When an operator is overloaded, that operator loses none of its original meaning. Instead, it gains additional meaning relative to the class for which it is defined.

To overload an operator, you create an *operator function*. Most often an operator function is a member or a friend of the class for which it is defined. However, there is a slight diference between a member operator function and a friend operator function. The first part of this chapter discusses creating member operator functions. Then friend operator functions are discussed.

The general form of a member operator function is shown here:

return-type class-name::operator#(arg-list)
{
    // operation to be performed
}

Often, the return type of an operator function is the class for which it is defined. (However, an operator function is free to return any type.) The operator being overloaded is substituted for the #. For example, if the + is being overloaded, then the function name would be **operator+**. The contents of *arg-list* vary depending upon how the operator function is implemented and the type of operator being overloaded.

There are two important restrictions to remember when overloading an operator. First, the precedence of the operator cannot be changed. Second, the number of operands that an operator takes cannot be altered. For example, you cannot overload the / operator so that it takes only one operand.

Most C++ operators can be overloaded. The only operators that you cannot overload are shown here:

.   ::   .*   ?

Also, you may not overload the preprocessor operators. (The .* operator is highly specialized and is beyond the scope of this book.)

Remember that C++ defines operators very broadly, including such things as the [ ] subscript operators and the ( ) function call operators. However, this chapter concentrates on overloading the most commonly used operators.

Except for the =, operator functions are inherited by any derived class. However, a derived class is free to overload any operator it chooses (including those overloaded by the base class) relative to itself.

You have been using two overloaded operators: << and >>. These operators have been overloaded to perform console I/O. As mentioned, overloading these operators to perform I/O does not prevent them from performing their traditional jobs of left shift and right shift.

While it is permissible for you to have an operator function perform *any* activity—whether related to the traditional use of the operator or not—it is best to have an overloaded operator's actions stay within the spirit of the operator's traditional use. When you create overloaded operators that stray from this principle, you run the risk of substantially destructuring your program. For example, overloading the / so that the phrase "I like C++" is written to a disk file 300 times is a fundamentally confusing misuse of operator overloading.

The preceding paragraph notwithstanding, there will be times when you need to use an operator in a way not related to its traditional usage. The two best examples of this are the << and >> operators, which are overloaded for console I/O. However, even in these cases, the left and right arrows provide a visual "clue" to their meaning. Therefore, if you need to overload an operator in a nonstandard way, make the greatest effort possible to use an appropriate operator.

One final point: operator functions may not have default arguments.

6.2 *O*VERLOADING BINARY OPERATORS

When a member operator function overloads a binary operator, the function will have only one parameter. This parameter will receive the object that is on the right side of the operator. The object on the left side is the object that generates the call to the operator function and is passed implicitly by **this**.

It is important to understand that operator functions can be written with many variations. The examples here and elsewhere in this chapter are not exhaustive, but they do illustrate several of the most common techniques.

EXAMPLES

1. The following program overloads the + operator relative to the **coord** class. This class is used to maintain X,Y coordinates.

```cpp
// Overload the + relative to coord class.
#include <iostream.h>

class coord {
  int x, y; // coordinate values
public:
  coord() { x=0; y=0; }
  coord(int i, int j) { x=i; y=j; }
  void get_xy(int &i, int &j) { i=x; j=y; }
  coord operator+(coord ob2);
};

// Overload + relative to coord class.
coord coord::operator+(coord ob2)
{
  coord temp;
  temp.x = x + ob2.x;
  temp.y = y + ob2.y;

  return temp;
}

main()
{
  coord o1(10, 10), o2(5, 3), o3;
  int x, y;

  o3 = o1 + o2; // add two objects - this calls operator+()

  o3.get_xy(x, y);
  cout << "(o1+o2) X: " << x << ", Y: " << y << "\n";

  return 0;
}
```

This program displays the following:

```
(o1+o2) X: 15, Y: 13
```

Let's look closely at this program. The **operator+( )** function returns an object of type **coord** that has the sum of each operand's X coordinates in **x** and the sum of the Y coordinates in **y**. Notice that a temporary object called **temp** is used inside **operator+( )** to hold the result, and it is this object that is returned. Notice also that neither operand is modified. The reason for **temp** is easy to understand. In this situation (as in most), the **+** has been overloaded in a manner consistent with its normal arithmetic use. Therefore, it was important that neither operand be changed. For example, when you add 10+4, the result is 14, but neither the 10 nor the 4 is modified. Thus, a temporary object is needed to hold the result.

The reason that the **operator+( )** function returns an object of type **coord** is that it allows the result of the addition of **coord** objects to be used in larger expressions. For example, the statement

```
o3 = o1 + o2;
```

is valid only because the result of **o1+o2** is a **coord** object that can be assigned to **o3**. If a different type had been returned, this statement would have been invalid. Further, by returning a **coord** object, the addition operator allows a string of additions. For example, this is a valid statement:

```
o3 = o1 + o2 + o1 + o3;
```

Although there will be situations in which you want an operator function to return something other than an object for which it is defined, most of the time operator functions that you create will return an object of the class for which they are defined. (The major exception to this rule is when the relational and logical operators are overloaded. This situation is examined in the section "Overloading the Relational and Logical Operators" later in this chapter.)

One final point about this example. Because a **coord** object is returned, the following statement is also perfectly valid:

```
(o1+o2).get_xy(x, y);
```

Here, the temporary object returned by **operator+( )** is used directly. Of course, after this statement has executed, the temporary object is destroyed.

2. The following version of the preceding program overloads the – and the = operators relative to the **coord** class.

```
// Overload the +, -, and = relative to coord class.
#include <iostream.h>

class coord {
  int x, y; // coordinate values
public:
  coord() { x=0; y=0; }
  coord(int i, int j) { x=i; y=j; }
  void get_xy(int &i, int &j) { i=x; j=y; }
  coord operator+(coord ob2);
  coord operator-(coord ob2);
  coord operator=(coord ob2);
};

// Overload + relative to coord class.
coord coord::operator+(coord ob2)
{
  coord temp;

  temp.x = x + ob2.x;
  temp.y = y + ob2.y;

  return temp;
}

// Overload - relative to coord class.
coord coord::operator-(coord ob2)
{
  coord temp;

  temp.x = x - ob2.x;
  temp.y = y - ob2.y;

  return temp;
}

// Overload = relative to coord.
coord coord::operator=(coord ob2)
{
  x = ob2.x;
  y = ob2.y;

  return *this; // return the object that is assigned
}

main()
{
  coord o1(10, 10), o2(5, 3), o3;
  int x, y;
```

```
o3 = o1 + o2; // add two objects - this calls operator+()
o3.get_xy(x, y);
cout << "(o1+o2) X: " << x << ", Y: " << y << "\n";

o3 = o1 - o2; // subtract two objects
o3.get_xy(x, y);
cout << "(o1-o2) X: " << x << ", Y: " << y << "\n";

o3 = o1; // assign an object
o3.get_xy(x, y);
cout << "(o3=o1) X: " << x << ", Y: " << y << "\n";

return 0;
}
```

The **operator–( )** function is implemented similarly to **operator+( )**. However, it illustrates a crucial point when overloading an operator in which the order of the operands is important. When the **operator+( )** function was created, it did not matter which order the operands were in. (That is, A+B is the same as B+A.) However, the subtraction operation is order dependent. Therefore, to correctly overload the subtraction operator, it is necessary to subtract the operand on the right from the operand on the left. Because it is the left operand that generates the call to **operator–( )**, the subtraction must be in this order:

```
x - ob2.x;
```

 REMEMBER *When a binary operator is overloaded, the left operand is passed implicitly to the function and the right operand is passed as an argument.*

Now, look at the assignment operator function. The first thing you should notice is that the left operand (that is, the object being assigned a value) is modified by the operation. This is in keeping with the normal meaning of assignment. The second thing to notice is that the function returns ***this**. That is, the **operator=( )** function returns the object that is being assigned to. The reason for this is to allow a series of assignments to be made. As you should know, in C++, the following statement is syntactically correct (and, indeed, very commonly used):

```
a = b = c = d = 0;
```

By returning ***this**, the overloaded assignment operator allows objects of type **coord** to be used in a similar fashion. For example, this is perfectly valid:

```
o3 = o2 = o1;
```

Keep in mind that there is no rule that requires an overloaded assignment function to return the object that receives the assignment. However, if you want the overloaded = to behave relative to its class the way it does for the built-in types, then it must return *this.

3. It is possible to overload an operator relative to a class so that the operand on the right side is an object of a built-in type, such as an integer, instead of the class for which the operator function is a member. For example, here the + operator is overloaded to add an integer value to a **coord** object:

```
// Overload + for ob + int as well as ob + ob.
#include <iostream.h>

class coord {
  int x, y; // coordinate values
public:
  coord() { x=0; y=0; }
  coord(int i, int j) { x=i; y=j; }
  void get_xy(int &i, int &j) { i=x; j=y; }
  coord operator+(coord ob2); // ob + ob
  coord operator+(int i); // ob + int
};

// Overload + relative to coord class.
coord coord::operator+(coord ob2)
{
  coord temp;

  temp.x = x + ob2.x;
  temp.y = y + ob2.y;

  return temp;
}

// Overload + for ob + int
coord coord::operator+(int i)
{
  coord temp;

  temp.x = x + i;
  temp.y = y + i;
  return temp;
}

main()
{
  coord o1(10, 10), o2(5, 3), o3;
```

```
    int x, y;

    o3 = o1 + o2; // add two objects - this calls operator+(coord)
    o3.get_xy(x, y);
    cout << "(o1+o2) X: " << x << ", Y: " << y << "\n";

    o3 = o1 + 100; // add object + int - this call  operator+(int)
    o3.get_xy(x, y);
    cout << "(o1+100) X: " << x << ", Y: " << y << "\n";

    return 0;
}
```

It is important to remember that when overloading a member operator function so an object can be used in an operation involving a built-in type, the built-in type must be on the right side of the operator. The reason for this is easy to understand: It is the object on the left that generates the call to the operator function. However, what happens when the compiler sees the following statement?

```
o3 = 19 + o1;  // int + ob
```

There is no built-in operation defined to handle the addition of an integer to an object. The overloaded **operator+(int i)** function works only when the object is on the left. Therefore, this statement generates a compile-time error. (Soon you will see one way around this restriction.)

4. You can use a reference parameter in an operator function. For example, this is a perfectly acceptable way to overload the + operator relative to the **coord** class:

```
// Overload + relative to coord class using references.
coord coord::operator+(coord &ob2)
{
  coord temp;

  temp.x = x + ob2.x;
  temp.y = y + ob2.y;

  return temp;
}
```

One reason for using a reference parameter in an operator function is efficiency. Passing objects as parameters to functions often incurs a large amount of overhead and consumes a significant number of CPU cycles. However, passing the address of an object is always quick and efficient. If the operator is going to be used often, using a reference parameter will generally improve performance significantly.

Another reason for using a reference parameter is to avoid the trouble caused when a copy of an operand is destroyed. As you know from previous chapters, when an argument is passed by value, a copy of that argument is made. If that object has a destructor function, then when the function terminates, the copy's destructor is called. In some cases it is possible for the destructor to destroy something needed by the calling object. If this is the case, using a reference parameter instead of a value parameter is an easy (and efficient) way around the problem. Keep in mind, however, that you could also define a copy constructor that would prevent this problem in the general case.

EXERCISES

1. Relative to **coord**, overload the * and / operators. Demonstrate that they work.

2. Why would the following be an inappropriate use of an overloaded operator?

```
coord coord::operator%(coord ob)
{
  double i;

  cout << "Enter a number: ";
  cin >> i;
  cout << "root of " << i << " is ";
  cout << sqr(i);
}
```

3. On your own, experiment by changing the return types of the operator functions to something other than **coord**. See what type of errors result.

OVERLOADING THE RELATIONAL AND LOGICAL OPERATORS

It is possible to overload the relational and logical operators. When you overload the relational and logical operators so that they behave in their traditional manner, you will not want the operator functions to return an object of the class for which they are defined. Instead, they will return an integer that indicates either true or false. This not only allows these operator functions to return a true/false value, it also allows the operators to be integrated into larger relational and logical expressions that involve other types of data.

EXAMPLE

1. In the following program, the **==** and **&&** operators are overloaded:

```
// Overload the == and && relative to coord class.
#include <iostream.h>

class coord {
   int x, y; // coordinate values
public:
   coord() { x=0; y=0; }
   coord(int i, int j) { x=i; y=j; }
   void get_xy(int &i, int &j) { i=x; j=y; }
   int operator==(coord ob2);
   int operator&&(coord ob2);
};

// Overload the == operator for coord.
int coord::operator==(coord ob2)
{
   if(x==ob2.x && y==ob2.y) return 1;
   else return 0;
}

// Overload the && operator for coord.
int coord::operator&&(coord ob2)
{
   return ((x && ob2.x) && (y && ob2.y));
}

main()
{
   coord o1(10, 10), o2(5, 3), o3(10, 10), o4(0, 0);
```

```
  if(o1==o2) cout << "o1 same as o2\n";
  else cout << "o1 and o2 differ\n";

  if(o1==o3) cout << "o1 same as o3\n";
  else cout << "o1 and o3 differ\n";

  if(o1&&o2) cout << "o1 && o2 is true\n";
  else cout << "o1 && o2 is false\n";

  if(o1&&o4) cout << "o1 && o4 is true\n";
  else cout << "o1 && o4 is false\n";

  return 0;
}
```

EXERCISE

1. Overload the < and > operators relative to the **coord** class.

6.4   *OVERLOADING A UNARY OPERATOR*

Overloading a unary operator is similar to overloading a binary operator except
that there is only one operand to deal with. When you overload a unary operator
using a member function, the function has no parameters. Since there is only one
operand, it is this operand that generates the call to the operator function. There is
no need for another parameter.

EXAMPLES

1. The following program overloads the increment operator (++) relative to
   the **coord** class:

```
// Overload ++ relative to coord class.
#include <iostream.h>

class coord {
  int x, y; // coordinate values
```

```
public:
  coord() { x=0; y=0; }
  coord(int i, int j) { x=i; y=j; }
  void get_xy(int &i, int &j) { i=x; j=y; }
  coord operator++();
};

// Overload ++ for coord class.
coord coord::operator++()
{
  x++;
  y++;

  return *this;
}

main()
{
  coord o1(10, 10);
  int x, y;

  ++o1; // increment an object
  o1.get_xy(x, y);
  cout << "(++o1) X: " << x << ", Y: " << y << "\n";

  return 0;
}
```

Since the increment operator is designed to increase its operand by one, the overloaded **++** modifies the object it operates upon. The function also returns the object that it increments. This allows the increment operator to be used as part of a larger statement, such as this:

```
o2 = o1++;
```

As with the binary operators, there is no rule that says you must overload a unary operator so that it reflects its normal meaning. However, most of the time, this is what you will want to do.

2. In early versions of C++, when overloading an increment or decrement operator, there was no way to determine whether an overloaded **++** or **− −** preceded or followed its operand. That is, assuming the preceding program, these two statements would have been identical:

```
o1++;
++o1;
```

However, the modern specification for C++ (including the proposed ANSI C++ standard) has defined a way by which the compiler can distinguish between these two statements. To accomplish this, create two versions of the **operator++( )** function. The first is defined as shown in the preceding example. The second is declared like this:

```
coord coord::operator++(int notused);
```

If the **++** precedes its operand, the **operator++( )** function is called. However, if the **++** follows its operand, the **operator++(int notused)** function is used. In this case, **notused** will always be passed the value 0. Therefore, if the difference between prefix and postfix increment or decrement is important to your class objects, you will need to implement both operator functions.

 NOTE *The feature that allows C++ to distinguish between a prefix and a postfix application of the increment operators may not be supported by older compilers.*

3. As you know, the minus sign is both a binary and a unary operator in C++. You might be wondering how you can overload it so that it retains both of these uses relative to a class that you create. The solution is actually quite easy: you simply overload it twice, once as a binary operator and once as a unary operator. This program shows how:

```
// Overload the - relative to coord class.
#include <iostream.h>

class coord {
  int x, y; // coordinate values
public:
  coord() { x=0; y=0; }
  coord(int i, int j) { x=i; y=j; }
  void get_xy(int &i, int &j) { i=x; j=y; }
  coord operator-(coord ob2); // binary minus
  coord operator-(); // unary minus
};

// Overload - relative to coord class.
coord coord::operator-(coord ob2)
{
  coord temp;

  temp.x = x - ob2.x;
  temp.y = y - ob2.y;

  return temp;
}
```

```
// Overload unary - for coord class.
coord coord::operator-()
{
  x = -x;
  y = -y;
  return *this;
}

main()
{
  coord o1(10, 10), o2(5, 7);
  int x, y;

  o1 = o1 - o2; // subtraction
  o1.get_xy(x, y);
  cout << "(o1-o2) X: " << x << ", Y: " << y << "\n";

  o1 = -o1; // negation
  o1.get_xy(x, y);
  cout << "(-o1) X: " << x << ", Y: " << y << "\n";

  return 0;
}
```

As you can see, when the minus is overloaded as a binary operator, it takes one parameter. When it is overloaded as a unary operator, it takes no parameter. This difference in the number of parameters is what makes it possible for the minus to be overloaded for both operations. As the program indicates, when the minus sign is used as a binary operator, the **operator–(coord ob2)** function is called. When it is used as a unary minus, the **operator–( )** function is called.

EXERCISES

1. Overload the – – operator for the **coord** class. Create both its prefix and postfix forms.

2. Overload the + operator for the **coord** class so that it is both a binary operator (as shown earlier) and a unary operator. When it is used as a unary operator, have the + make any negative coordinate value positive.

USING FRIEND OPERATOR FUNCTIONS

As mentioned at the start of this chapter, it is possible to overload an operator relative to a class by using a friend rather than a member function. As you know, a friend function does not have a **this** pointer. In the case of a binary operator, this means that a friend operator function is passed both operands explicitly. For unary operators, the single operand is passed. All other things being equal, there is no reason to use a friend rather than a member operator function, with one important exception, which is discussed in the examples.

 REMEMBER *You cannot use a friend to overload the assigment operator. The assignment operator can be overloaded only by a member operator function.*

EXAMPLES

1. Here, **operator+( )** is overloaded for the **coord** class by using a friend function:

```
// Overload the + relative to coord class using a friend.
#include <iostream.h>

class coord {
  int x, y; // coordinate values
public:
  coord() { x=0; y=0; }
  coord(int i, int j) { x=i; y=j; }
  void get_xy(int &i, int &j) { i=x; j=y; }
  friend coord operator+(coord ob1, coord ob2);
};

// Overload + using a friend.
coord operator+(coord ob1, coord ob2)
{
  coord temp;

  temp.x = ob1.x + ob2.x;
  temp.y = ob1.y + ob2.y;

  return temp;
}

main()
```

```
{
  coord o1(10, 10), o2(5, 3), o3;
  int x, y;

  o3 = o1 + o2; // add two objects - this calls operator+()
  o3.get_xy(x, y);
  cout << "(o1+o2) X: " << x << ", Y: " << y << "\n";

  return 0;
}
```

Notice that the left operand is passed to the first parameter and the right operand is passed to the second parameter.

2. Overloading an operator by using a friend provides one very important feature that a member function does not have. Using a friend operator function, you can allow objects to be used in operations involving built-in types where the built-in type is on the left side of the operator. As you saw earlier in this chapter, it is possible to overload a binary member operator function such that the left operand is an object and the right operand is a built-in type. But it is not possible to use a member function to allow the built-in type to occur on the left side of the operator. For example, assuming an overloaded member operator function, the first statement shown here is legal; the second is not:

```
ob1 = ob2 + 10; // legal
ob1 = 10 + ob2; // illegal
```

While it is possible to organize such statements like the first, always having to make sure that the object is on the left side of the operand and the built-in type on the right can be a cumbersome restriction. The solution to this problem is to make the overloaded operator functions friends and define both possible situations.

As you know, a friend operator function is explicitly passed *both* operands. Thus, it is possible to define one overloaded friend function so that the left operand is an object and the right operand is the other type. Then, overload the operator again with the left operand being the built-in type and the right operand being the object. The following program illustrates this method:

```
// Use friend operator functions to add flexibility.
#include <iostream.h>

class coord {
  int x, y; // coordinate values
```

```
public:
  coord() { x=0; y=0; }
  coord(int i, int j) { x=i; y=j; }
  void get_xy(int &i, int &j) { i=x; j=y; }
  friend coord operator+(coord ob1, int i);
  friend coord operator+(int i, coord ob1);
};

// Overload for ob + int.
coord operator+(coord ob1, int i)
{
  coord temp;

  temp.x = ob1.x + i;
  temp.y = ob1.y + i;

  return temp;
}

// Overload for int + ob.
coord operator+(int i, coord ob1)
{
  coord temp;

  temp.x = ob1.x + i;
  temp.y = ob1.y + i;

  return temp;
}

main()
{
  coord o1(10, 10);
  int x, y;


  o1 = o1 + 10; // object + integer
  o1.get_xy(x, y);
  cout << "(o1+10) X: " << x << ", Y: " << y << "\n";

  o1 = 99 + o1; // integer + object
  o1.get_xy(x, y);
  cout << "(99+o1) X: " << x << ", Y: " << y << "\n";

  return 0;
}
```

As a result of overloading friend operator functions for both situations, both of these statements are now valid:

```
o1 = o1 + 10;
o1 = 99 + o1;
```

3. If you want to use a friend operator function to overload either the **++** or **− −** unary operator, you must pass the operand to the function as a reference parameter. This is because friend functions do not have **this** pointers. Remember that the increment and decrement operators imply that the operand will be modified. However, if you overload these operators by using a friend, the operand is passed by value as a parameter. Thus, any modifications that occur to the parameter inside the friend operator function will not affect the object that generated the call. And since no pointer to the object is passed implicitly (that is, there is no **this** pointer) when a friend is used, there is no way for the increment or decrement to affect the operand.

   However, by passing the operand to the friend as a reference parameter, changes that occur inside the friend function affect the object that generates the call. For example, here is a program that overloads the **++** operator by using a friend function:

```
// Overload the ++ using a friend.
#include <iostream.h>

class coord {
  int x, y; // coordinate values
public:
  coord() { x=0; y=0; }
  coord(int i, int j) { x=i; y=j; }
  void get_xy(int &i, int &j) { i=x; j=y; }
  friend coord operator++(coord &ob);
};

// Overload ++ using a friend.
coord operator++(coord &ob) // use reference parameter
{
  ob.x++;
  ob.y++;

  return ob; // return object generating the call
}

main()
{
  coord o1(10, 10);
  int x, y;

  ++o1;  // o1 is passed by reference
  o1.get_xy(x, y);
```

```
    cout << "(++o1) X: " << x << ", Y: " << y << "\n";

    return 0;
}
```

If you are using a modern compiler, you can also distinquish between the prefix and postfix forms of the increment or decrement operators when using a **friend** operator function in much the same way as you did when using member functions. You simply add an integer parameter when defining the postfix version. For example, here are the prototypes for both the prefix and postfix versions of the increment operator relative to the **coord** class.

```
coord operator++(coord &ob); // prefix
coord operator++(coord &ob, int notused); // postfix
```

If the **++** precedes its operand, the **operator++(coord &ob)** function is called. However, if the **++** follows its operand, the **operator++(coord &ob, int notused)** function is used. In this case, **notused** will be passed the value 0.

EXERCISES

1. Overload the – and the / operators for the **coord** class, using friend functions.

2. Overload the **coord** class so it can use **coord** objects in operations in which an integer value may be multiplied by each coordinate. Allow the operations to use either order: *ob * int* or *int * ob*.

3. Explain why the solution to Exercise 2 requires the use of friend operator functions.

4. Using a friend, show how to overload the – – relative to the **coord** class. Define both the prefix and postfix forms.

A CLOSER LOOK AT THE ASSIGNMENT OPERATOR

As you have seen, it is possible to overload the assignment operator relative to a class. By default, when the assignment operator is applied to an object, a bitwise copy of the object on the right is put into the object on the left. If this is what you want, there is no reason to provide your own **operator=( )** function. However, there are cases in which a strict bitwise copy is not desirable. You saw some examples of this in Chapter 3, in cases when an object allocates memory. In these types of situations, you will want to provide a special assignment operation.

EXAMPLE

1. Here is another version of the **strtype** class that you have seen in various forms in the preceding chapters. However, this version overloads the = operator so that the pointer **p** is not overwritten by an assignment operation.

```
#include <iostream.h>
#include <string.h>
#include <stdlib.h>

class strtype {
  char *p;
  int len;
public:
  strtype(char *s);
  ~strtype() {
    cout << "Freeing " << (unsigned) p << '\n';
    delete [] p;
  }
  char *get() { return p; }
  strtype &operator=(strtype &ob);
};

strtype::strtype(char *s)
{
  int l;

  l = strlen(s);

  p = new char [l];
  if(!p) {
```

```
      cout << "Allocation error\n";
      exit(1);
    }

  len = 1;
  strcpy(p, s);
}

// Assign an object.
strtype &strtype::operator=(strtype &ob)
{
  // see if more memory is needed
  if(len < ob.len) { // need to allocate more memory
    delete [] p;
    p = new char [ob.len];
    if(!p) {
      cout << "Allocation error\n";
      exit(1);
    }
  }
  len = ob.len;
  strcpy(p, ob.p);
  return *this;
}

main()
{
  strtype a("Hello"), b("There");

  cout << a.get() << '\n';
  cout << b.get() << '\n';

  a = b; // now p is not overwritten

  cout << a.get() << '\n';
  cout << b.get() << '\n';

  return 0;
}
```

As you can see, the overloaded assignment operator prevents **p** from being
overwritten. It first checks to see if the object on the left has allocated
enough memory to hold the string that is being assigned to it. If it hasn't,
that memory is freed and another portion is allocated. Then the string is
copied to that memory and the length is copied into **len**.

Notice two other important features about the **operator=( )** function.
First, it takes a reference parameter. This prevents a copy of the object on
the right side of the assignment from being made. As you know from
previous chapters, when a copy of an object is made when passed to a
function, that copy is destroyed when the function terminates. In this

case, destroying the copy would call the destructor function, which would free **p**. However, this is the same **p** still needed by the object used as an argument. Using a reference parameter prevents this problem.

The second important feature of the **operator=( )** function is that it returns a reference, not an object. The reason for this is the same as the reason it used a reference parameter. When a function returns an object, a temporary is created that is destroyed after the return is complete. However, this means that the temporary's destructor will be called, causing **p** to be freed, but **p** (and the memory it points to) is still needed by the object being assigned a value. Therefore, by returning a reference, you prevent a temporary object from being created.

NOTE _As you learned in Chapter 5, creating a copy constructor is another way to prevent both of the problems described in the preceding two paragraphs. But the copy constructor may not be as efficient a solution as using a reference parameter and a reference return type. This is because using a reference prevents the overhead associated with copying an object in either circumstance. As you can see, there are often several ways to accomplish the same end in C++. Learning to choose between them is part of becoming an excellent C++ programmer._

EXERCISE

1. Given the following class declaration, fill in all the details that will create a "safe" array type. Also, overload the assignment operator so that the allocated memory of each array is not accidentally destroyed. (Refer to Chapter 4 if you can't remember how to create a "safe" array.)

```
class dynarray {
  int *p;
  int size;
public:
  dynarray(int s);
  int &put(int i);
  int get(int i);
  // create operator=() function
};
```

mastery
skills check

At this point, you should be able to perform the following exercises and answer the questions.

1. Overload the >> and << operators relative to the **coord** class so that the following types of operations are allowed:

```
ob << integer
ob >> integer
```

Make sure your operators shift the **x** and **y** values by the amount specified.

2. Given the class

```
class three_d {
  int x, y, z;
public:
  three_d(int i, int j, int k)
  {
    x = i; y = j; z = k;
  }
  three_d() { x=0; y=0; z=0; }
  void get(int &i, int &j, int &k)
  {
    i = x; j = y; k = z;
  }
};
```

overload the +, −, ++, and −− operators for this class. (For the increment and decrement operators, overload only the prefix form.)

3. Rewrite your answer to Question 2 so it uses reference parameters instead of value parameters to the operator functions. (Hint: You will need to use friend functions for the increment and decrement operators.)

4. How do friend operator functions differ from member operator functions?

5. Explain why you may need to overload the assignment operator.

6. Can **operator=( )** be a friend function?

7. Overload the + for the **three_d** class so that it accepts the following types of operations:

```
ob + double;
double + ob;
```

8. Overload the ==, !=, and || operators relative to the **three_d** class.

cumulative
skills check

This section checks how well you have integrated material in this chapter with that from the preceding chapters.

1. Create a **strtype** class that allows the following types of operators:

   ▼ string concatenation using the + operator

   ▼ string assignment using the = operator

   ▼ string comparisons using <, >, and ==

   Feel free to use fixed-length strings. This is a challenging assignment, but with some thought (and experimentation), you should be able to accomplish it.

7

Inheritance

Y O U were introduced to the concept of inheritance earlier in this book. Now it is time to explore it more thoroughly. Inheritance is one of the three principles of OOP and, as such, it is an important feature of C++. Inheritance, in C++, not only supports the concept of hierarchical classification; in Chapter 10 you will learn how inheritance provides support for polymorphism, another principal feature of OOP. The topics covered in this chapter include base class access control and the **protected** access specifier, inheriting multiple base classes, passing arguments to base class constructors, and virtual base classes.

review

skills check

Before proceeding, you should be able to correctly answer the following questions and do the exercises.

1. When an operator is overloaded, does it lose any of its original functionality?

2. Must an operator be overloaded relative to a class?

3. Can the precedence of an overloaded operator be changed? Can the number of operands be altered?

4. Given the following partially completed program, fill in the needed operator functions:

```cpp
#include <iostream.h>

class array {
  int nums[10];
public:
  array();
  void set(int n[10]);
  void show();
  array operator+(array ob2);
  array operator-(array ob2);
  int operator==(array ob2);
};

array::array()
{
  int i;
```

```
  for(i=0; i<10; i++) nums[i] = 0;
}

void array::set(int *n)
{
  int i;

  for(i=0; i<10; i++) nums[i] = n[i];
}

void array::show()
{
  int i;

  for(i=0; i<10; i++)
    cout << nums[i] << ' ';

  cout << "\n";
}

// Fill in operator functions.

main()
{
  array o1, o2, o3;

  int i[10] = {1, 2, 3, 4, 5, 6, 7, 8, 9, 10 };

  o1.set(i);
  o2.set(i);

  o3 = o1 + o2;
  o3.show();

  o3 = o1 - o3;
  o3.show();

  if(o1==o2) cout << "o1 equals o2\n";
  else cout << "o1 does not equal o2\n";

  if(o1==o3) cout << "o1 equals o3\n";
  else cout << "o1 does not equal o3\n";

  return 0;
}
```

Have the overloaded + add each element of each operand. Have the overloaded − subtract each element of the right operand from the left. Have the overloaded = = return true if each element of each operand is the same and return false otherwise.

5. Convert the solution to Exercise 4 so it overloads the operators by using friend functions.

6. Using the class and support functions from Exercise 4, overload the **++** operator by using a member function and overload the **– –** operator by using a friend. (Overload only the prefix forms of **++** and **– –**.)

7. Can the assignment operator be overloaded by using a friend function?

7.1 *B*ASE CLASS ACCESS CONTROL

When one class inherits another, it uses this general form:

class *derived-class-name* : *access base-class-name* {
  // ...
}

Here, *access* is one of three keywords: **public**, **private**, or **protected**. A discussion of the **protected** access specifier is deferred until the next section of this chapter. The other two are discussed here.

The access specifier determines how elements of the base class are inherited by the derived class. When the access specifier for the inherited base class is **public**, all public members of the base become public members of the derived class. If the access specifier is **private**, all public members of the base class become private members of the derived class. In either case, any private members of the base remain private to it and are inaccessible by the derived class.

It is important to understand that if the access specifier is **private**, then public members of the base become private members of the derived class, but these members are still accessible by member functions of the derived class.

EXAMPLES

1. Here is a short base class and a derived class that inherits it (as public):

```
#include <iostream.h>

class base {
  int x;
public:
  void setx(int n) { x = n; }
  void showx() { cout << x << '\n'; }
};
```

```
// Inherit as public.
class derived : public base {
  int y;
public:
  void sety(int n) { y = n; }
  void showy() { cout << y << '\n'; }
};

main()
{
  derived ob;

  ob.setx(10); // access member of base class
  ob.sety(20); // access member of derived class

  ob.showx(); // access member of base class
  ob.showy(); // access member of derived class

  return 0;
}
```

As this program illustrates, because **base** is inherited as public, the public members of **base** – – **setx( )** and **showx( )** – – become public members of **derived** and are, therefore, accessible by any other part of the program. Specifically, they are legally called within **main( )**.

2. It is important to understand that just because a derived class inherits a base as public, it does not mean that the derived class has access to the base's private members. For example, this addition to **derived** from the preceding example is incorrect:

```
class base {
  int x;
public:
  void setx(int n) { x = n; }
  void showx() { cout << x << '\n'; }
};

// Inherit as public - this has an error!
class derived : public base {
  int y;
public:
  void sety(int n) { y = n; }

  /* Cannot access private member of base class.
     x is a private member of base and not available
     within derived. */
  void show_sum() { cout << x+y << '\n'; } // Error!
```

```
void showy() { cout << y << '\n'; }
};
```

In this example, the **derived** class attempts to access **x**, which is a private member of **base**. However, this is an error because the private parts of the base class remain private to it *no matter how it is inherited.*

3. Here is the program shown in Example 1 that inherits **base** as private. This change causes the program to be in error, as indicated in the comments.

```
// This program contains an error.
#include <iostream.h>

class base {
  int x;
public:
  void setx(int n) { x = n; }
  void showx() { cout << x << '\n'; }
};

// Inherit base as private.
class derived : private base {
  int y;
public:
  void sety(int n) { y = n; }
  void showy() { cout << y << '\n'; }
};

main()
{
  derived ob;

  ob.setx(10); // ERROR - now private to derived class
  ob.sety(20); // access member of derived class - OK

  ob.showx(); // ERROR - now private to derived class
  ob.showy(); // access member of derived class - OK

  return 0;
}
```

As the comments in this (incorrect) program illustrate, both **showx( )** and **setx( )** become private to **derived** and are not accessible outside of it.

It is important to understand that **showx( )** and **setx( )** are still public within **base** no matter how they are inherited by some derived class. This means that an object of type **base** could access these functions anywhere.

However, relative to objects of type **derived**, they become private. For example, given this fragment:

```
base base_ob;

base_ob.setx(1); // is legal because base_ob is of type base
```

the call to **setx( )** is legal because **setx( )** is public within **base**.

4. As stated, even though public members of a base class become private members of a derived class when inherited using the **private** specifier, they are still accessible *within* the derived class. For example, here is a "fixed" version of the preceding program:

```
// This program is fixed.
#include <iostream.h>

class base {
  int x;
public:
  void setx(int n) { x = n; }
  void showx() { cout << x << '\n'; }
};

// Inherit base as private.
class derived : private base {
  int y;
public:
  // setx is accessible from within derived
  void setxy(int n, int m) { setx(n); y = m; }
  // showx is accessible from within derived
  void showxy() { showx(); cout << y << '\n'; }
};

main()
{
  derived ob;

  ob.setxy(10, 20);

  ob.showxy();

  return 0;
}
```

In this case, the functions **setx( )** and **showx( )** are accessed inside the derived class, which is perfectly legal because they are private members of that class.

EXERCISES

1. Examine this skeleton:

```cpp
#include <iostream.h>

class mybase {
  int a, b;
public:
  int c;
  void setab(int i, int j) { a = i; b = j; }
  void getab(int &i, int &j) { i = a; j = b; }
};

class derived1 : public mybase {
// ...
};

class derived2 : private mybase {
// ...
};

main()
{
  derived1 o1;
  derived2 o2;
  int i, j;

  // ...
}
```

Within **main( )**, which of the following statements are legal?

A. `o1.getab(i, j)`
B. `o2.getab(i, j);`
C. `o1.c = 10;`
D. `o2.c = 10;`

2. What happens when a public member is inherited as public? What happens when it is inherited as private?

3. If you have not done so, try all the examples presented in this section. On your own, try various changes relative to the access specifiers and observe the results.

7.2   USING PROTECTED MEMBERS

As you know from the preceding section, a derived class does not have access to the private members of the base class. This means that if the derived class needs access to some member of the base, then that member must be public. However, there will be times when you want to keep a member of a base class private but still allow a derived class access to it. To accomplish this goal, C++ includes the **protected** access specifier.

The **protected** access specifier is equivalent to the **private** specifier with the sole exception that protected members of a base class are accessible to members of any class derived from that base. Outside the base or derived classes, protected members are not accessible.

The **protected** access specifer may occur anywhere in the class declaration, although typically it occurs after the (default) private members are declared and before the public members. The full general form of a class declaration is shown here:

```
class class-name {
  // private members
protected: // optional
  // protected members
public:
  // public members
};
```

When a protected member of a base class is inherited as **public** by the derived class, it becomes a protected member of the derived class. If the base is inherited as **private**, then a protected member of the base becomes a private member of the derived class.

A base class may also be inherited as **protected** by a derived class. When this is the case, public and protected members of the base class become protected members of the derived class. (Of course, private members of the base class remain private to it, and are not accessible by the derived class.)

The **protected** access specifier may also be used with structures and unions.

1. This program illustrates how public, private, and protected members of a class may be accessed:

```
#include <iostream.h>

class samp {
  // private by default
  int a;
protected: // still private relative to samp
  int b;
public:
  int c;

  samp(int n, int m) { a = n; b = m; }
  int geta() { return a; }
  int getb() { return b; }
};

main()
{
  samp ob(10, 20);

  // ob.b = 99;  Error! b is protected and thus private
  ob.c = 30; // OK, c is public

  cout << ob.geta() << ' ';
  cout << ob.getb() << ' ' << ob.c << '\n';

  return 0;
}
```

As you can see, the commented-out line is not permissible in **main( )** because **b** is protected and is thus still private to **samp**.

2. The following program illustrates what occurs when protected members are inherited as public:

```
#include <iostream.h>

class base {
protected:  // private to base
  int a, b; // but still accessible by derived
public:
  void setab(int n, int m) { a = n; b = m; }
};

class derived : public base {
```

```
    int c;
  public:
    void setc(int n) { c = n; }

    // this function has access to a and b from base
    void showabc() {
      cout << a << ' ' << b << ' ' << c << '\n';
    }
};

main()
{
  derived ob;

  /* a and b are not accessible here because they are
     private to both base and derived. */

  ob.setab(1, 2);
  ob.setc(3);

  ob.showabc();

  return 0;
}
```

Because **a** and **b** are protected in **base** and inherited as public by **derived**, they are available for use by member functions of **derived**. However, outside of these two classes, **a** and **b** are effectively private and unaccessible.

3. As mentioned earlier, when a base class is inherited as **protected**, public and protected members of the base class become protected members of the derived class. For example, here the preceding program is changed slightly, inheriting **base** as **protected** instead of **public**:

```
// This program will not compile.
#include <iostream.h>

class base {
protected:  // private to base
  int a, b; // but still accessible by derived
public:
  void setab(int n, int m) { a = n; b = m; }
};

class derived : protected base { // inherit as protected
  int c;
public:
  void setc(int n) { c = n; }

  // this function has access to a and b from base
```

```
    void showabc() {
      cout << a << ' ' << b << ' ' << c << '\n';
    }
};

main()
{
  derived ob;

  // ERROR: setab() is now a protected member of base.
  ob.setab(1, 2); // setab() is not accessible here.

  ob.setc(3);

  ob.showabc();

  return 0;
}
```

As the comments now describe, because **base** is inherited as **protected**, its public and protected elements become protected members of **derived** and are therefore inaccessible within **main( )**.

1. What happens when a protected member is inherited as public? What happens when it is inherited as private? What happens when it is inherited as protected?

2. Explain why the protected category is needed.

3. In Exercise 1 from Section 7.1, if the **a** and **b** inside **myclass** were made into protected instead of private (by default) members, would any of your answers to that exercise change? If so, how?

7.3   CONSTRUCTORS, DESTRUCTORS, AND INHERITANCE

It is possible for the base class, the derived class, or both to have constructor and/or destructor functions. Several issues that relate to these situations are examined in this section.

When a base and derived class both have constructor and destructor functions, the constructor functions are executed in order of derivation. The destructor functions are executed in reverse order. That is, the base class constructor is executed before the constructor in the derived class. The reverse is true for destructor functions: the derived class's destructor is executed before the base class's destructor.

If you think about it, it makes sense that constructor functions are executed in order of derivation. Because a base class has no knowledge of any derived class, any initialization it performs is separate from and possibly prerequisite to any initialization performed by the derived class. Therefore, it must be executed first.

On the other hand, a derived class's destructor must be executed before the destructor of the base class because the base class underlies the derived class. If the base class's destructor were executed first, it would imply the destruction of the derived class. Thus, the derived class's destructor must be called before the object goes out of existence.

So far, none of the preceding examples have passed arguments to either a derived or base class constructor. However, it is possible to do this. When only the derived class takes an initialization, arguments are passed to the derived class's constructor in the normal fashion. However, if you need to pass an argument to the constructor of the base class, a little more effort is needed. To accomplish this, a chain of argument passing is established. First, all necessary arguments to both the base and derived class are passed to the derived class's constructor. Using an expanded form of the derived class's constructor declaration, the appropriate arguments are then passed along to the base class. The syntax for passing along an argument from the derived to the base class is shown here:

```
derived-constructor (arg-list) : base(arg-list) {
    // body of derived class constructor
}
```

It is permissible for both the derived class and the base class to use the same argument. It is also possible for the derived class to ignore all arguments and just pass them along to the base.

1. Here is a very short program that illustrates when base class and derived class constructor and destructor functions are executed:

```
#include <iostream.h>

class base {
public:
  base() { cout << "Constructing base class\n"; }
  ~base() { cout << "Destructing base class\n"; }
};

class derived : public base {
public:
  derived() { cout << "Constructing derived class\n"; }
  ~derived() { cout << "Destructing derived class\n"; }
};

main()
{
  derived o;

  return 0;
}
```

This program displays the following output:

```
Constructing base class
Constructing derived class
Destructing derived class
Destructing base class
```

As you can see, the constructors are executed in order of derivation and the destructors are executed in reverse order.

2. This program shows how to pass an argument to a derived class's constructor:

```
#include <iostream.h>

class base {
public:
  base() { cout << "Constructing base class\n"; }
  ~base() { cout << "Destructing base class\n"; }
};
```

```
class derived : public base {
  int j;
public:
  derived(int n) {
    cout << "Constructing derived class\n";
    j = n;
  }
  ~derived() { cout << "Destructing derived class\n"; }
  void showj() { cout << j << '\n'; }
};

main()
{
  derived o(10);

  o.showj();

  return 0;
}
```

Notice that the argument is passed to the derived class's constructor in the normal fashion.

3. In the following example, both the derived class and the base class constructor take an argument. In this specific case, both use the same argument, and the derived class simply passes along the argument to the base.

```
#include <iostream.h>

class base {
  int i;
public:
  base(int n) {
    cout << "Constructing base class\n";
    i = n;
  }
  ~base() { cout << "Destructing base class\n"; }
  void showi() { cout << i << '\n'; }
};

class derived : public base {
  int j;
public:
  derived(int n) : base(n) { // pass arg to base class
    cout << "Constructing derived class\n";
    j = n;
  }
  ~derived() { cout << "Destructing derived class\n"; }
  void showj() { cout << j << '\n'; }
};
```

```
main()
{
  derived o(10);

  o.showi();
  o.showj();

  return 0;
}
```

Pay special attention to the declaration of **derived**'s constructor. Notice how the parameter **n** (which receives the initialization argument) is both used by **derived( )** and passed to **base( )**.

4. In most cases, the constructor functions for the base and derived class will *not* use the same argument. When this is the case and you need to pass one or more arguments to each, you must pass to the derived class's constructor *all* arguments needed by *both* the derived class and the base class. Then, the derived class simply passes along to the base those arguments required by it. For example, this program shows how to pass an argument to the derived class's constructor and another one to the base class:

```
#include <iostream.h>

class base {
  int i;
public:
  base(int n) {
    cout << "Constructing base class\n";
    i = n;
  }
  ~base() { cout << "Destructing base class\n"; }
  void showi() { cout << i << '\n'; }
};

class derived : public base {
  int j;
public:
  derived(int n, int m) : base(m) { // pass arg to base class
    cout << "Constructing derived class\n";
    j = n;
  }
  ~derived() { cout << "Destructing derived class\n"; }
  void showj() { cout << j << '\n'; }
};

main()
{
```

```
    derived o(10, 20);

    o.showi();
    o.showj();

    return 0;
}
```

5. It is important to understand that it is not necessary for the derived class's constructor to take an argument in order to pass one to the base class. If the derived class does not need an argument, it ignores the argument and simply passes it along to the base. For example, in this fragment, parameter **n** is not used by **derived( )**. Instead, it is simply passed to **base( )**:

```
class base {
  int i;
public:
  base(int n) {
    cout << "Constructing base class\n";
    i = n;
  }
  ~base() { cout << "Destructing base class\n"; }
  void showi() { cout << i << '\n'; }
};

class derived : public base {
  int j;
public:
  derived(int n) : base(n) { // pass arg to base class
    cout << "Constructing derived class\n";
    j = 0; // n not used here
  }
  ~derived() { cout << "Destructing derived class\n"; }
  void showj() { cout << j << '\n'; }
};
```

EXERCISES

1. Given the following skeleton, fill in the constructor function for **myderived**. Have it pass along a pointer to an initialization string to **mybase**. Also, have **myderived( )** initialize **len** to the length of string.

```
#include <iostream.h>
#include <string.h>
```

```
        class mybase {
          char str[80];
        public:
          mybase(char *s) { strcpy(str, s); }
          char *get() { return str; }
        };

        class myderived : public mybase {
          int len;
        public:
          // add myderived() here
          int getlen() { return len; }
          void show() { cout << get() << '\n'; }
        };

        main()
        {
          myderived ob("hello");

          ob.show();
          cout << ob.getlen() << '\n';

          return 0;
        }
```

2. Using the following skeleton, create appropriate **car( )** and **truck( )** constructor functions. Have each pass along appropriate arguments to **vehicle**. In addition, have **car( )** initialize **passengers** as specified when an object is created. Have **truck( )** initialize **loadlimit** as specified when an object is created.

```
  #include <iostream.h>

// A base class for various types of vehicles.
class vehicle {
  int num_wheels;
  int range;
public:
  vehicle(int w, int r)
  {
    num_wheels = w; range = r;
  }
  void showv()
  {
    cout << "Wheels: " << num_wheels << '\n';
    cout << "Range: " << range << '\n';
  }
};

class car : public vehicle {
  int passengers;
```

```
public:
  // insert car() constructor here
  void show()
  {
    showv();
    cout << "Passengers: " << passengers << '\n';
  }
};

class truck : public vehicle {
  int loadlimit;
public:
  // insert truck() constructor here
  void show()
  {
    showv();
    cout << "loadlimit " << loadlimit << '\n';
  }
};

main()
{
  car c(5, 4, 500);
  truck t(30000, 12, 1200);

  cout << "Car: \n";
  c.show();
  cout << "\nTruck:\n";
  t.show();

  return 0;
}
```

Have **car( )** and **truck( )** declare objects like this:

```
car ob(passengers, wheels, range);
truck ob(loadlimit, wheels, range);
```

---

*M*ULTIPLE INHERITANCE

There are two ways that a derived class may inherit more than one base class. First, a derived class may be used as a base class for another derived class, creating a multilevel class hierarchy. In this case, the original base class is said to be an *indirect* base class of the second derived class. (Keep in mind that any class—no matter how it is created—can be used as a base class.) Second, a derived class may directly inherit more than one base class. In this situation, two or more base classes are combined to help create the derived class. There are several issues that arise when multiple base classes are involved, and these issues are examined in this section.

When a base class is used to derive a class that is used as a base class for another derived class, the constructor functions of all three classes are called in order of derivation. (This is a generalization of the principle you learned earlier in this chapter.) Also, destructor functions are called in reverse order. Thus, if class *B1* is inherited by *D1*, and *D1* is inherited by *D2*, then *B1*'s constructor is called first, followed by *D1*'s, followed by *D2*'s. The destructors are called in reverse order.

When a derived class directly inherits multiple base classes, it uses this expanded declaration:

```
class derived-class-name : access base1,
                           access base2,
                           ..., access baseN
{
    // ... body of class
}
```

Here, *base1* through *baseN* are the base class names and *access* is the access specifier, which may be different for each base class. When multiple base classes are inherited, constructors are executed in the order, left to right, that the base classes are specified. Destructors are executed in the opposite order.

When a class inherits multiple base classes that have constructors that require arguments, the derived class passes the necessary arguments to them by using this expanded form of the derived class's constructor function:

```
derived-constructor(arg-list) : base1(arg-list),
                                base2(arg-list),
                                ...,
                                baseN(arg-list)
{
    // body of derived class constructor
}
```

Here, *base1* through *baseN* are the names of the base classes.

When a derived class inherits a hierarchy of classes, each derived class in the chain must pass back to its preceding base any arguments it needs.

EXAMPLES

1. Here is an example of a derived class that inherits a class derived from another class. Notice how arguments are passed along the chain from **D2** to **B1**.

```
// Multiple Inheritance
#include <iostream.h>

class B1 {
  int a;
public:
  B1(int x) { a = x; }
  int geta() { return a; }
};

// Inherit direct base class.
class D1 : public B1 {
  int b;
public:
  D1(int x, int y) : B1(y) // pass y to B1
  {
    b = x;
  }
  int getb() { return b; }
};

// Inherit a derived class and an indirect base.
class D2 : public D1 {
  int c;
public:
  D2(int x, int y, int z) : D1(y, z) // pass args to D1
  {
    c = x;
  }

  /* Because bases inherited as public, D2 has access
     to public elements of both B1 and D1. */
  void show() {
    cout << geta() << ' ' << getb() << ' ';
    cout << c << '\n';
  }
};

main()
{
  D2 ob(1, 2, 3);

  ob.show();
  // geta() and getb() are still public here
```

```
        cout << ob.geta() << ' ' << ob.getb() << '\n';

   return 0;
}
```

The call to **ob.show( )** displays **3 2 1**. In this example, **B1** is an indirect
base class of **D2**. Notice that **D2** has access to the public members of
both **D1** and **B1**. As you should remember, when public members of a
base class are inherited, they become public members of a derived class.
Therefore, when **D1** inherits **B1**, **geta( )** becomes a public member of **D1**,
which became a public member of **D2**.

   As the program illustrates, each class in a class hierarchy must pass all
arguments required by each preceding base class. Failure to do so will
generate a compile-time error.

   The class hierarchy created in this program is illustrated here:

B1

D1

D2

2. Here is a reworked version of the preceding program in which a derived
   class directly inherits two base classes:

```
#include <iostream.h>

// Create first base class.
class B1 {
  int a;
public:
  B1(int x) { a = x; }
  int geta() { return a; }
};

// Create second base class.
class B2 {
  int b;
public:
  B2(int x)
  {
    b = x;
  }
  int getb() { return b; }
};
```

```
// Directly inherit two base classes.
class D : public B1, public B2 {
  int c;
public:
  // here, z and y are passed directly to B1 and B2
  D(int x, int y, int z) : B1(z), B2(y)
  {
    c = x;
  }

  /* Because bases inherited as public, D has access
     to public elements of both B1 and B2. */
  void show() {
    cout << geta() << ' ' << getb() << ' ';
    cout << c << '\n';
  }
};

main()
{
  D ob(1, 2, 3);

  ob.show();

  return 0;
}
```

In this version, the arguments to **B1** and **B2** are passed individually to these classes by **D**.

This program creates a class that looks like this:

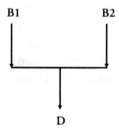

3. The following program illustrates the order in which constructor and destructor functions are called when a derived class directly inherits multiple base classes:

```
#include <iostream.h>

class B1 {
public:
```

```
      B1() { cout << "Constructing B1\n"; }
      ~B1() { cout << "Destructing B1\n"; }
    };

    class B2 {
      int b;
    public:
      B2() { cout << "Constructing B2\n"; }
      ~B2() { cout << "Destructing B2\n"; }
    };

    // Inherit two base classes.
    class D : public B1, public B2 {
    public:
      D() { cout << "Constructing D\n"; }
      ~D() { cout << "Destructing D\n"; }
    };

    main()
    {
      D ob;

      return 0;
    }
```

This program displays the following:

```
Constructing B1
Constructing B2
Constructing D
Destructing D
Destructing B2
Destructing B1
```

As you have learned, when multiple direct base classes are inherited, constructors are called in order, left to right, as specified in the inheritance list. Destructors are called in reverse order.

EXERCISES

1. What does the following program display? (Try to determine this without actually running the program.)

```
#include <iostream.h>
```

```cpp
class A {
public:
  A() { cout << "Constructing A\n"; }
  ~A() { cout << "Destructing A\n"; }
};

class B {
public:
  B() { cout << "Constructing B\n"; }
  ~B() { cout << "Destructing B\n"; }
};

class C : public A, public B {
public:
  C() { cout << "Constructing C\n"; }
  ~C() { cout << "Destructing C\n"; }
};

main()
{
  C ob;

  return 0;
}
```

2. Using the following class hierarchy, create **C**'s constructor so it initializes **k** and passes on arguments to **A( )** and **B( )**.

```cpp
#include <iostream.h>

class A {
  int i;
public:
  A(int a) { i = a; }
};

class B {
  int j;
public:
  B(int a) { j = a; }
};

class C : public A, public B {
  int k;
public:
  /* Create C() so that it initializes k
     and passes arguments to both A() and B() */
};
```

| 7.5 | # V*IRTUAL BASE CLASSES* |

A potential problem exists when multiple base classes are directly inherited by a derived class. To understand what this problem is, consider the following class hierarchy:

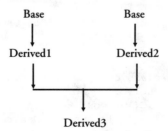

Here, the base class *Base* is inherited by both *Derived1* and *Derived2*. *Derived3* directly inherits both *Derived1* and *Derived2*. However, this implies that *Base* is actually inherited twice by *Derived3*—first, it is inherited through *Derived1,* and second, through *Derived2*. However, this causes ambiguity when a member of *Base* is referenced by *Derived3*. Since two copies of *Base* are included in *Derived3*, is a reference to a member of *Base* referring to the *Base* inherited indirectly through *Derived1* or to the *Base* inherited indirectly through *Derived2*? To resolve this ambiguity, C++ includes a mechanism by which only one copy of *Base* will be included in *Derived3*. This feature is called a *virtual base class.*

In situations like those just described in which a derived class indirectly inherits the same base class more than once, it is possible to prevent two copies of the base from being present in the derived object by having that base class inherited as **virtual** by any derived classes. Doing this prevents two (or more) copies of the base from being present in any subsequent derived class that inherits the base class indirectly. The **virtual** keyword precedes the base class access specifier when it is inherited by a derived class.

EXAMPLES

1. Here is an example that uses a virtual base class to prevent two copies of **base** from being present in **derived3**.

```
// This program uses a virtual base class.
#include <iostream.h>
```

```
class base {
public:
  int i;
};

// Inherit base as virtual.
class derived1 : virtual public base {
public:
  int j;
};

// Inherit base as virtual, here too.
class derived2 : virtual public base {
public:
  int k;
};

/* Here, derived3 inherits both derived1 and derived2.
   However, only one copy of base is present.
*/
class derived3 : public derived1, public derived2 {
public:
  int product() { return i * j * k; }
};

main()
{
  derived3 ob;

  ob.i = 10; // unambiguous because only one copy present
  ob.j = 3;
  ob.k = 5;

  cout << "Product is " << ob.product() << '\n';

  return 0;
}
```

If **derived1** and **derived2** had not inherited **base** as virtual, then the statement

```
ob.i = 10;
```

would have been ambiguous and a compile-time error would have resulted. (See Exercise 1, below.)

2. It is important to understand that when a base class is inherited as virtual by a derived class, that base class still exists within that derived class. For example, assuming the preceding program, this fragment is perfectly valid:

```
derived1 ob;
ob.i = 100;
```

The only difference between a normal base class and a virtual one occurs when an object inherits the base more than once. If virtual base classes are used, then only one base class is present in the object. Otherwise, multiple copies will be found.

EXERCISES

1. Using the program in Example 1, remove the **virtual** keyword and try to compile the program. See what types of errors result.
2. Explain why a virtual base class may be necessary.

**mastery
skills check**

At this point you should be able to perform the following exercises and answer the questions.

1. Create a generic base class called **building** that stores the number of floors a building has, the number of rooms, and its total square footage. Create a derived class called **house** that inherits **building** and also stores the following: the number of bedrooms and bathrooms. Also, create a derived class called **office** that inherits **building** and also stores the number of fire extinguishers and telephones. Note: Your solution may differ from the answer given in the back of this book. However, if it is functionally the same, count it as correct.

2. When a public member of a base class is inherited as public by the derived class, what happens to its public members? What happens to its

private members? If the base is inherited as private by the derived class, what happens to its public and private members?

3. Explain what **protected** means. (Be sure to explain what it means both when referring to members of a class and when it is used as an inheritance access specifier.)

4. When one class inherits another, when are the classes' constructors called? When are their destructors called?

5. Given this skeleton, fill in the details as indicated in the comments:

```
#include <iostream.h>

class planet {
protected:
  double distance; // miles from the sun
  int revolve;   // in days
public:
  planet(double d, int r) { distance = d; revolve = r; }
};

class earth : public planet {
  double circumference; // circumference of orbit
public:
  /* Create earth(double d, int r). Have it pass the
     distance and days of revolution back to planet. Have
     it compute the circumference of the orbit. (Hint:
     circumference = 2r*3.1416.)
  */
  /* Create a function called show() that displays the
     information. */
};

main()
{
  earth ob(93000000, 365);

  ob.show();

  return 0;
}
```

6. Fix the following program:

```
/* A variation on the vehicle hierarchy. But
   this program contains an error. Fix it. Hint:
   try compiling it as is and observe the error messages.
*/
#include <iostream.h>
```

```
// A base class for various types of vehicles.
class vehicle {
  int num_wheels;
  int range;
public:
  vehicle(int w, int r)
  {
    num_wheels = w; range = r;
  }
  void showv()
  {
    cout << "Wheels: " << num_wheels << '\n';
    cout << "Range: " << range << '\n';
  }
};

enum motor {gas, electric, diesel};

class motorized : public vehicle {
  enum motor mtr;
public:
  motorized(enum motor m, int w, int r) : vehicle(w, r)
  {
    mtr = m;
  }
  void showm() {
    cout << "Motor: ";
    switch(mtr) {
      case gas : cout << "Gas\n";
        break;
      case electric : cout << "Electric\n";
        break;
      case diesel : cout << "Diesel\n";
        break;
    }
  }
};

class road_use : public vehicle {
  int passengers;
public:
  road_use(int p, int w, int r) : vehicle(w, r)
  {
    passengers = p;
  }
  void showr()
  {
    cout << "Passengers: " << passengers << '\n';
  }
```

```
  };

  enum steering { power, rack_pinion, manual };

  class car : public motorized, public road_use {
    enum steering strng;
  public:
    car(enum steering s, enum motor m, int w, int r, int p) :
      road_use(p, w, r), motorized(m, w, r), vehicle(w, r)
    {
      strng = s;
    }
    void show() {
      showv(); showr(); showm();
      cout << "Steering: ";
      switch(strng) {
        case power : cout << "Power\n";
          break;
        case rack_pinion : cout << "Rack and Pinion\n";
          break;
        case manual : cout << "Manual\n";
          break;
      }
    }
  };

main()
{
  car c(power, gas, 4, 500, 5);

  c.show();

  return 0;
}
```

Teach Yourself

**cumulative
skills check**

This section checks how well you have integrated material in this chapter with
that from the preceding chapters.

1. In Exercise 6 from the preceding Mastery Skills Check section, you might
have seen a warning message (or perhaps an error message) concerning
the use of the **switch** statement within **car( )** and **motor( )**. Why?

2. As you know from the preceding chapter, most operators overloaded in a base class are available for use in a derived class. Which one or ones are not? Can you offer a reason why this is the case?

3. Following is a reworked version of the **coord** class from the previous chapter. This time, it is used as a base for another class called **quad**, which also maintains which quadrant the specific point is in. On your own, run this program and try to understand its output.

```
/* Overload the +, -, and = relative to coord class. Then,
   use coord as a base for quad. */
#include <iostream.h>

class coord {
public:
  int x, y; // coordinate values
  coord() { x=0; y=0; }
  coord(int i, int j) { x=i; y=j; }
  void get_xy(int &i, int &j) { i=x; j=y; }
  coord operator+(coord ob2);
  coord operator-(coord ob2);
  coord operator=(coord ob2);
};

// Overload + relative to coord class.
coord coord::operator+(coord ob2)
{
  coord temp;

  cout << "Using coord operator+()\n";

  temp.x = x + ob2.x;
  temp.y = y + ob2.y;

  return temp;
}

// Overload - relative to coord class.
coord coord::operator-(coord ob2)
{
  coord temp;

  cout << "Using coord operator-()\n";

  temp.x = x - ob2.x;
  temp.y = y - ob2.y;

  return temp;
}
```

```
// Overload = relative to coord.
coord coord::operator=(coord ob2)
{
  cout << "Using coord operator=()\n";

  x = ob2.x;
  y = ob2.y;

  return *this; // return the object that is assigned to
}

class quad : public coord {
  int quadrant;
public:
  quad() { x = 0; y = 0; quadrant = 0; }
  quad(int x, int y) : coord(x, y)
  {
    if(x>=0 && y>=0) quadrant = 1;
    else if(x<0 && y>=0) quadrant = 2;
    else if(x<0 && y<0) quadrant = 3;
    else quadrant = 4;
  }
  void showq()
  {
    cout << "Point in Quadrant: " << quadrant << '\n';
  }
  quad operator=(coord ob2);
};

quad quad::operator=(coord ob2)
{
  cout << "Using quad operator=()\n";

  x = ob2.x;
  y = ob2.y;
  if(x>=0 && y>=0) quadrant = 1;
  else if(x<0 && y>=0) quadrant = 2;
  else if(x<0 && y<0) quadrant = 3;
  else quadrant = 4;

  return *this;
}

main()
{
  quad o1(10, 10), o2(15, 3), o3;
  int x, y;

  o3 = o1 + o2; // add two objects - this calls operator+()
```

```
    o3.get_xy(x, y);
    o3.showq();
    cout << "(o1+o2) X: " << x << ", Y: " << y << "\n";

    o3 = o1 - o2; // subtract two objects
    o3.get_xy(x, y);
    o3.showq();
    cout << "(o1-o2) X: " << x << ", Y: " << y << "\n";

    o3 = o1; // assign an object
    o3.get_xy(x, y);
    o3.showq();
    cout << "(o3=o1) X: " << x << ", Y: " << y << "\n";

    return 0;
}
```

4. Again on your own, convert the program shown in Exercise 3 so that it uses friend operator functions.

8

Introducing the
C++ I/O System

chapter objectives

8.1 Some C++ I/O basics

8.2 Formatted I/O

8.3 Using **width( )**, **precision( )**, and **fill( )**

8.4 Using I/O manipulators

8.5 Creating your own inserters

8.6 Creating extractors

A L T H O U G H you have been using C++ style I/O since the first chapter of this book, it is time to explore it more fully. Like its predecessor, C, the C++ language includes a rich I/O system that is both flexible and powerful. It is important to understand that C++ still supports the entire C I/O system. However, C++ supplies a complete set of object-oriented I/O routines. The major advantage of the C++ I/O system is that it can be overloaded relative to classes that you create. Put differently, the C++ I/O system allows you to seamlessly integrate into the I/O system new types that you create.

Like C, the C++ object-oriented I/O system makes little distinction between console and file I/O. File and console I/O are really just different perspectives on the same mechanism. The examples in this chapter use console I/O, but the information presented is applicable to file I/O, as well. (File I/O is examined in detail in Chapter 9.)

This chapter covers several aspects of C++'s I/O system, including formatted I/O, I/O manipulators, and creating your own I/O inserters and extractors. As you will see, the C++ I/O system shares many features with the C I/O system.

review

skills check

Before proceeding, you should be able to correctly answer the following questions and do the exercises.

1. Create a class hierarchy that stores information about airships. Start with a general base class called **airship** that stores the number of passengers that can be carried and the amount of cargo (in pounds) that can be carried. Then create two derived classes called **airplane** and **balloon** from **airship**. Have **airplane** store the type of engine used (propeller or jet) and range, in miles. Have **balloon** store information about the type of gas used to lift the balloon (hydrogen or helium) and its maximum altitude (in feet). Create a short program that demonstrates this class hierarchy.

NOTE *Your solution will, no doubt, differ slightly from the answer shown in the back of this book. If it is functionally similar, count it as correct.*

2. What is **protected** used for?

3. Given the following class hierarchy, in what order are the constructor functions called? In what order are the destructor functions called?

```cpp
#include <iostream.h>

class A {
public:
  A() { cout << "Constructing A\n"; }
  ~A() { cout << "Destructing A\n"; }
};

class B : public A {
public:
  B() { cout << "Constructing B\n"; }
  ~B() { cout << "Destructing B\n"; }
};

class C : public B {
public:
  C() { cout << "Constructing C\n"; }
  ~C() { cout << "Destructing C\n"; }
};

main()
{
  C ob;

  return 0;
}
```

4. Given the following fragment, in what order are the constructor functions called?

```cpp
class myclass : public A, public B, public C { ...
```

5. Fill in the missing constructor functions in this program:

```cpp
#include <iostream.h>

class base {
  int i, j;
public:
  // need constructor
  void showij() { cout << i << ' ' << j << '\n'; }
};

class derived : public base {
  int k;
```

```
public:
  // need constructor
  void show() { cout << k << ' '; showij(); }
};

main()
{
  derived ob(1, 2, 3);

  ob.show();

  return 0;
}
```

6. In general, when you define a class hierarchy, you begin with the most
   _____ class and move to the most _____ class.
   (Fill in the missing words.)

SOME C++ I/O BASICS

Before we begin our discussion of C++ I/O, a few general comments are in order.

The C++ I/O system, like the C I/O system, operates through *streams*. Because of your C programming experience, you should already know what a stream is, but the next few sentences will summarize. A stream is a logical device that either produces or consumes information. A stream is linked to a physical device by the C++ I/O system. All streams behave in the same manner, even if the actual physical devices they are linked to differ. Because all streams act the same, the I/O system can operate on virtually any type of device. For example, the same method that you use to write to the screen can be used to write to a disk file or to the printer.

As you know, when a C program begins execution, three predefined streams are automatically opened: **stdin**, **stdout**, and **stderr**. A similar thing happens when a C++ program starts running. When a C++ program begins, these four streams are automatically opened:

Stream	Meaning	Default Device
cin	Standard input	Keyboard
cout	Standard output	Screen
cerr	Standard error	Screen
clog	Buffered version of cerr	Screen

As you have probably guessed, the streams **cin**, **cout**, and **cerr** correspond to C's **stdin**, **stdout**, and **stderr**. You have already been using **cin** and **cout**. The stream **clog** is simply a buffered version of **cerr**.

By default, the standard streams are used to communicate with the console. However, in environments that support I/O redirection, these streams can be redirected to other devices.

As you learned in Chapter 1, C++ provides support for its I/O system in the header file **iostream.h**. In this file, class hierarchies are defined that support I/O operations. There are two related, but different, I/O class hierarchies. The first is derived from the low-level I/O class called **streambuf**. This class supplies the basic, low-level input and output operations, and provides the underlying support for the entire C++ I/O system. Unless you are doing advanced I/O programming, you will not need to use **streambuf** directly. The class hierarchy that you will most commonly be working with is derived from **ios**. This is a high-level I/O class that provides formatting, error-checking, and status information related to stream I/O. **ios** is used as a base for several derived classes, including **istream**, **ostream**, and **iostream**. These classes are used to create streams capable of input, output, and input/output, respectively.

The **ios** class contains many member functions and variables that control or monitor the fundamental operation of a stream. It will be referred to frequently. Just remember that if you include **iostream.h** in your program, you will have access to this important class.

| 8.2 | ## FORMATTED I/O |

Until now, all examples in this book displayed information to the screen using C++'s default formats. However, it is possible to output information in a wide variety of forms. In fact, you can format data using C++'s I/O system in much the same way that you do using C's **printf( )** function. Also, you can alter certain aspects of the way information is input.

Each C++ stream has associated with it a number of format flags that determine how data is displayed. They are encoded into a long integer. (The proposed ANSI C++ standard suggests the type name **fmtflags** for variables holding format flags, but no compilers currently support this type.) These flags are named and given values within the **ios** class, typically using an enumeration, as shown here:

```
// ios format flags
enum {
  skipws = 0x0001,
  left = 0x0002,
  right = 0x0004,
```

```
      internal = 0x0008,
      dec = 0x0010,
      oct = 0x0020,
      hex = 0x0040,
      showbase = 0x0080,
      showpoint = 0x0100,
      uppercase = 0x0200,
      showpos = 0x0400,
      scientific = 0x0800,
      fixed = 0x1000,
      unitbuf = 0x2000,
      stdio = 0x4000
};
```

Generally, when a format flag is set, that feature is turned on. When a flag is cleared, the default format is used. Following is a description of these flags.

When the **skipws** flag is set, leading whitespace characters (spaces, tabs, and newlines) are discarded when you are performing input on a stream. When **skipws** is cleared, whitespace characters are not discarded. Generally, you will need to alter this flag only when reading certain types of disk files.

When the **left** flag is set, output is left justified. When **right** is set, output is right justified. When the **internal** flag is set, a numeric value is padded to fill a field by the insertion of spaces between any signs or base characters. (You will learn how to specify a field width shortly.) If none of these flags is set, output is right justified by default.

By default, integer values are output in decimal. However, it is possible to change the number base. Setting the **oct** flag causes output to be displayed in octal. Setting the **hex** flag causes output to be displayed in hexadecimal. To return output to decimal, set the **dec** flag.

Setting **showbase** causes the base of numeric values to be shown. For example, if the conversion base is hexadecimal, the value 1F will be displayed as 0x1F.

Setting **showpoint** causes a decimal point and trailing zeros to be displayed for all floating-point output—whether needed or not.

By default, when scientific notation is displayed, the "e" is in lowercase. Also, when a hexadecimal value is displayed, the "x" is in lowercase. When **uppercase** is set, these characters are displayed in uppercase.

Setting **showpos** causes a leading plus sign to be displayed before positive decimal values.

Setting the **scientific** flag causes floating-point numeric values to be displayed in scientific notation. When **fixed** is set, floating-point values are displayed in normal notation. By default, when **fixed** is set, six decimal places are displayed. When neither flag is set, the compiler chooses an appropriate method.

When **unitbuf** is set, the C++ I/O system flushes its output streams after each output operation. (Check your compiler manual for details on this format flag.)

When **stdio** is set, **stdout** and **stderr** are automatically flushed after each output operation. However, this flag is not defined by the proposed ANSI C++ standard and may not be applicable to your compiler.

To set a format flag, use the **setf( )** function. This function is a member of **ios**. Its most common form is shown here:

long setf(long *flags*);

This function returns the previous settings of the format flags and turns on those flags specified by *flags*. (All other flags are unaffected.) For example, to turn on the **showpos** flag, you can use this statement:

stream.setf(ios::showpos);

Here, *stream* is the stream you wish to affect. Notice the use of the scope resolution operator. Remember, **showpos** is an enumerated constant within the **ios** class. Therefore, it is necessary to tell the compiler this fact by preceding **showpos** with the class name and the scope resolution operator. If you don't, the constant **showpos** will simply not be recognized.

It is important to understand that **setf( )** is a member function of the **ios** class and affects streams created by that class. Therefore, any call to **setf( )** is done relative to a specific stream. There is no concept of calling **setf( )** by itself. Put differently, there is no concept in C++ of global format status. Each stream maintains its own format status information individually.

It is possible to set more than one flag in one call to **setf( )**, rather than making multiple calls to **setf( )**. To do this, OR together the values of the flags you want set. For example, this single call sets the **showbase** and **hex** flags for **cout**:

```
cout.setf(ios::showbase | ios::hex);
```

 REMEMBER *Because the format flags are defined within the* **ios** *class, you must access their values by using* **ios** *and the scope resolution operator. For example,* **showbase** *by itself will not be recognized; you must specify* **ios::showbase**.

The complement of **setf( )** is **unsetf( )**. This member function of **ios** clears one or more format flags. Its most common prototype form is shown here:

long unsetf(long *flags*);

The flags specified by *flags* are cleared. (All other flags are unaffected.) The previous flag settings are returned.

There will be times when you only want to know the current format settings but not alter any. Since both **setf( )** and **unsetf( )** alter the setting of one or more flags, **ios** also includes the member function **flags( )**, which simply returns the current setting of each format flag encoded into a **long int**. Its prototype is shown here:

long flags( );

The **flags( )** function has a second form that allows you to set *all* format flags associated with a stream to those specified in the argument to **flags( )**. The prototype for this version of **flags( )** is shown here:

long flags(long *f*);

When you use this version, the bit pattern found in *f* is copied to the variable used to hold the format flags associated with the stream, thus overwriting all previous flag settings. The function returns the previous settings.

EXAMPLES

1. Here is an example that illustrates **setf( )**:

```
#include <iostream.h>

main()
{

  // display using default settings
  cout << 123.23 << " hello " << 100 << '\n';
  cout << 10 << ' ' << -10 << '\n';
  cout << 100.0 << "\n\n";

  // now, change formats
  cout.setf(ios::hex | ios::scientific);
  cout << 123.23 << " hello " << 100 << '\n';

  cout.setf(ios::showpos);
```

```
cout << 10 << ' ' << -10 << '\n';

cout. setf(ios::showpoint | ios::fixed);
cout << 100.0;

return 0;
}
```

This program displays the following output:

```
123.23 hello 100
10 -10
100

1.232300e+02 hello 64
a fffffff6
+100.000000
```

Notice that the **showpos** flag only affects decimal output. It does not affect the value 10 when output in hexadecimal.

2. The following program illustrates **unsetf( )**. It first sets the **uppercase**, **showbase**, and **hex** flags. It then outputs 88 using scientific notation. In this case, the "X" used in the hexadecimal notation is in uppercase. Next, it clears the **uppercase** flag by using **unsetf( )**, and again outputs 88 in hexadecimal. This time, the "x" is in lowercase.

```
#include <iostream.h>

main()
{
  cout.setf(ios::uppercase | ios::showbase | ios::hex);

  cout << 88 << '\n';

  cout.unsetf(ios::uppercase);

  cout << 88 << '\n';

  return 0;
}
```

3. The following program uses **flags( )** to display the setting of the format flags relative to **cout**. Pay special attention to the **showflags( )** function. You might find it useful in programs you write.

```
#include <iostream.h>

void showflags();
```

```
main()
{
  // show default condition of format flags
  showflags();

  cout.setf(ios::oct | ios::showbase | ios::fixed);

  showflags();

  return 0;
}

// This function displays the status of the format flags.
void showflags()
{
  long f, i;
  int j;

  char flgs[15][12] = {
    "skipws",
    "left",
    "right",
    "internal",
    "dec",
    "oct",
    "hex",
    "showbase",
    "showpoint",
    "uppercase",
    "showpos",
    "scientific",
    "fixed",
    "unitbuf",
    "stdio"
  };

  f = cout.flags();  // get flag settings

  // check each flag
  for(i=1, j=0; i<=0x4000; i = i<<1, j++)
    if(i & f) cout << flgs[j] << " is on\n";
    else cout << flgs[j] << " is off\n";

  cout << "\n";
}
```

The output from the program is shown here:

```
skipws is on
left is off
```

```
right is off
internal is off
dec is off
oct is off
hex is off
showbase is off
showpoint is off
uppercase is off
showpos is off
scientific is off
fixed is off
unitbuf is off
stdio is off

skipws is on
left is off
right is off
internal is off
dec is off
oct is on
hex is off
showbase is on
showpoint is off
uppercase is off
showpos is off
scientific is off
fixed is on
unitbuf is off
stdio is off
```

4. The next program illustrates the second version of **flags( )**. It first constructs a flag mask that turns on **showpos**, **showbase**, **oct**, and **right**. These flags have the values 0x0400, 0x0080, 0x0020, and 0x0004. When added together they produce the value used in the program, 0x04A4. All other flags are turned off. It then uses **flags( )** to set the flag variable associated with **cout** to these settings. The function **showflags( )** verifies that the flags are set as indicated. (It is the same as the one used in the previous program.)

```
#include <iostream.h>

void showflags() ;

main()
{
  // show default condition of format flags
  showflags();

  // showpos, showbase, oct, right are on, others off
  long f = 0x04A4;
```

```
        cout.flags(f);  // set all flags

        showflags();

        return 0;
    }
```

EXERCISES

1. Write a program that sets **cout**'s flags so that integers display a + sign when positive values are displayed. Demonstrate that you have set the format flags correctly.

2. Write a program that sets **cout**'s flags so that the decimal point is always shown when floating-point values are displayed. Also, have all floating-point values be displayed in scientific notation with an uppercase E.

3. What call to **flags( )** resets the format flags to their default condition?

4. Write a program that saves the current state of the format flags, sets **showbase** and **hex**, and displays the value 100. Next, reset the flags to their previous values.

8.3 *USING width( ), precision( ), AND fill( )*

In addition to the formatting flags, there are three member functions defined by **ios** that set these format parameters: the field width, the precision, and the fill character. The functions that do these things are **width( )**, **precision( )**, and **fill( )**, respectively.

By default, when a value is output, it occupies only as much space as the number of characters it takes to display it. However, you can specify a minimum field width by using the **width( )** function. Its prototype is shown here:

int width(int *w*);

Here, *w* becomes the field width, and the previous field width is returned. In some implementations, each time an output operation is performed, the field width returns to its default setting, so it may be necessary to set the minimum field width before each output statement.

After you set a mininum field width, when a value uses less than the specified width, the field is padded with the current fill character (the space, by default) so that the field width is reached. However, keep in mind that if the size of the value output exceeds the minimum field width, the field will be overrun. No values are truncated.

By default, six digits of precision are used. However, you can set this number by using the **precision( )** function. Its prototype is shown here:

```
int precision(int p);
```

Here, the precision is set to *p* and the old value is returned.

By default, when a field needs to be filled, it is filled with spaces. However, you can specify the fill character by using the **fill( )** function. Its prototype is shown here:

```
char fill(char ch);
```

After a call to **fill( )**, *ch* becomes the new fill character, and the old one is returned.

EXAMPLES

1. Here is a program that illustrates these functions:

```
#include <iostream.h>

main()
{
  cout.width(10); // set minimum field width
  cout << "hello" << '\n';  // right justify by default
  cout.fill('%'); // set fill character
  cout.width(10); // set width
  cout << "hello" << '\n'; // right justify by default
  cout.setf(ios::left); // left justify
  cout.width(10); // set width
  cout << "hello" << '\n'; // output left justified

  cout.width(10); // set width
  cout.precision(10); // set 10 digits of precision
```

```
cout << 123.234567 << '\n';
cout.width(10);   // set width
cout.precision(6);   // set 6 digits of precision
cout << 123.234567 << '\n';

return 0;
}
```

This program displays the following output:

```
    hello
%%%%%hello
hello%%%%%
123.234567
123.235%%%
```

Notice that the field width is set before each output statement.

2. The following program shows how to use the C++ I/O format functions to create an aligned table of numbers:

```
// Create a table of square roots and squares.
#include <iostream.h>
#include <math.h>

main()
{
  double x;

  cout.precision(4);
  cout << "     x    sqrt(x)      x^2\n\n";

  for(x = 2.0; x <= 20.0; x++) {
    cout.width(7);
    cout << x << "  ";
    cout.width(7);
    cout << sqrt(x) << "  ";
    cout.width(7);
    cout << x*x << '\n';
  }

  return 0;
}
```

This program creates the following table:

```
    x    sqrt(x)      x^2

    2    1.414        4
    3    1.732        9
    4       2        16
```

5	2.236	25
6	2.449	36
7	2.646	49
8	2.828	64
9	3	81
10	3.162	100
11	3.317	121
12	3.464	144
13	3.606	169
14	3.742	196
15	3.873	225
16	4	256
17	4.123	289
18	4.243	324
19	4.359	361
20	4.472	400

EXERCISES

1. Create a program that prints the natural log and base 10 log of the numbers from 2 to 100. Format the table so the numbers are right-justified within a field width of 10, using a precision of 5 decimal places.

2. Create a function called **center( )** that has this prototype:

   void center(char *s);

   Have this function center the specified string on the screen. To accomplish this, use the **width( )** function. Assume that the screen is 80 characters wide. (For simplicity, you may assume that no string exceeds 80 characters.) Write a program that demonstrates that your function works.

3. On your own, experiment with the format flags and the format functions. Once you become familar with the C++ I/O system, you will have no trouble using it to format output any way you like.

8.4 USING I/O MANIPULATORS

There is a second way that you can format information using C++'s I/O system. This method uses special functions called *I/O manipulators*. As you will see, I/O manipulators are, in some situations, easier to use than the **ios** format flags and functions.

I/O manipulators are special I/O format functions that may occur *within* an I/O statement, instead of separate from it the way the **ios** member functions must. The standard manipulators are shown in Table 8-1. As you can see, many of the I/O manipulators parallel member functions of the **ios** class.

NOTE *To access manipulators that take parameters (such as **setw( )**), you must include **iomanip.h** in your program. This is not necessary when you are using a manipulator that does not require an argument.*

As stated above, the manipulators may occur in the chain of I/O operations. For example:

```
cout << oct << 100 << hex << 100;
cout << setw(10) << 100;
```

The first statement tells **cout** to display integers in octal and then outputs 100 in octal. It then tells the stream to display integers in hexadecimal and then outputs 100 in hexadecimal format. The second statement sets the field width to 10 and

Manipulator	Purpose	Input/Output
dec	Format numeric data in decimal	Output
endl	Output a newline character and flush the stream	Output
ends	Output a null	Output
flush	Flush a stream	Output
hex	Format numeric data in hexadecimal	Output
oct	Format numeric data in octal	Output
resetiosflags (long *f*)	Turn off the flags specified in *f*	Input and output
setbase (int *base*)	Set the number base to *base*	Output
setfill (int *ch*)	Set the fill character to *ch*	Output
setiosflags (long *f*)	Turn on the flags specified in *f*	Input and output
setprecision (int *p*)	Set the number of digits of precision	Output
setw (int *w*)	Set the field width to *w*	Output
ws	Skip leading whitespace	Input

TABLE 8-1   *The C++ I/O Manipulators* ▼

then displays 100 in hexadecimal format, again. Notice that when a manipulator does not take an argument, such as **oct** in the example, it is not followed by parentheses. This is because it is the address of the manipulator that is passed to the overloaded << operator.

Keep in mind that an I/O manipulator affects only the stream of which the I/O expression is a part. I/O manipulators do *not* affect all streams currently opened for use.

As the preceding example suggests, the main advatanges of using manipulators over the **ios** member functions is that they are often easier to use and allow more compact code to be written.

If you wish to set specific format flags manually by using a manipulator, use **setiosflags( )**. This manipulator performs the same function as the member function **setf( )**. To turn off flags, use the **resetiosflags( )** manipulator. This manipulator is equivalent to **unsetf( )**.

EXAMPLES

1. This program demonstrates several of the I/O manipulators:

```
#include <iostream.h>
#include <iomanip.h>

main()
{
  cout << hex << 100 << endl;
  cout << oct << 10 << endl;

  cout << setfill('X') << setw(10);
  cout << 100 << " hi " << endl;

  return 0;
}
```

This program displays the following:

```
64
12
XXXXXXX144 hi
```

2. Here is another version of the program that displays a table of the squares and square roots of the numbers 2 through 20. This version uses I/O manipulators instead of member functions and format flags.

```
/* This version uses I/O manipulators to display
   the table of squares and square roots. */
#include <iostream.h>
#include <iomanip.h>
#include <math.h>

main()
{
  double x;

  cout << setprecision(4);
  cout << "      x      sqrt(x)      x^2\n\n";

  for(x = 2.0; x <= 20.0; x++) {
    cout << setw(7) << x << "   ";
    cout << setw(7) << sqrt(x) << "   ";
    cout << setw(7) << x*x << '\n';
  }

  return 0;
}
```

EXERCISES

1. Redo Exercises 1 and 2 from Section 8.3, only this time, use I/O manipulators instead of member functions and format flags.

2. Show the I/O statement that outputs the value 100 in hexadecimal with the base indicator (the 0x) shown. Use the **setiosflags( )** manipulator to accomplish this.

8.5	

CREATING YOUR OWN INSERTERS

As stated earlier in this book, one of the reasons to use C++ I/O statements rather than C-like I/O functions is that you can overload the I/O operators for classes that you create. By doing so, you can seamlessly incorporate your classes into your C++ programs. In this section you learn how to overload C++'s output operator <<.

In the language of C++, the output operation is called an *insertion* and the << is called the *insertion operator*. When you overload the << for output, you are creating an *inserter function,* or *inserter* for short. The rationale for these terms comes from the fact that an output operator *inserts* information into a stream.

All inserter functions have this general form:

```
ostream &operator <<(ostream &stream, class-name ob)
{
  // body of inserter
  return stream;
}
```

The first parameter is a reference to an object of type **ostream**. This means that *stream* must be an output stream. (Remember, **ostream** is defined within the **ios** class.) The second parameter receives the object that will be output. (This may also be a reference parameter, if that is more suitable to your application.) Notice that the inserter function returns a reference to *stream,* which is of type **ostream**. This is required if the overloaded << is going to be used in complex I/O expressions, such as

```
cout << ob1 << ob2 << ob2;
```

Within an inserter you may perform any type of procedure. What an inserter does is completely up to you. However, for the inserter to be consistent with good programming practices, you should limit its operations to outputting information to a stream.

Although surprising at first, an inserter *cannot* be a member of the class on which it is designed to operate. Here is why: When an operator function of any type is a member of a class, the left operand, which is passed implicitly through the **this** pointer, is the object that generates the call to the operator function. This implies that the left operand is an object of that class. Therefore, if an overloaded operator function is a member of a class, then the left operand must be an object of that class. However, when you create an inserter, the left operand is a stream, not a class object, and the right operand is the object that you want output. Therefore, an inserter cannot be a member function.

The fact that an inserter cannot be a member function may appear to be a serious flaw in C++ because it seems to imply that all data of a class that will be output using an inserter will need to be public, thus violating the key principle of encapsulation. However, this is not the case. Even though inserters cannot be members of the class upon which they are designed to operate, they can be friends of the class. In fact, in most programming situations you will encounter, an overloaded inserter will be a friend of the class it was created for.

EXAMPLES

1. As a simple first example, this program contains an inserter for the **coord** class, developed in a previous chapter:

```cpp
// Use a friend inserter for objects of type coord.
#include <iostream.h>

class coord {
  int x, y;
public:
  coord() { x = 0; y = 0; }
  coord(int i, int j) { x = i; y = j; }
  friend ostream &operator<<(ostream &stream, coord ob);
};

ostream &operator<<(ostream &stream, coord ob)
{
  stream << ob.x << ", " << ob.y << '\n';
  return stream;
}

main()
{
  coord a(1, 1), b(10, 23);

  cout << a << b;

  return 0;
}
```

This program displays the following:

```
1, 1
10, 23
```

The inserter in this program illustrates one very important point about creating your own inserters: make them as general as possible. In this case, the I/O statement inside the inserter outputs the values of **x** and **y** to **stream**, which is whatever stream is passed to the function.

As you will see in the following chapter, the same inserter that outputs to the screen can be used to output to *any* stream. Sometimes beginners are tempted to write the **coord** inserter like this:

```
ostream &operator<<(ostream &stream, coord ob)
{
  cout << ob.x << ", " << ob.y << '\n';
  return stream;
}
```

In this case, the output statement is hard-coded to display information on the standard output device linked to **cout**. However, this prevents the inserter from being used by other streams. The point is that you should make your inserters as general as possible because there is no disadvantage to doing so.

2. For the sake of illustration, here is the preceding program revised so that the inserter is *not* a friend of the **coord** class. Because the inserter does not have access to the private parts of **coord**, the variables **x** and **y** have to be made public.

```
/* Create an inserter for objects of type coord, using
   a non-friend inserter. */

#include <iostream.h>

class coord {
public:
  int x, y;  // must be public
  coord() { x = 0; y = 0; }
  coord(int i, int j) { x = i; y = j; }
};

// An inserter for the coord class.
ostream &operator<<(ostream &stream, coord ob)
{
  stream << ob.x << ", " << ob.y << '\n';
  return stream;
}

main()
{
  coord a(1, 1), b(10, 23);
```

```
    cout << a << b;
    return 0;
}
```

3. An inserter is not limited to displaying only textual information. An inserter can perform any operation or conversion necessary to output information in a form needed by a particular device or situation. For example, it is perfectly valid to create an inserter that sends information to a plotter. In this case, the inserter will need to send appropriate plotter codes in addition to the information. To allow you to taste the flavor of this type of inserter, the following program creates a class called **triangle**, which stores the width and height of a right triangle. The inserter for this class displays the triangle on the screen.

```
// This program draws right triangles
#include <iostream.h>

class triangle {
  int height, base;
public:
  triangle(int h, int b) { height = h; base = b; }
  friend ostream &operator<<(ostream &stream, triangle ob);
};

// Draw a triangle.
ostream &operator<<(ostream &stream, triangle ob)
{
  int i, j, h, k;

  i = j = ob.base-1;
  for(h=ob.height-1; h; h--) {
    for(k=i; k; k--)
      stream << ' ';
    stream << '*';

    if(j!=i) {
      for(k=j-i-1; k; k--)
        stream << ' ';
      stream << '*';
    }

    i--;
    stream << '\n';
  }
  for(k=0; k<ob.base; k++) stream << '*';
  stream << '\n';

  return stream;
```

```
}

main()
{
  triangle t1(5, 5), t2(10, 10), t3(12, 12);

  cout << t1;
  cout << endl << t2 << endl << t3;

  return 0;
}
```

Notice that this program illustrates how a properly designed inserter can be fully integrated into a "normal" I/O expression. This program displays the following:

```
    *
   **
  * *
 *   *
*****


         *
        **
       * *
      *   *
     *     *
    *       *
   *         *
  *           *
 *             *
*********


          *
         **
        * *
       *   *
      *     *
     *       *
    *         *
   *           *
  *             *
 *               *
*           *
***********
```

1. Given the following **strtype** class and partial program, create an inserter that displays a string:

```
#include <iostream.h>
#include <string.h>
#include <stdlib.h>

class strtype {
  char *p;
  int len;
public:
  strtype(char *ptr);
  ~strtype();
  friend ostream &operator<<(ostream &stream, strtype &ob);
};

strtype::strtype(char *ptr)
{
  len = strlen(ptr);
  p = new char [len+1];
  if(!p) {
    cout << "Allocation error\n";
    exit(1);
  }
  strcpy(p, ptr);
}

strtype::~strtype()
{
  delete p;
}

// Create operator<< inserter function here.

main()
{
  strtype s1("This is a test"), s2("I like C++");

  cout<< s1 << '\n' << s2;

  return 0;
}
```

2. Replace the **show( )** function in the following program with an inserter function:

```
#include <iostream.h>

class planet {
protected:
  double distance; // miles from the sun
  int revolve;   // in days
public:
  planet(double d, int r) { distance = d; revolve = r; }
};

class earth : public planet {
  double circumference; // circumference of orbit
public:
  earth(double d, int r) : planet(d, r) {
    circumference = 2*distance*3.1416;
  }

  /*
    Rewrite this so that it displays the information using
    an inserter function. */
  void show() {
    cout << "Distance from sun: " << distance << '\n';
    cout << "Days in obit: " << revolve << '\n';
    cout << "Circumference of orbit: " << circumference << '\n';
  }
};

main()
{
  earth ob(93000000, 365);

  cout << ob;

  return 0;
}
```

3. On your own, review why an inserter cannot be a member function.

---

*C*REATING EXTRACTORS

Just as you can overload the << output operator, you can overload the >> input operator. In C++, the >> is referred to as the *extraction operator* and a function that overloads it is called an *extractor*. The reason for this term is that the act of inputting information from a stream removes (that is, extracts) data from it.

The general form of an extractor function is shown here:

```
istream &operator>>(istream &stream, class-name &ob)
{
  // body of extractor
  return stream;
}
```

Extractors return a reference to **istream**, which is an input stream. The first parameter must be a reference to an input stream. The second parameter is a reference to the object that is receiving input.

For the same reason that an inserter cannot be a member function, an extractor may not be a member function. While you may perform any operation within an extractor, it is best to limit its activity to inputting information.

EXAMPLES

1. This program adds an extractor to the **coord** class:

```
// Add a friend extractor for objects of type coord.
#include <iostream.h>

class coord {
  int x, y;
public:
  coord() { x = 0; y = 0; }
  coord(int i, int j) { x = i; y = j; }
  friend ostream &operator<<(ostream &stream, coord ob);
  friend istream &operator>>(istream &stream, coord &ob);
};

ostream &operator<<(ostream &stream, coord ob)
{
  stream << ob.x << ", " << ob.y << '\n';
  return stream;
}

istream &operator>>(istream &stream, coord &ob)
{
```

```
    cout << "Enter coordinates: ";
    stream >> ob.x >> ob.y;
    return stream;
  }

main()
{
  coord a(1, 1), b(10, 23);

  cout << a << b;

  cin >> a;
  cout << a;


  return 0;
}
```

Notice how the extractor also prompts the user for input. While not required (or even desired) for most situations, this function shows how customized extractor can simplify coding when a prompting message is needed.

2. Here, an inventory class is created that stores the name of an item, the number on hand, and its cost. The program includes both an inserter and an extractor for this class.

```
#include <iostream.h>
#include <string.h>

class inventory {
  char item[40]; // name of item
  int onhand; // number on hand
  double cost;  // cost of item
public:
  inventory(char *i, int o, double c)
  {
    strcpy(item, i);
    onhand = o;
    cost = c;
  }
  friend ostream &operator<<(ostream &stream, inventory ob);
  friend istream &operator>>(istream &stream, inventory &ob);
};

ostream &operator<<(ostream &stream, inventory ob)
```

```
   {
     stream << ob.item << ": " << ob.onhand;
     stream << " on hand at $" << ob.cost << '\n';

     return stream;
   }

   istream &operator>>(istream &stream, inventory &ob)
   {
     cout << "Enter item name: ";
     stream >> ob.item;
     cout << "Enter number on hand: ";
     stream >> ob.onhand;
     cout << "Enter cost: ";
     stream >> ob.cost;

     return stream;
   }
main()
{
   inventory ob("hammer", 4, 12.55);

   cout << ob;

   cin >> ob;

   cout << ob;

   return 0;
}
```

EXERCISES

1. Add an extractor to the **strtype** class from Exercise 1 in the preceding section.

2. Create a class that stores an integer value and its lowest factor. Create both an inserter and an extractor for this class.

At this point, you should be able to perform the following exercises and answer the questions.

1. Write a program that displays the number 100 in decimal, hexadecimal, and octal. (Use the **ios** format flags.)

2. Write a program that displays the value 1000.5364 in a 20-character field, left justified, with two decimal places, and using * as a fill character. (Use the **ios** format flags.)

3. Rewrite your answers to Exercises 1 and 2 so that they use I/O manipulators.

4. Show how to save the format flags for **cout** and how to restore them. Use either member functions or manipulators.

5. Create an inserter and an extractor for this class:

```
class pwr {
  int base;
  int exponent;
  double result; // base to the exponent power
public:
  pwr(int b, int e);
};

pwr::pwr(int b, int e)
{
  base = b;
  exponent = e;

  result = 1;
  for( ; e; e--) result = result * base;
}
```

6. Create a class called **box** that stores the dimensions of a square. Create an inserter that displays a square box on the screen. (Use any method you like to display the box.)

This section checks how well you have integrated material in this chapter with that from the preceding chapters.

1. Using the **stack** class shown here, create an inserter that displays the contents of the stack. Demonstrate that your inserter works.

```cpp
#include <iostream.h>

#define SIZE 10

// Declare a stack class for characters
class stack {
  char stck[SIZE]; // holds the stack
  int tos; // index of top-of-stack
public:
  stack();
  void push(char ch); // push character on stack
  char pop(); // pop character from stack
};

// Initialize the stack
stack::stack()
{
  tos = 0;
}

// Push a character.
void stack::push(char ch)
{
  if(tos==SIZE) {
    cout << "Stack is full";
    return;
  }
  stck[tos] = ch;
  tos++;
}

// Pop a character.
char stack::pop()
{
```

```
    if(tos==0) {
      cout << "Stack is empty";
      return 0; // return null on empty stack
    }
    tos--;
    return stck[tos];
}
```

2. Write a program that contains a class called **watch**. Using the standard time functions, have this class's constructor read the system time and store it. Create an inserter that displays the time.

3. Using the following class, which converts feet to inches, create an extractor that prompts the user for feet. Also, create an inserter that displays the number of feet and inches. Include a program that demonstrates that your inserter and extractor work.

```
class ft_to_inches {
  double feet;
  double inches;
public:
  void set(double f) {
    feet = f;
    inches = f * 12;
  }
};
```

9

Advanced C++ I/O

chapter objectives

9.1 Creating your own manipulators

9.2 File I/O basics

9.3 Unformatted, binary I/O

9.4 More binary I/O functions

9.5 Random access

9.6 Checking the I/O status

9.7 Customized I/O and files

THIS chapter continues the examination of the C++ I/O system. In it you will learn to create your own I/O manipulators and how to perform file I/O. Keep in mind that the C++ I/O system is very rich and flexible and contains many functions. While it is beyond the scope of this book to include all of them, the most important ones are discussed here. A complete description of the C++ I/O system can be found in my book *C++: The Complete Reference* (Berkeley: Osborne/McGraw-Hill, 1991).

NOTE *The C++ I/O system described in this chapter reflects the proposed ANSI C++ standard and is compatible with all major C++ compilers. If you have an older or nonconforming version, its I/O system will not have all the capabilities described here.*

review

skills check

Before proceeding, you should be able to correctly answer the following questions and do the exercises.

1. Write a program that displays the sentence: "C++ is fun" in a 40-character-wide field using a colon (:) as the fill character.

2. Write a program that displays the outcome of 10/3 to four decimal places. Use **ios** member functions to do this.

3. Redo the preceding program using I/O manipulators.

4. What is an inserter? What is an extractor?

5. Given the following class, create an inserter and an extractor for it.

```
class date {
  char date[9]; // store date as string: mm/dd/yy
public:
  // add inserter and extractor
};
```

6. What header file must be included to use I/O manipulators that take parameters?

7. What predefined streams are created when a C++ program begins execution?

9.1 | CREATING YOUR OWN MANIPULATORS

In addition to overloading the insertion and extraction operators, you can further customize C++'s I/O system by creating your own manipulator functions. Custom manipulators are important for two main reasons. First, a manipulator can consolidate a sequence of several separate I/O operations into one manipulator. For example, it is not uncommon to have situations in which the same sequence of I/O operations occurs frequently within a program. In these cases you can use a custom manipulator to perform these actions, thus simplifying your source code and preventing accidental errors. Second, a custom manipulator can be important when you need to perform I/O operations on a nonstandard device. For example, you might use a manipulator to send control codes to a special type of printer or an optical recognition system.

Custom manipulators are a feature of C++ that supports OOP, but they can also benefit programs that aren't object oriented. As you will see, custom manipulators can help make any I/O-intensive program clearer and more efficient.

As you know, there are two basic types of manipulators: those that operate on input streams and those that operate on output streams. However, in addition to these two broad categories, there is a secondary division: those manipulators that take an argument and those that don't. There are some significant differences between the way a parameterless manipulator and a parameterized manipulator are created. Further, creating parameterized manipulators is substantially more difficult than creating parameterless ones and is beyond the scope of this book. However, writing your own parameterless manipulators is quite easy and is examined here.

All parameterless manipulator output functions have this skeleton:

```
ostream &manip-name(ostream &stream)
{
  // your code here

  return stream;
}
```

Here, *manip-name* is the name of the manipulator. Notice that a reference to a stream of type **ostream** is returned. This is necessary if a manipulator is used as part of a larger I/O expression. It is important to understand that even though the manipulator has as its single argument a reference to the stream upon which it is operating, no argument is used when the manipulator is called in an output operation.

All parameterless input manipulator functions have this skeleton:

```
istream &manip-name(istream &stream)
{
    // your code here

    return stream;
}
```

An input manipulator receives a reference to the stream for which it was invoked. This stream must be returned by the manipulator.

It is crucial that your manipulators return *stream*. If this is not done, your manipulators cannot be used in a series of input or output operations.

EXAMPLES

1. As a simple first example, the following program creates a manipulator called **setup( )** that sets the field width to 10, the precision to 4, and the fill character to *.

```
#include <iostream.h>

ostream &setup(ostream &stream)
{
  stream.width(10);
  stream.precision(4);
  stream.fill('*');

  return stream;
}

main()
{
  cout << setup << 123.123456;

  return 0;
}
```

As you can see, **setup** is used as part of an I/O expression in the same way that any of the built-in manipulators are used.

2. Custom manipulators need not be complex to be useful. For example, the simple manipulators **atn( )** and **note( )** provide a shorter way to output frequently used words or phrases.

```
#include <iostream.h>
#include <iomanip.h>

// Attention:
ostream &atn(ostream &stream)
{
  stream << "Attention: ";
  return stream;
}

// Please note:
ostream &note(ostream &stream)
{
  stream << "Please Note: ";
  return stream;
}

main()
{
  cout << atn << "High voltage circuit\n";
  cout << note << "Turn off all lights\n";

  return 0;
}
```

Even though simple, if used frequently, these manipulators save you from some tedious typing.

3. This program creates the **getpass( )** input manipulator that rings the bell and then prompts for a password:

```
#include <iostream.h>
#include <string.h>

// A simple input manipulator
istream &getpass(istream &stream)
{
  cout << '\a';  // sound bell
  cout << "Enter password: ";

  return stream;
}

main()
```

```
    {
      char pw[80];

      do {
        cin >> getpass >> pw;
      } while (strcmp(pw, "password"));

      cout << "Logon complete\n";

      return 0;
    }
```

EXERCISES

1. Create an output manipulator that displays the current system time and date. Call this manipulator **td( )**.

2. Create an output manipulator called **sethex( )** that sets output to hexadecimal and turns on the **uppercase** and **showbase** flags. Also, create an output manipulator called **reset( )** that undoes the changes made by **sethex( )**.

3. Create an input manipulator called **skipchar( )** that reads and ignores the next ten characters from the input stream.

9.2 **_FILE I/O BASICS_**

To perform file I/O, you must include the header file **fstream.h** in your program. It defines several classes, including **ifstream**, **ofstream**, and **fstream**. These classes are derived from **istream** and **ostream**. Remember, **istream** and **ostream** are derived from **ios**, so **ifstream**, **ofstream**, and **fstream** also have access to all operations defined by **ios** (discussed in the preceding chapter).

In C++, a file is opened by linking it to a stream. There are three types of streams: input, output, and input/output. Before you can open a file, you must first obtain a stream. To create an input stream, you must declare the stream to be of class **ifstream**. To create an output stream, it must be declared as class **ofstream**.

Streams that will be performing both input and output operations must be declared as class **fstream**. For example, this fragment creates one input stream, one output stream, and one stream capable of both input and output:

```
ifstream in;  // input
ofstream out; // output
fstream io; // input and output
```

Once you have created a stream, one way to associate it with a file is by using the function **open( )**. This function is a member of each of the three stream classes. Its prototype is shown here:

void open(const char *filename, int mode, int access);

Here, *filename* is the name of the file, which may include a path specifier. The value of *mode* determines how the file is opened. It must be one (or more) of these values (inherited by **fstream.h**):

ios::app
ios::ate
ios::binary
ios::in
ios::nocreate
ios::noreplace
ios::out
ios::trunc

You can combine two or more of these values by ORing them together. Let's see what each of these values means.

Including **ios::app** causes all output to that file to be appended to the end. This value can be used only with files capable of output. Including **ios::ate** causes a seek to the end of the file to occur when the file is opened. Although **ios::ate** causes a seek to end-of-file, I/O operations can still occur anywhere within the file.

The **ios::in** value specifies that the file is capable of input. The **ios::out** value specifies that the file is capable of output. However, creating a stream by using **ifstream** implies input, and creating a stream by using **ofstream** implies output, so in these cases, it is unnecessary to supply these values.

The **ios::binary** value causes a file to be opened in binary mode. By default, all files are opened in text mode. In text mode, various character translations may take place, such as carriage return, linefeed sequences being converted into newlines. However, when a file is opened in binary mode, no such character translations will occur. Keep in mind that any file, whether it contains formatted text or raw data, can be opened in either binary or text mode. The only difference is whether character translations take place.

Including **ios::nocreate** causes the **open( )** function to fail if the file does not already exist. The **ios::noreplace** value causes the **open( )** function to fail if the file does already exist.

The **ios::trunc** value causes the contents of a preexisting file by the same name to be destroyed, and the file is truncated to zero length.

The value of *access* determines how the file can be accessed. Its default value is **filebuf::openprot** (**filebuf** is a parent class of the stream classes), which is 0x644 for UNIX environments and means a normal file. In DOS/Windows environments, the *access* value generally corresponds to DOS/Windows' file attribute codes. They are

Attribute	Meaning
0	normal file: open access
1	read-only file
2	hidden file
4	system file
8	archive bit set

You can OR two or more of these together. For DOS/Windows, a normal file has an *access* value of zero. For other operating systems, check your compiler user manual for the valid values of *access*.

The following fragment opens a normal output file in a DOS/Windows environment:

```
ofstream out;
out.open("test", ios::out, 0);
```

However, you will seldom (if ever) see **open( )** called as shown because both the *mode* and *access* parameters have default values. For **ifstream**, *mode* is **ios::in**, and for **ofstream**, it is **ios::out**. By default, *access* has a value that creates a normal file. Therefore, the preceding statement will usually look like this:

```
out.open("test");  // defaults to output and normal file
```

To open a stream for input and output, you must specify both the **ios::in** and the **ios::out** *mode* values, as shown in this example. (No default value for *mode* is supplied for this situation.)

```
fstream mystream;
mystream.open("test", ios::in | ios::out);
```

If **open( )** fails, the stream will be zero. Therefore, before using a file, you should test to make sure the open operation succeeded by using a statement like this:

```
if(!mystream) {
  cout << "Cannot open file\n";
  // handle error
}
```

Although it is entirely proper to open a file by using the **open( )** function, most of the time you will not do so because the **ifstream**, **ofstream**, and **fstream** classes have constructor functions that automatically open the file. The constructor functions have the same parameters and defaults as the **open( )** function. Therefore, the most common way you will see a file opened is shown in this example:

```
ifstream  mystream("myfile"); // open file for input
```

As stated, if for some reason the file cannot be opened, the value of the associated stream variable will be zero. Therefore, whether you use a constructor function to open the file or an explicit call to **open( )**, you will want to confirm that the file has actually been opened by testing the value of the stream.

To close a file, use the member function **close( )**. For example, to close the file linked to a stream called **mystream**, use this statement:

```
mystream.close( );
```

The **close( )** function takes no parameters and returns no value.

You can detect when the end of an input file has been reached by using the **eof( )** member function. It has this prototype:

　　int eof( );

It returns nonzero when the end of the file has been encountered and zero otherwise.

Once a file has been opened, it is very easy to read textual data from it or write formatted, textual data to it. Simply use the << and >> operators the same way you do when performing console I/O, except that instead of using **cin** and **cout**, you substitute a stream that is linked to a file. In a way, reading and writing files by using >> and << is like using C's **fprintf( )** and **fscanf( )** functions. All information is stored in the file in the same format as it would be displayed on the screen. Therefore, a file produced by using << is a formatted text file, and any file read by >> must be a formatted text file.

REMEMBER *When I/O is performed on text files, some character translations may occur. For example, newline characters may turn into carriage-return/ linefeed combinations. However, opening a file for binary operations prevents these translations from occurring.*

EXAMPLES

---

1. Here is a program that creates an output file, writes information to it, closes the file and opens it again as an input file, and reads in the information:

```
#include <iostream.h>
#include <fstream.h>

main()
{
  ofstream fout("test");  // create normal output file

  if(!fout) {
    cout << "Cannot open output file.\n";
    return 1;
  }

  fout << "Hello!\n";
  fout << 100 << ' ' << hex << 100 << endl;

  fout.close();

  ifstream fin("test"); // open normal input file

  if(!fin) {
    cout << "Cannot open input file.\n";
    return 1;
  }

  char str[80];
  int i;

  fin >> str >> i;
  cout << str << ' ' << i << endl;

  fin.close();
```

```
    return 0;
}
```

After you run this program, examine the contents of **test**. It will contain the following:

```
Hello!
100 64
```

As stated earlier, when the **<<** and **>>** operators are used to perform file I/O, information is formatted exactly as it would appear on the screen.

2. Following is another example of disk I/O. This program reads strings entered at the keyboard and writes them to disk. The program stops when the user enters a blank line. To use the program, specify the name of the output file on the command line.

```
#include <iostream.h>
#include <fstream.h>
#include <stdio.h>

main(int argc, char *argv[])
{
  if(argc!=2) {
    cout << "Usage: WRITE <filename>\n";
    return 1;
  }

  ofstream out(argv[1]); // output, normal file

  if(!out) {
    cout << "Cannot open output file.\n";
    return 1;
  }

  char str[80];
  cout << "Write strings to disk, RETURN to stop\n";

  do {
    cout << ": ";
    gets(str);
    out << str << endl;
  } while (*str);

  out.close();
  return 0;
}
```

3. Following is a program that copies a text file and, in the process, converts all spaces into | symbols. Notice how **eof( )** is used to check for the end of the input file. Notice also how the input stream **fin** has its **skipws** turned off. This prevents leading spaces from being skipped.

```
// Convert spaces to |s.
#include <iostream.h>
#include <fstream.h>

main(int argc, char *argv[])
{
  if(argc!=3) {
    cout << "Usage: CONVERT <input> <output>\n";
    return 1;
  }

  ifstream fin(argv[1]); // open input file
  ofstream fout(argv[2]);  // create output file
  if(!fout) {
    cout << "Cannot open output file.\n";
    return 1;
  }
  if(!fin) {
    cout << "Cannot open input file.\n";
    return 1;
  }

  char ch;

  fin.unsetf(ios::skipws);  // do not skip spaces
  while(!fin.eof()) {
    fin >> ch;
    if(ch==' ') ch = '|';
    fout << ch;
  }

  return 0;
}
```

EXERCISES

1. Write a program that will copy a text file. Have this program count the number of characters copied and display this result. Why does the number displayed differ from that shown when you list the output file in the directory?

2. Write a program that writes the following table of information to a file called **phone**.

```
Issac Newton, 415 555-3423
Robert Goddard, 213 555-2312
Enrico Fermi, 202 555-1111
```

3. Write a program that counts the number of words in a file.

9.3 *U*NFORMATTED, BINARY I/O

Although formatted text files like those produced by the preceding examples are useful in a variety of situations, they do not have the flexibility of unformatted, binary files. For this reason, C++ supports a wide range of binary (or "raw") file I/O functions.

The lowest level binary I/O functions are **get( )** and **put( )**. You may write a byte by using the member function **put( )** and read a byte by using the member function **get( )**. The **get( )** function has many forms, but the most commonly used version is shown here along with **put( )**:

```
istream &get(char &ch);
ostream &put(char ch);
```

The **get( )** function reads a single character from the associated stream and puts that value in *ch*. It returns a reference to the stream which will be null if EOF is encountered. The **put( )** function writes *ch* to the stream and returns the stream.

To read and write blocks of binary data, use C++'s **read( )** and **write( )** functions. Their prototypes are shown here:

istream &read(unsigned char *buf, int *num*);
ostream &write(const unsigned char *buf, int *num*);

The **read( )** function reads *num* bytes from the associated stream and puts them in the buffer pointed to by *buf*. The **write( )** function writes *num* bytes to the associated stream from the buffer pointed to by *buf*.

If the end of the file is reached before *num* characters have been read, **read( )** simply stops, and the buffer contains as many characters as were available. You can find out how many characters have been read by using another member function, called **gcount( )**, that has this prototype:

int gcount();

It returns the number of characters read by the last binary input operation.

 NOTE *It is not necessary to open a file using* **ios::binary** *in order to use the unformatted, binary file functions. These functions can be used to access either type of file. Specifying* **ios::binary** *simply prevents any character translations from occurring. Since character translations are not an issue in the examples in this book,* **ios::binary** *is not needed.*

■ **EXAMPLES**

1. The next program will display the contents of any file on the screen. It uses the **get( )** function.

```
#include <iostream.h>
#include <fstream.h>

main(int argc, char *argv[])
{
  char ch;

  if(argc!=2) {
    cout << "Usage: PR <filename>\n";
    return 1;
  }
  ifstream in(argv[1]);
```

```
      if(!in) {
        cout << "Cannot open file";
        return 1;
      }

      while(!in.eof()) {
        in.get(ch);
        cout << ch;
      }

      return 0;
    }
```

2. This program uses **put( )** to write characters to a file until the user enters a dollar sign:

```
#include <iostream.h>
#include <fstream.h>

main(int argc, char *argv[])
{
  char ch;

  if(argc!=2) {
    cout << "Usage: WRITE <filename>\n";
    return 1;
  }

  ofstream out(argv[1]);
  if(!out) {
    cout << "Cannot open file";
    return 1;
  }

  cout << "Enter a $ to stop\n";
  do {
    cout << ": ";
    cin.get(ch);
    out.put(ch);
  } while (ch!='$');

  out.close();

  return 0;
}
```

Notice that the program uses **get( )** to read characters from **cin**. This is necessary because using >> causes leading whitespace to be skipped. However, **get( )** does not discard spaces.

3. Here is a program that uses **write( )** to write a **double** and a string to a file called **test**:

```
#include <iostream.h>
#include <fstream.h>
#include <string.h>

main()
{
  ofstream out("test");
  if(!out) {
    cout << "Cannot open output file.\n";
    return 1;
  }

  double num = 100.45;
  char str[] = "This is a test";

  out.write((char *) &num, sizeof(double));
  out.write(str, strlen(str));

  out.close();

  return 0;
}
```

 NOTE *The type cast to* **(char *)** *inside the call to* **write( )** *is necessary when outputting a buffer that is not defined as a character array. Because of C++'s strong type checking, a pointer of one type will not automatically be converted into a pointer of another type.*

4. This program uses **read( )** to read the file created by the program in Example 3:

```
#include <iostream.h>
#include <fstream.h>

main()
{
  ifstream in("test");
  if(!in) {
    cout << "Cannot open input file.\n";
    return 1;
  }

  double num;
  char str[80];
```

```
    in.read((char *) &num, sizeof(double));
    in.read(str, 15);

    cout << num << ' ' << str;

    in.close();

    return 0;
}
```

As is the case with the program in the preceding example, the type cast inside **read()** is necessary because C++ will not automatically convert a pointer of one type to another.

5. The following program first writes an array of **double** values to a file and then reads them back. It also reports the number of characters read.

```
// Demonstrate gcount().
#include <iostream.h>
#include <fstream.h>

main()
{
  ofstream out("test");
  if(!out) {
    cout << "Cannot open output file.\n";
    return 1;
  }

  double nums[4] = {1.1, 2.2, 3.3, 4.4 };

  out.write((char *) nums, sizeof(nums));
  out.close();

  ifstream in("test");
  if(!in) {
    cout << "Cannot open input file.\n";
    return 1;
  }

  in.read((char *) &nums, sizeof(nums));

  int i;
  for(i=0; i<4; i++)
    cout << nums[i] << ' ';

  cout << '\n';

  cout << in.gcount() << " characters read\n";
```

```
    in.close();

    return 0;
}
```

EXERCISES

1. Rewrite your answers to Exercises 1 and 3 in the preceding section (9.2) so they use **get( )**, **put( )**, **read( )**, and/or **write( )**. (Use whichever of these functions you deem most appropriate.)

2. Given the following class, write a program that outputs the contents of the class to a file. Create an inserter function for this purpose.

```
class account {
    int custnum;
    char name[80];
    double balance;
public:
    account(int c, char *n, double b)
    {
        custnum = c;
        strcpy(name, n);
        balance = b;
    }
    // create inserter here
};
```

9.4 *M*ORE BINARY I/O FUNCTIONS

In addition to the form shown earlier, the **get( )** function is overloaded several different ways. The prototypes for the two most commonly used overloaded forms are shown here:

istream &get(char *buf*, int *num*, char *delim*='\n');
int get( );

The first overloaded form reads characters into the array pointed to by *buf* until either *num* characters have been read or the character specified by *delim* has been encountered. The array pointed to by *buf* will be null terminated by **get**( ). If no *delim* parameter is specified, by default a newline character acts as a delimiter. If the delimiter character is encountered in the input stream, it is *not* extracted. Instead, it remains in the stream until the next input operation.

The second overloaded form of **get**( ) returns the next character from the stream. It returns EOF if the end of the file is encountered. This form of **get**( ) is similar to C's **getc**( ) function.

Another member function that performs input is **getline**( ). Its prototype is shown here:

```
istream &getline(char *buf, int num, char delim='\n');
```

As you can see, this function is virtually identical to the **get(buf, num, delim)** version of **get**( ). It reads characters from input and puts them into the array pointed to by *buf* until either *num* characters have been read or until the character specified by *delim* is encountered. If not specified, *delim* defaults to the newline character. The array pointed to by *buf* is null terminated. The difference between **get(buf, num, delim)** and **getline**( ) is that **getline**( ) reads and removes the delimiter from the input stream.

You can obtain the next character in the input stream without removing it from that stream by using **peek**( ). It has this prototype:

```
int peek( );
```

It returns the next character in the stream or EOF if the end of the file is encountered.

You can return the last character read from a stream to that stream by using **putback**( ). Its prototype is shown here:

```
istream &putback(char c);
```

where *c* is the last character read.

When output is performed, data is not immediately written to the physical device linked to the stream. Instead, information is stored in an internal buffer until the buffer is full. Only then are the contents of that buffer written to disk. However, you can force the information to be physically written to disk before the buffer is full by calling **flush**( ). Its prototype is shown here:

```
ostream &flush( );
```

Calls to **flush( )** might be warranted when a program is going to be used in adverse environments (in situations where power outages occur frequently, for example).

EXAMPLES

1. As you know, when you use **>>** to read a string, it stops reading when the first whitespace character is encountered. This makes it useless for reading a string containing spaces. However, you can overcome this problem by using **getline( )**, as this program illustrates:

```
// Use getline() to read a string that contains spaces.
#include <iostream.h>
#include <fstream.h>

main()
{
  char str[80];

  cout << "Enter your name: ";
  cin.getline(str, 79);

  cout << str << '\n';

  return 0;
}
```

In this case, the final parameter to **getline( )** is allowed to default to a newline. This makes **getline( )** act much like the standard **gets( )** function.

2. In real programming situations, the functions **peek( )** and **putback( )** are especially useful because they let you more easily handle situations in which you do not know what type of information is being input at any point in time. The following program gives the flavor of this. It reads either strings or integers from a file. The strings and integers may occur in any order.

```
// Demonstrate peek().
#include <iostream.h>
#include <fstream.h>
```

```
#include <ctype.h>
#include <stdlib.h>

main()
{
  char ch;
  ofstream out("test");
  if(!out) {
    cout << "Cannot open output file.\n";
    return 1;
  }

  char str[80], *p;

  out << 123 << "this is a test" << 23;
  out << "Hello there!" << 99 << "sdf" << endl;
  out.close();

  ifstream in("test");
  if(!in) {
    cout << "Cannot open input file.\n";
    return 1;
  }

  do {
    p = str;
    ch = in.peek(); // see what type of char is next
    if(isdigit(ch)) {
      while(isdigit(*p=in.get())) p++; // read integer
      in.putback(*p); // return char to stream
      *p = '\0'; // null terminate the string
      cout << "Integer: " << atoi(str);
    }
    else if(isalpha(ch)) { // read a string
      while(isalpha(*p=in.get())) p++;
      in.putback(*p); // return char to stream
      *p = '\0'; // null terminate the string
      cout << "String: " << str;
    }
    else in.get(); // ignore
    cout << '\n';
  } while(!in.eof());

  in.close();
  return 0;
}
```

EXERCISES

1. Rewrite the program in Example 1 so it uses **get( )** instead of **getline( )**. Does the program function differently?

2. Write a program that reads a text file one line at a time and displays each line on the screen. Use **getline( )**.

3. On your own, think about why there may be cases in which a call to **flush( )** is appropriate.

9.5 RANDOM ACCESS

In C++'s I/O system, you perform random access by using the **seekg( )** and **seekp( )** functions. Their most common forms are shown here:

```
istream &seekg(streamoff offset, seek_dir origin);
ostream &seekp(streamoff offset, seek_dir origin);
```

Here, **streamoff** is a type defined in **iostream.h** that is capable of containing the largest valid value that *offset* can have. **seek_dir** is an enumeration that has these values:

Value	Meaning
ios::beg	seek from beginning
ios::cur	seek from current location
ios::end	seek from end

The C++ I/O system manages two pointers associated with a file. One is the *get pointer*, which specifies where in the file the next input operation will occur. The other is the *put pointer*, which specifies where in the file the next output operation will occur. Each time an input or output operation takes place, the appropriate pointer is automatically sequentially advanced. However, by using the **seekg( )** and **seekp( )** functions, it is possible to access the file in a nonsequential fashion.

The **seekg( )** function moves the associated file's current get pointer *offset* number of bytes from the specified *origin*. The **seekp( )** function moves the associated file's current put pointer *offset* number of bytes from the specified *origin*.

You can determine the current position of each file pointer by using these functions:

```
streampos tellg();
streampos tellp();
```

Here, **streampos** is a type defined in **iostream.h** that is capable of holding the largest value that either function can return.

EXAMPLES

1. The following program demonstrates the **seekp( )** function. It allows you to change a specific character in a file. Specify a file name on the command line, followed by the number of the byte in the file you want to change, followed by the new character. Notice that the file is opened for read/write operations.

```
#include <iostream.h>
#include <fstream.h>
#include <stdlib.h>

main(int argc, char *argv[])
{
  if(argc!=4) {
    cout << "Usage: CHANGE <filename> <byte> <char>\n";
    return 1;
  }

  fstream out(argv[1], ios::in|ios::out);
  if(!out) {
    cout << "Cannot open file";
    return 1;
  }

  out.seekp(atoi(argv[2]), ios::beg);

  out.put(*argv[3]);
  out.close();

  return 0;
}
```

2. The next program uses **seekg( )** to position the get pointer into the middle of a file and then displays the contents of that file from that point. The name of the file and the location to begin reading from are specified on the command line.

```cpp
// Demonstrate seekg().
#include <iostream.h>
#include <fstream.h>
#include <stdlib.h>

main(int argc, char *argv[])
{
  char ch;

  if(argc!=3) {
    cout << "Usage: LOCATE <filename> <loc>\n";
    return 1;
  }

  ifstream in(argv[1]);
  if(!in) {
    cout << "Cannot open input file.\n";
    return 1;
  }

  in.seekg(atoi(argv[2]), ios::beg);

  while(!in.eof()) {
    in.get(ch);
    cout << ch;
  }

  in.close();

  return 0;
}
```

EXERCISES

1. Write a program that displays a text file backwards. Hint: Think about this before creating your program. The solution is easier than you may imagine.

2. Write a program that swaps each character pair in a text file. For example, if the file contains "1234", then after the program is run, the file will contain "2143". (For simplicity, you may assume that the file contains an even number of characters.)

9.6   *C*HECKING THE I/O STATUS

The C++ I/O system maintains status information about the outcome of each I/O operation. The current state of the I/O system is held in an integer, in which the following flags are encoded:

Name	Meaning
goodbit	0 when no errors occur 1 when an error is flagged
eofbit	1 when end of file is encountered 0 otherwise
failbit	1 when a nonfatal I/O error has occurred 0 otherwise
badbit	1 when a fatal I/O error has occurred 0 otherwise

These flags are enumerated inside **ios**.

There are two ways in which you can obtain I/O status information. First, you can call the **rdstate( )** member function. It has this prototype:

```
int rdstate( );
```

It returns the current status of the error flags encoded into an integer. As you can probably guess from looking at the preceding list of flags, **rdstate( )** returns zero when no error has occurred. Otherwise, an error bit is turned on.

The other way you can determine if an error has occurred is by using one or more of these functions:

```
int   bad()
int   eof()
int   fail()
int   good()
```

The **eof( )** function was discussed earlier. The **bad( )** function returns true if **badbit** is set. The **fail( )** function returns true if **failbit** is set. The **good( )** function returns true if there are no errors. Otherwise they return false.

Once an error has occurred, it may need to be cleared before your program continues. To do this, use the **clear( )** function, whose prototype is shown here:

```
void clear(int flags=0);
```

If *flags* is zero (as it is by default), all error flags are cleared (reset to zero). Otherwise, set *flags* to the flags or settings you desire.

NOTE *The proposed ANSI C++ standard defines the type* **iostate***, which is an integer type capable of holding the I/O system's status. It uses this type, rather than* **int***, to represent the I/O status when it defines such functions as* **rdstate( )** *and* **clear( )***. However, at the time of this writing, no compilers support this type. But, for practical purposes, this distinction is irrelevant.*

EXAMPLES

1. The following program illustrates **rdstate( )**. It displays the contents of a text file. If an error occurs, the function reports it by using **checkstatus( )**.

```
#include <iostream.h>
#include <fstream.h>

void checkstatus(ifstream &in);

main(int argc, char *argv[])
{
```

```
    if(argc!=2) {
      cout << "Usage: DISPLAY <filename>\n";
      return 1;
    }

    ifstream in(argv[1]);

    if(!in) {
      cout << "Cannot open input file.\n";
      return 1;
    }

    char c;
    while(in.get(c)) {
      cout << c;
      checkstatus(in);
    }

    checkstatus(in);   // check final status
    in.close();
    return 0;
  }

  void checkstatus(ifstream &in)
  {
    int i;

    i = in.rdstate();

    if(i & ios::eofbit)
      cout << "EOF encountered\n";
    else if(i & ios::failbit)
      cout << "Non-Fatal I/O error\n";
    else if(i & ios::badbit)
      cout << "Fatal I/O error\n";
  }
```

The preceding program will always report one "error." After the **while** loop ends, the final call to **checkstatus( )** reports, as expected, that an EOF has been encountered.

2. This program uses **good( )** to detect a file error:

```
#include <iostream.h>
#include <fstream.h>
```

```
main(int argc, char *argv[])
{
  char ch;

  if(argc!=2) {
    cout << "PR: <filename>\n";
    return 1;
  }

  ifstream in(argv[1]);
  if(!in) {
    cout << "Cannot open input file.\n";
    return 1;
  }

  while(!in.eof()) {
    in.get(ch);
    // check for error
    if(!in.good() && !in.eof()) {
      cout << "I/O Error...terminating\n";
      return 1;
    }
    cout << ch;
  }

  in.close();

  return 0;
}
```

EXERCISE

1. Add error checking to your answers to questions from the preceding section.

9.7 CUSTOMIZED I/O AND FILES

In the preceding chapter, you learned how to overload the insertion and extraction operators relative to your own classes. In that chapter, only console I/O was performed. However, because all C++ streams are the same, the same overloaded inserter function, for example, can be used to output to the screen or to a file with no changes whatsoever. This is one of the most important and useful features of C++'s approach to I/O.

As stated in the previous chapter, overloaded inserters and extractors, as well as I/O manipulators, can be used with any stream provided they are written in a general manner. If you "hardcode" a specific stream into an I/O function, its use is, of course, limited to only that stream. This is why you were urged to generalize your I/O functions whenever possible.

EXAMPLES

1. In the following program, the **coord** class overloads the **<<** and **>>** operators. Notice that you can use the operator functions to write both to the screen and to a file.

```cpp
#include <iostream.h>
#include <fstream.h>

class coord {
  int x, y;
public:
  coord(int i, int j) { x = i; y = j; }
  friend ostream &operator<<(ostream &stream, coord ob);
  friend istream &operator>>(istream &stream, coord &ob);
};

ostream &operator<<(ostream &stream, coord ob)
{
  stream << ob.x << ' ' << ob.y << '\n';

  return stream;
}

istream &operator>>(istream &stream, coord &ob)
{
  stream >> ob.x >> ob.y;

  return stream;
}

main()
{
  coord o1(1, 2), o2(3, 4);
```

```
      ofstream out("test");

      if(!out) {
        cout << "Cannot open output file\n";
        return 1;
      }

      out << o1 << o2;

      out.close();

      ifstream in("test");
      if(!in) {
        cout << "Cannot open input file\n";
        return 1;
      }

      coord o3(0, 0), o4(0, 0);
      in >> o3 >> o4;

      cout << o3 << o4;

      return 0;
    }
```

2. All of the I/O manipulators can be used with files. For example, in this reworked version of a program presented earlier in this chapter, the same manipulator that writes to the screen will also write to a file:

```
#include <iostream.h>
#include <fstream.h>
#include <iomanip.h>

// Attention:
ostream &atn(ostream &stream)
{
  stream << "Attention: ";
  return stream;
}

// Please note:
ostream &note(ostream &stream)
{
  stream << "Please Note: ";
  return stream;
}

main()
{
  ofstream out("test");
```

```
        if(!out) {
          cout << "Cannot open output file\n";
          return 1;
        }

        // write to screen
        cout << atn << "High voltage circuit\n";
        cout << note << "Turn off all lights\n";

        // write to file
        out << atn << "High voltage circuit\n";
        out << note << "Turn off all lights\n";

        out.close();

        return 0;
      }
```

EXERCISE

1. On your own, experiment with the programs from the preceding chapter, trying each on a disk file.

mastery

skills check

At this point you should be able to perform the following exercises and answer the questions.

1. Create an output manipulator that outputs three tabs and then sets the field width to 20. Demonstrate that your manipulator works.

2. Create an input manipulator that reads and discards all nonalphabetical characters. When the first alphabetical character is read, have the manipulator return it to the input stream and return. Call this manipulator **findalpha**.

3. Write a program that copies a text file. In the process, reverse the case of all letters.

4. Write a program that reads a text file and then reports the number of times each letter in the alphabet occurs in the file.

5. If you have not done so, add complete error checking to your solutions to Exercises 3 and 4 above.

6. What function positions the get pointer? What function positions the put pointer?

**cumulative
skills check**

This section checks how well you have integrated material in this chapter with that from the preceding chapters.

1. Following is a reworked version of the **inventory** class presented in the preceding chapter. Write a program that fills in the functions **store( )** and **retrieve( )**. Next, create a small inventory file on disk containing a few entries. Then, using random I/O, allow the user to display the information about any item by specifying its record number.

```cpp
#include <fstream.h>
#include <iostream.h>
#include <string.h>

#define SIZE 40

class inventory {
  char item[SIZE]; // name of item
  int onhand; // number on hand
  double cost;  // cost of item
public:
  inventory(char *i, int o, double c)
  {
    strcpy(item, i);
```

```
      onhand = o;
      cost = c;
    }
    void store(fstream &stream);
    void retrieve(fstream &stream);
    friend ostream &operator<<(ostream &stream, inventory ob);
    friend istream &operator>>(istream &stream, inventory &ob);
};

ostream &operator<<(ostream &stream, inventory ob)
{
  stream << ob.item << ": " << ob.onhand;
  stream << " on hand at $" << ob.cost << '\n';

  return stream;
}

istream &operator>>(istream &stream, inventory &ob)
{
  cout << "Enter item name: ";
  stream >> ob.item;
  cout << "Enter number on hand: ";
  stream >> ob.onhand;
  cout << "Enter cost: ";
  stream >> ob.cost;

  return stream;
}
```

2. As a special challenge on your own, create a **stack** class for characters that stores them in a disk file rather than in an array in memory.

10

Virtual Functions

chapter objectives

10.1 Pointers to derived classes

10.2 Introducing virtual functions

10.3 More about virtual functions

10.4 Applying polymorphism

THIS chapter examines another important aspect of C++: the virtual function. What makes virtual functions important is that they are used to support run-time polymorphism. As you know, polymorphism is supported by C++ in two ways. First, it is supported at compile time, through the use of overloaded operators and functions. Second, it is supported at run time, through the use of virtual functions. As you will learn, run-time polymorphism provides the greatest flexibility.

At the foundation of virtual functions and run-time polymorphism are pointers to derived classes. For this reason this chapter begins with a discussion of pointers to derived classes.

review

skills check

Before proceeding, you should be able to correctly answer the following questions and do the exercises.

1. Create a manipulator that causes numbers to be displayed in scientific notation, using a capital E.

2. Write a program that copies a text file. During the copy process, convert all tabs into the correct number of spaces.

3. Write a program that searches a text file for a word specified on the command line. Have the program display how many times the specified word is found.

4. Show the statement that sets the put pointer to the 234th byte in a file linked to a stream called **out**.

5. What functions report status information about the C++ I/O system?

6. Give one advantage of using the C++ I/O functions instead of the C-like I/O system.

10.1 *P*OINTERS TO DERIVED CLASSES

Although Chapter 4 discussed C++ pointers at some length, one special aspect was deferred until now because it relates specifically to virtual functions. The feature is this: A pointer declared as a pointer to a base class can also be used to point to any class derived from that base. For example, assume two classes called **base** and **derived**, where **derived** inherits **base**. Given this situation, the following statements are correct:

```
base *p; // base class pointer

base base_ob; // object of type base
derived derived_ob; // object of type derived

// p can, of course, point to base objects
p = &base_ob; // p points to base object

// p can also point to derived objects without error
p = &derived_ob; // p points to derived object
```

As the comments suggest, a base pointer can point to an object of any class derived from that base without generating a type mismatch error.

Although you can use a base pointer to point to a derived object, you can access only those members of the derived object that were inherited from the base. This is because the base pointer has knowledge only of the base class. It knows nothing about the members added by the derived class.

While it is permissible for a base pointer to point to a derived object, the reverse is not true. A pointer of the derived type cannot be used to access an object of the base class. (A type cast can be used to overcome this restriction, but its use is not recommended practice.)

One final point: Remember that pointer arithmetic is relative to the data type the pointer is declared as pointing to. Thus, if you point a base pointer to a derived object and then increment that pointer, it will not be pointing to the next derived object. It will be pointing to (what it thinks is) the next base object. Be careful about this.

EXAMPLE

1. Here is a short program that illustrates how a base class pointer can be used to access a derived class:

```
// Demonstrate pointer to derived class.
#include <iostream.h>
```

```
class base {
  int x;
public:
  void setx(int i) { x = i; }
  int getx() { return x; }
};

class derived : public base {
  int y;
public:
  void sety(int i) { y = i; }
  int gety() { return y; }
};

main()
{
  base *p; // pointer to base type
  base b_ob; // object of base
  derived d_ob; // object of derived

  // use p to access base object
  p = &b_ob;
  p->setx(10); // access base object
  cout << "Base object x: " << p->getx() << '\n';

  // use p to access derived object
  p = &d_ob; // point to derived object
  p->setx(99); // access derived object

  // can't use p to set y, so do it directly
  d_ob.sety(88);
  cout << "Derived object x: " << p->getx() << ' ';
  cout << "Derived object y: " << d_ob.gety() << '\n';

  return 0;
}
```

Aside from illustrating pointers to derived classes, there is no value in using a base class pointer in the way shown in this example. However, in the next section you will see why base class pointers to derived objects are so important.

1. On your own, try the preceding example and experiment with it. For example, try declaring a derived pointer and having it access an object of the base class.

10.2 INTRODUCING VIRTUAL FUNCTIONS

A *virtual function* is a class member function that is declared within a base class and redefined by a derived class. To create a virtual function, precede the function's declaration with the keyword **virtual**. When a class containing a virtual function is inherited, the derived class redefines the virtual function relative to the derived class. In essence, virtual functions implement the "one interface, multiple methods" philosophy that underlies polymorphism. The virtual function within the base class defines the *form* of the *interface* to that function. Each redefinition of the virtual function by a derived class implements its operation as it relates specifically to the derived class. That is, the redefinition creates a *specific method*. When a virtual function is redefined by a derived class, the keyword **virtual** is not needed.

A virtual function can be called just like any other member function. However, what makes a virtual function interesting—and capable of supporting run-time polymorphism—is what happens when a virtual function is called by using a pointer. From the preceding section you know that a base class pointer can be used to point to a derived class object. When a base pointer points to a derived object that contains a virtual function and that virtual function is called through that pointer, the compiler determines which version of that function to call based upon the type of object being pointed to by the pointer. Put differently, it is the type of the object pointed to that determines which version of the virtual function will be executed. Therefore, if two or more different classes are derived from a base class that contains a virtual function, then when different objects are pointed to by a base pointer, different versions of the virtual function are executed. This process is the way that run-time polymorphism is achieved. In fact, a class that contains a virtual function is referred to as a *polymorphic class*.

1. Here is a short example that uses a virtual function:

```cpp
// A simple example using a virtual function.
#include <iostream.h>

class base {
public:
  int i;
  base(int x) { i = x; }
  virtual void func()
  {
    cout << "Using base version of func(): ";
    cout << i << '\n';
  }
};

class derived1 : public base {
public:
  derived1(int x) : base(x) {}
  void func()
  {
    cout << "Using derived1's version of func(): ";
    cout << i*i << '\n';
  }
};

class derived2 : public base {
public:
  derived2(int x) : base(x) {}
  void func()
  {
    cout << "Using derived2's version of func(): ";
    cout << i+i << '\n';
  }
};

main()
{
  base *p;
  base ob(10);
  derived1 d_ob1(10);
  derived2 d_ob2(10);

  p = &ob;
  p->func(); // use base's func()
```

```
   p = &d_ob1;
   p->func(); // use derived1's func()

   p = &d_ob2;
   p->func(); // use derived2's func()

   return 0;
}
```

This program displays the following output:

```
Using base version of func(): 10
Using derived1's version of func(): 100
Using derived2's version of func(): 20
```

The redefinition of a virtual function inside a derived class may, at first, seem somewhat similar to function overloading. However, the two processes are distinctly different. First, an overloaded function must differ in type and/or number of parameters, while a redefined virtual function must have precisely the same type and number of parameters and the same return type. (In fact, if you change either the number or type of parameters when redefining a virtual function, it simply becomes an overloaded function, and its virtual nature is lost.) Further, virtual functions must be class members. This is not the case for overloaded functions. Also, while destructor functions may be virtual, constructors may not. Because of the differences between overloaded functions and redefined virtual functions, the term *overriding* is used to describe virtual function redefinition.

As you can see, the example program creates three classes. The **base** class defines the virtual function **func( )**. This class is then inherited by both **derived1** and **derived2**. Each of these classes overrides **func( )** with its individual implementation. Inside **main( )**, the base class pointer **p** is declared along with objects of type **base**, **derived1**, and **derived2**. First, **p** is assigned the address of **ob** (an object of type **base**). When **func( )** is called by using **p**, it is the version in **base** that is used. Next, **p** is assigned the address of **d_ob1** and **func( )** is called again. Because it is the type of the object pointed to that determines which virtual function will be called, this time it is the overridden version in **derived1** that is executed. Finally, **p** is assigned the address of **d_ob2** and **func( )** is called again. This time, it is the version of **func( )** defined inside **derived2** that is executed.

The key points to understand from the preceding example are that the type of the object being pointed to determines which version of an overridden virtual function will be executed when accessed via a base class pointer, and that this decision is made at run time.

2. Virtual functions are hierarchical in order of inheritance. Further, when a derived class does *not* override a virtual function, the function defined within its base class is used. For example, here is a slightly different version of the preceding program:

```
// Virtual functions are hierarchical.
#include <iostream.h>

class base {
public:
  int i;
  base(int x) { i = x; }
  virtual void func()
  {
    cout << "Using base version of func(): ";
    cout << i << '\n';
  }
};

class derived1 : public base {
public:
  derived1(int x) : base(x) {}
  void func()
  {
    cout << "Using derived1's version of func(): ";
    cout << i*i << '\n';
  }
};

class derived2 : public base {
public:
  derived2(int x) : base(x) {}
  // derived2 does not override func()
};

main()
{
  base *p;
  base ob(10);
  derived1 d_ob1(10);
  derived2 d_ob2(10);
  p = &ob;
  p->func(); // use base's func()

  p = &d_ob1;
  p->func(); // use derived1's func()
```

```
    p = &d_ob2;
    p->func(); // use base's func()

    return 0;
}
```

This program displays the following output:

```
Using base version of func(): 10
Using derived1's version of func(): 100
Using base version of func(): 10
```

In this version, **derived2** does not override **func( )**. When **p** is assigned **d_ob2** and **func( )** is called, **base**'s version is used because it is next up in the class hierarchy. In general, when a derived class does not override a virtual function, the base class's version is used.

3. The next example shows how a virtual function can respond to random events occurring at run time. This program selects between **d_ob1** and **d_ob2** based upon the value returned by the standard random number generator **rand( )**. Keep in mind that the version of **func( )** executed is resolved at run time. (Indeed, it is impossible to resolve the calls to **func( )** at compile time.)

```
/* This example illustrates how a virtual function
   can be used to respond to random events occurring
   at run time.
*/
#include <iostream.h>
#include <stdlib.h>

class base {
public:
  int i;
  base(int x) { i = x; }
  virtual void func()
  {
    cout << "Using base version of func(): ";
    cout << i << '\n';
  }
};

class derived1 : public base {
public:
  derived1(int x) : base(x) {}
  void func()
  {
    cout << "Using derived1's version of func(): ";
    cout << i*i << '\n';
```

```
    }
};

class derived2 : public base {
public:
  derived2(int x) : base(x) {}
  void func()
  {
    cout << "Using derived2's version of func(): ";
    cout << i+i << '\n';
  }
};

main()
{
  base *p;
  derived1 d_ob1(10);
  derived2 d_ob2(10);
  int i, j;

  for(i=0; i<10; i++) {
    j = rand();
    if((j%2)) p = &d_ob1; // if odd use d_ob1
    else p = &d_ob2; // if even use d_ob2
    p->func(); // call appropriate function
  }

  return 0;
}
```

4. Here is a more practical example of how a virtual function can be used. This program creates a generic base class called **area** that holds two dimensions of a figure. It also declares a virtual function called **getarea( )** that, when overridden by derived classes, returns the area of the type of figure defined by the derived class. In this case, the declaration of **getarea( )** inside the base class determines the nature of the interface. The actual implementation is left to the classes that inherit it. In this example, the area of a triangle and a rectangle are computed.

```
// Use virtual function to define interface.
#include <iostream.h>

class area {
  double dim1, dim2; // dimensions of figure
public:
  void setarea(double d1, double d2)
  {
    dim1 = d1;
```

```
      dim2 = d2;
    }
    void getdim(double &d1, double &d2)
    {
      d1 = dim1;
      d2 = dim2;
    }
    virtual double getarea()
    {
      cout << "You must override this function\n";
      return 0.0;
    }
};

class rectangle : public area {
public:
  double getarea()
  {
    double d1, d2;
    getdim(d1, d2);
    return d1 * d2;
  }
};

class triangle : public area {
public:
  double getarea()
  {
    double d1, d2;

    getdim(d1, d2);
    return 0.5 * d1 * d2;
  }
};

main()
{
  area *p;
  rectangle r;
  triangle t;

  r.setarea(3.3, 4.5);
  t.setarea(4.0, 5.0);

  p = &r;
  cout << "Rectangle has area: " << p->getarea() << '\n';

  p = &t;
  cout << "Triangle has area: " << p->getarea() << '\n';
```

```
        return 0;
}
```

Notice that the definition of **getarea( )** inside **area** is just a placeholder and performs no real function. Because **area** is not linked to any specific type of figure, there is no meaningful definition that can be given to **getarea( )** inside **area**. In fact, **getarea( )** must be overridden by a derived class in order to be useful. In the next section, you will see a way to enforce this.

---

1. Write a program that creates a base class called **num**. Have this class hold an integer value and contain a virtual function called **shownum( )**. Create two derived classes called **outhex** and **outoct** that inherit **num**. Have the derived classes override **shownum( )** so that it displays the value in hexadecimal and octal, respectively.

2. Write a program that creates a base class called **distance** that stores the distance between two points in a **double** variable. In **distance**, create a virtual function called **trav_time( )** that outputs the time it takes to travel that distance, assuming that the distance is in miles and the speed is 60 miles per hour. In a derived class called **metric**, override **trav_time( )** so that it outputs the travel time assuming that the distance is in kilometers and the speed is 100 kilometers per hour.

10.3   *M*ORE ABOUT VIRTUAL FUNCTIONS

As Example 4 from the preceding section illustrates, sometimes when a virtual function is declared in the base class, there is no meaningful operation for it to perform. This situation is common because often a base class does not define a complete class by itself. Instead, it simply supplies a core set of member functions and variables to which the derived class supplies the remainder. When there is no meaningful action for a base class virtual function to perform, the implication is that any derived class *must* override this function. To ensure that this will occur, C++ supports *pure virtual functions.*

A pure virtual function has no definition relative to the base class. Only the function's prototype is included. To make a pure virtual function, use this general form:

virtual *type func-name(parameter-list)* = 0;

The key part of this declaration is the setting of the function equal to zero. This tells the compiler that no body exists for this function relative to the base class. When a virtual function is made pure, it forces any derived class to override it. If a derived class does not, a compile-time error results. Thus, making a virtual function pure is a way to guarantee that a derived class will provide its own redefinition.

When a class contains at least one pure virtual function, it is referred to as an *abstract class.* Since an abstract class contains at least one function for which no body exists, it is, technically, an incomplete type, and no objects of that class can be created. Thus, abstract classes exist only to be inherited. They are neither intended nor able to stand alone. It is important to understand, however, that you can still create a pointer to an abstract class since it is through the use of base class pointers that run-time polymorphism is achieved. (It is also permissible to have a reference to an abstract class.)

When a virtual function is inherited, so is its virtual nature. This means that when a derived class inherits a virtual function from a base class and then the derived class is used as a base for yet another derived class, the virtual function may be overridden by the final derived class (as well as the first derived class). For example, if base class B contains a virtual function called f( ), and D1 inherits B and D2 inherits D1, then both D1 and D2 may override f( ) relative to their respective classes.

EXAMPLES

1. Here is an improved version of the program shown in Example 4 in the preceding section. In this version, the function **getarea( )** is declared as pure in the base class **area**.

```
// Create an abstract class.
#include <iostream.h>

class area {
  double dim1, dim2; // dimensions of figure
public:
  void setarea(double d1, double d2)
  {
    dim1 = d1;
    dim2 = d2;
  }
  void getdim(double &d1, double &d2)
  {
    d1 = dim1;
    d2 = dim2;
  }
  virtual double getarea() = 0; // pure virtual function
};

class rectangle : public area {
public:
  double getarea()
  {
    double d1, d2;

    getdim(d1, d2);
    return d1 * d2;
  }
};

class triangle : public area {
public:
  double getarea()
  {
    double d1, d2;

    getdim(d1, d2);
    return 0.5 * d1 * d2;
  }
};

main()
{
  area *p;
  rectangle r;
  triangle t;

  r.setarea(3.3, 4.5);
  t.setarea(4.0, 5.0);
```

```
   p = &r;
   cout << "Rectangle has area: " << p->getarea() << '\n';

   p = &t;
   cout << "Triangle has area: " << p->getarea() << '\n';

   return 0;
}
```

Now that **getarea( )** is pure, it ensures that each derived class will override it.

2. The following program illustrates how a function's virtual nature is preserved when inherited:

```
// Virtual functions retain their virtual nature when inherited.
#include <iostream.h>

class base {
public:
  virtual void func()
  {
    cout << "Using base version of func()\n";
  }
};

class derived1 : public base {
public:
  void func()
  {
    cout << "Using derived1's version of func()\n";
  }
};

// Derived2 inherits derived1.
class derived2 : public derived1 {
public:
  void func()
  {
    cout << "Using derived2's version of func()\n";
  }
};

main()
{
  base *p;
  base ob;
  derived1 d_ob1;
  derived2 d_ob2;
```

```
    p = &ob;
    p->func(); // use base's func()

    p = &d_ob1;
    p->func(); // use derived1's func()

    p = &d_ob2;
    p->func(); // use derived2's func()

    return 0;
}
```

In this program, the virtual function **func( )** is first inherited by **derived1**, which overrides it relative to itself. Next, **derived2** inherits **derived1**. In **derived2**, **func( )** is again overridden.

Because virtual functions are hierarchical, if **derived2** did not override **func( )**, then when **d_ob2** was accessed, **derived1**'s **func( )** would have been used. If neither **derived1** nor **derived2** had overridden **func( )**, all references to it would have been routed to the one defined in **base**.

EXERCISES

1. On your own, experiment with the two example programs. Specifically, try creating an object by using **area** from Example 1 and observe the error message. In Example 2, try removing the redefinition of **func( )** within **derived2**. Confirm that, indeed, the version inside **derived1** is used.

2. Why can't an object be created by using an abstract class?

3. In Example 2, what happens if you remove only the redefinition of **func( )** inside **derived1**? Does the program still compile and run? If so, why?

10.4 ▲PPLYING POLYMORPHISM

Now that you know how to use a virtual function to achieve run-time polymorphism, it is time to consider how and why to use it. As has been stated many times in this book, polymorphism is the process by which a common interface is applied to two or more similar (but technically different) situations, thus implementing the "one interface, multiple methods" philosophy.

Polymorphism is important because it can greatly simplify complex systems. A single, well-defined interface is used to access a number of different but related actions, and artificial complexity is removed. In essence, polymorphism allows the logical relationship of similar actions to become apparent; thus, the program is easier to understand and maintain. When related actions are accessed through a common interface, you have less to remember.

There are two terms that are often linked to OOP in general and to C++ specifically. They are *early binding* and *late binding*. It is important that you know what they mean. Early binding essentially refers to those events that can be known at compile time. Specifically, it refers to those function calls that can be resolved during compilation. Early bound entities include "normal" functions, overloaded functions, and nonvirtual member and friend functions. When these types of functions are compiled, all address information necessary to call them is known at compile time. The main advantage of early binding (and the reason that it is so widely used) is that it is very efficient. Calls to functions bound at compile time are the fastest types of function calls. The main disadvantage is lack of flexibility.

Late binding refers to events that must occur at run time. A late bound function call is one in which the address of the function to be called is not known until the program runs. In C++, a virtual function is a late bound object. When a virtual function is accessed via a base class pointer, the program must determine at run time what type of object is being pointed to and then select which version of the overridden function to execute. The main advantage of late binding is flexibility at run time. Your program is free to respond to random events without having to contain large amounts of "contingency code." Its primary disadvantage is that there is more overhead associated with a function call. This generally makes such calls slower than those that occur with early binding.

Because of the potential efficiency trade-offs, you must decide when it is appropriate to use early binding and when to use late binding.

EXAMPLES

1. Here is a program that illustrates "one interface, multiple methods." It implements a generic singly linked list class for integer values. It also declares the nature of the interface to a list. To store a value, call the

store( ) function. To retrieve a value from the list, call **retrieve( )**. The
base class **list** does not define any default methods for these actions.
Instead, each derived class defines exactly what type of list will be
maintained. In the program, two types of lists are created: a queue and a
stack. However, although the two lists operate completely differently,
each is accessed using the same interface. You should study this program
carefully.

```cpp
// Create a generic list class for integers.
#include <iostream.h>
#include <stdlib.h>
#include <ctype.h>

class list {
public:
  list *head; // pointer to start of list
  list *tail; // pointer to end of list
  list *next; // pointer to next item
  int num; // value to be stored
  list() { head = tail = next = NULL; }
  virtual void store(int i) = 0;
  virtual int retrieve() = 0;
};

// Create a queue type list.
class queue : public list {
public:
  void store(int i);
  int retrieve();
};

void queue::store(int i)
{
  list *item;

  item = new queue;
  if(!item) {
    cout << "Allocation error\n";
    exit(1);
  }
  item->num = i;

  // put on end of list
  if(tail) tail->next = item;
  tail = item;
  item->next = NULL;
  if(!head) head = tail;
}
```

```cpp
int queue::retrieve()
{
  int i;
  list *p;

  if(!head) {
    cout << "List empty\n";
    return 0;
  }

  // remove from start of list
  i = head->num;
  p = head;
  head = head->next;
  delete p;

  return i;
}

// Create a stack type list.
class stack : public list {
public:
  void store(int i);
  int retrieve();
};

void stack::store(int i)
{
  list *item;

  item = new stack;
  if(!item) {
    cout << "Allocation error\n";
    exit(1);
  }
  item->num = i;

  // put on front of list for stack-like operation
  if(head) item->next = head;
  head = item;
  if(!tail) tail = head;
}

int stack::retrieve()
{
  int i;
  list *p;

  if(!head) {
    cout << "List empty\n";
```

```
      return 0;
    }

    // remove from start of list
    i = head->num;
    p = head;
    head = head->next;
    delete p;

    return i;
}

main()
{
  list *p;

  // demonstrate queue
  queue q_ob;

  p = &q_ob; // point to queue

  p->store(1);
  p->store(2);
  p->store(3);

  cout << "Queue: ";
  cout << p->retrieve();
  cout << p->retrieve();
  cout << p->retrieve();

  cout << '\n';

  // demonstrate stack
  stack s_ob;

  p = &s_ob; // point to stack

  p->store(1);
  p->store(2);
  p->store(3);

  cout << "Stack: ";
  cout << p->retrieve();
  cout << p->retrieve();
  cout << p->retrieve();

  cout << '\n';

  return 0;
}
```

2. The **main( )** function in the list program just shown simply illustrates that the list classes do, indeed, work. However, to begin to see why run-time polymorphism is so powerful, try using this **main( )** instead:

```
main()
{
  list *p;
  stack s_ob;
  queue q_ob;
  char ch;
  int i;

  for(i=0; i<10; i++) {
    cout << "Stack or Queue? (S/Q): ";
    cin >> ch;
    ch = tolower(ch);
    if(ch=='q') p = &q_ob;
    else p = &s_ob;
    p->store(i);
  }

  cout << "Enter T to terminate\n";
  for(;;) {
    cout << "Remove from Stack or Queue? (S/Q): ";
    cin >> ch;
    ch = tolower(ch);
    if(ch=='t') break;
    if(ch=='q') p = &q_ob;
    else p = &s_ob;
    cout << p->retrieve() << '\n';
  }

  cout << '\n';

  return 0;
}
```

This **main( )** illustrates how random events that occur at run time can be easily handled by using virtual functions and run-time polymorphism. The program executes a **for** loop running from 0 to 9. Each iteration through the loop, you are asked to choose into which type of list—the stack or the queue—you want to put the value. According to your answer, the base pointer **p** is set to point to the correct object and the value is stored. Once the loop is finished, another loop begins that prompts you to indicate from which list to remove a value. Once again, it is your response that determines which list is selected.

While this example is trivial, you should be able to see how run-time polymorphism can simplify a program that must respond to random events. As you may know, most windows-based operating systems, such as Windows and OS/2, interface to a program by sending it messages. These messages are generated at random, and your program must respond to each one as it is received. As you can guess, run-time polymorphism is quite useful in programs written for these operating systems.

EXERCISES

1. Add another type of list to the program in Example 1. Have this version maintain a sorted list (in ascending order). Call this list **sorted**.

2. On your own, think about ways in which you can apply run-time polymorphism to simplify the solutions to certain types of problems.

mastery
skills check

At this point you should be able to perform the following exercises and answer the questions.

1. What is a virtual function?

2. What types of functions may not be made virtual?

3. How does a virtual function help achieve run-time polymorphism? Be specific.

4. What is a pure virtual function?

5. What is an abstract class? What is a polymorphic class?

6. Is the following fragment correct? If not, why not?

```
class base {
public:
  virtual int f(int a) = 0;
  // ...
};

class derived : public base {
public:
  int f(int a, int b) { return a*b; }
  // ...
};
```

7. Is the virtual quality inherited?

8. On your own, experiment with virtual functions at this time. This is an important concept and you should master the technique.

cumulative skills check

This section checks how well you have integrated material in this chapter with that from the preceding chapters.

1. Enhance the list example from Section 10.4, Example 1, so it overloads the + and -- operators. Have the + store an element and the -- retrieve an element.

2. How do virtual functions differ from overloaded functions?

3. On your own, reexamine some of the function overloading examples presented earlier in this book. Determine which can be converted to virtual functions. Also, think about ways in which a virtual function can solve some of your own programming problems.

Teach Yourself

11

Templates and Exception Handling

chapter objectives

11.1 Generic functions

11.2 Generic classes

11.3 Exception handling

11.4 More about exception handling

THERE are two important new features that have recently been added to C++: *templates* and *exception handling*. While neither was part of the original specification for C++, both are defined by the proposed ANSI C++ standard and are supported by most C++ compilers available today. However, if you have an older compiler, it may not support one or both of these features. (You will need to check your user manual.)

Using templates, it is possible to create generic functions and classes. In a generic function or class, the type of data that is used is specified as a parameter. Thus, one function or class can be used with several different types of data without having to explicitly recode a specific version for each different data type. Both generic functions and generic classes are discussed here.

Exception handling is the subsystem of C++ that allows you to handle errors that occur at run time in a structured and controlled manner. Using C++ exception handling, your program can automatically invoke an error handling routine when an error occurs. The principal advantage of exception handling is that it automates much of the error-handling code that previously had to be coded "by hand" in any large program.

review

skills check

Before proceeding, you should be able to correctly answer the following questions and do the exercises.

1. What is a virtual function?

2. What is a pure virtual function? If a class declaration contains a pure virtual function, what is that class called, and what restrictions apply to its usage?

3. Run-time polymorphism is achieved through the use of _____ functions and _____ class pointers. (Fill in the missing words.)

4. If, in a class hierarchy, a derived class neglects to override a (non-pure) virtual function, what happens when an object of that derived class references that function?

5. What is the main advantage of run-time polymorphism? What is its potential disadvantage?

11.1   *GENERIC FUNCTIONS*

A generic function defines a general set of operations that will be applied to various types of data. A generic function has the type of data that it will operate upon passed to it as a parameter. Using this mechanism, the same general procedure can be applied to a wide range of data. As you know, many algorithms are logically the same no matter what type of data is being operated upon. For example, the Quicksort algorithm is the same whether it is applied to an array of integers or an array of floats. It is just that the type of the data being sorted is different. By creating a generic function, you can define, independent of any data, the nature of the algorithm. Once this is done, the compiler automatically generates the correct code for the type of data that is actually used when you execute the function. In essence, when you create a generic function you are creating a function that can automatically overload itself.

A generic function is created using the keyword **template**. The normal meaning of the word "template" accurately reflects its use in C++. It is used to create a template (or framework) which describes what a function will do, leaving it to the compiler to fill in the details, as needed. The general form of a **template** function definition is shown here:

```
template <class Ttype> ret-type func-name( parameter list)
{
    // body of function
}
```

Here, *Ttype* is a placeholder name for a data type used by the function. This name may be used within the function definition. However, it is only a placeholder which the compiler will automatically replace with an actual data type when it creates a specific version of the function.

EXAMPLES

1. The following program creates a generic function that swaps the values of the two variables it is called with. Because the general process of exchanging two values is independent of the type of the variables, this process is a good choice to be made into a generic function.

```
// Function template example.
#include <iostream.h>

// This is a function template.
template <class X> void swap(X &a, X &b)
{
  X temp;

  temp = a;
  a = b;
  b = temp;
}

main()
{
  int i=10, j=20;
  float x=10.1, y=23.3;

  cout << "Original i, j: " << i << ' ' << j << endl;
  cout << "Original x, y: " << x << ' ' << y << endl;

  swap(i, j); // swap integers
  swap(x, y); // swap floats

  cout << "Original i, j: " << i << ' ' << j << endl;
  cout << "Original x, y: " << x << ' ' << y << endl;

  return 0;
}
```

The keyword **template** is used to define a generic function. The line:

```
template <class X> void swap(X &a, X &b)
```

tells the compiler two things: that a template is being created and that a
generic definition is beginning. Here, **X** is a generic type that is used as a
placeholder. After the **template** portion, the function **swap( )** is declared,
using **X** as the data type of the values that will be swapped. In **main( )**, the
swap( ) function is called using two different types of data: integers and
floats. Because **swap( )** is a generic function, the compiler automatically
creates two versions of **swap( )**—one that will exchange integer values and
one that will exchange floating point values. You should compile and try
this program now.

Here are some other terms that are sometimes used when discussing
templates and that you may encounter in other C++ literature. First, a
generic function (that is, a function definition preceded by a **template**
statement) is also called a *template function*. When the compiler creates a

specific version of this function, it is said to have created a *generated function*. The act of generating a function is referred to as *instantiating* it. Put differently, a generated function is a specific instance of a template function.

2. Technically, the **template** portion of a generic function definition does not have to be on the same line as the function's name. For example, the following is also a common way to format the **swap( )** function:

```
template <class X>
void swap(X &a, X &b)
{
  X temp;

  temp = a;
  a = b;
  b = temp;
}
```

If you use this form, it is important to understand that no other statements may occur between the **template** statement and the start of the generic function definition. For example, the following fragment will not compile:

```
// This will not compile.
template <class X>
int i; // this is an error
void swap(X &a, X &b)
{
  X temp;

  temp = a;
  a = b;
  b = temp;
}
```

As the comments imply, the **template** specification must directly precede the function definition.

3. You may define more than one generic data type using the **template** statement, using a comma-separated list. For example, this program creates a generic function that has two generic types:

```
#include <iostream.h>

template <class type1, class type2>
void myfunc(type1 x, type2 y)
{
  cout << x << ' ' << y << endl;
}
```

```
main()
{
  myfunc(10, "hi");

  myfunc(0.23, 10L);

  return 0;
}
```

In this example, the placeholder types **type1** and **type2** are replaced by the compiler with the data types **int** and **char *** and **double** and **long**, respectively, when the compiler generates the specific instances of **myfunc( )**.

 REMEMBER _When you create a generic function, you are, in essence, allowing the compiler to generate as many different versions of that function as necessary to handle the various ways that your program calls that function._

4. Generic functions are similar to overloaded functions except that they are more restrictive. When functions are overloaded, you may have different actions performed within the body of each function. But a generic function must perform the same general action for all versions. For example, the following overloaded functions could _not_ be replaced by a generic function because they do not do the same thing.

```
void outdata(int i)
{
  cout << i;
}

void outdata(double d)
{
  cout << setprecision(10) << setfill('#');
  cout << d;
  cout << setprecision(6) << setfill(' ');
}
```

5. Even though a template function overloads itself as needed, you can explicitly overload one, too. If you overload a generic function, then that overloaded function overrides (or "hides") the generic function relative to that specific version. For example, consider this version of Example 1:

```
// Overriding a template function.
#include <iostream.h>
```

```
template <class X> void swap(X &a, X &b)
{
  X temp;

  temp = a;
  a = b;
  b = temp;
}

// This overrides the generic version of swap().
void swap(int a, int b)
{
  cout << "this is inside swap(int,int)\n";
}

main()
{
  int i=10, j=20;
  float x=10.1, y=23.3;

  cout << "Original i, j: " << i << ' ' << j << endl;
  cout << "Original x, y: " << x << ' ' << y << endl;

  swap(i, j); // this calls the explicitly overloaded swap()
  swap(x, y); // swap floats

  cout << "Original i, j: " << i << ' ' << j << endl;
  cout << "Original x, y: " << x << ' ' << y << endl;

  return 0;
}
```

As the comments indicate, when **swap(i, j)** is called, it invokes the explicitly overloaded version of **swap( )** defined in the program. Thus, the compiler does not generate this version of the generic **swap( )** function because the generic function is overridden by the explicit overloading.

Manual overloading of a template, as shown in this example, allows you to tailor a version of a generic function to accommodate a special situation. However, in general, if you need to have different versions of a function for different data types, you should use overloaded functions rather than templates.

---

1. If you have not done so, try each of the preceding examples.

2. Write a generic function, called **min( )**, that returns the lesser of its two arguments. For example, **min(3, 4)** will return **3** and **min('c', 'a')** will return **a**. Demonstrate your function in a program.

3. A good candidate for a template function is called **find( )**. This function searches an array for an object. It returns either the index of the matching object (if one is found) or −1 if no match is found. Here is the prototype for a specific version of **find( )**. Convert **find( )** into a generic function and demonstrate your solution within a program. (The **size** parameter specifies the number of elements in the array.)

```
int find(int object, int *list, int size)
{
  // ...
}
```

4. In your own words, explain why generic functions are valuable and may help simplify the source code to programs that you create.

11.2 GENERIC CLASSES

In addition to generic functions, you may also define a generic class. When you do this, you create a class that defines all algorithms used by that class, but the actual type of the data being manipulated will be specified as a parameter when objects of that class are created.

Generic classes are useful when a class contains generalizable logic. For example, the same algorithm that maintains a queue of integers will also work for a queue of characters. Also, the same mechanism that maintains a linked list of mailing addresses will also maintain a linked list of auto part information. By using a generic class, you can create a class that will maintain a queue, linked list, and so on for any type of data. The compiler will automatically generate the correct type of object based upon the type you specify when the object is created.

The general form of a generic class declaration is shown here:

template <class *Ttype*> class *class-name* {

   .

   .

   .

}

Here, *Ttype* is the placeholder type name which will be specified when a class is instantiated. If necessary, you may define more than one generic data type using a comma-separated list.

Once you have created a generic class, you create a specific instance of that class using the following general form:

class-name <*type*> *ob*;

Here, *type* is the type name of the data that the class will be operating upon.

Member functions of a generic class are, themselves, automatically generic. They need not be explicitly specified as such using **template**.

EXAMPLES

1. This program creates a very simple generic singly linked list class. It then demonstrates the class by creating a linked list that stores characters.

```cpp
// A simple generic linked list.
#include <iostream.h>

template <class data_t> class list {
  data_t data;
  list *next;
public:
  list(data_t d);
  void add(list *node) {node->next = this; next = 0; }
  list *getnext() { return next; }
  data_t getdata() { return data; }
};

template <class data_t> list<data_t>::list(data_t d)
{
  data = d;
  next = 0;
```

```
   }

main()
{
  list<char> start('a');
  list<char> *p, *last;
  int i;

  // build a list
  last = &start;
  for(i=1; i<26; i++) {
    p = new list<char> ('a' + i);
    p->add(last);
    last = p;
  }

  // follow the list
  p = &start;
  while(p) {
    cout << p->getdata();
    p = p->getnext();
  }

  return 0;
}
```

As you can see, the declaration of a generic class is similar to that of a generic function. The actual type of data stored by the list is generic in the class declaration. It is not until an object of the list is declared that the actual data type is determined. In this example, objects and pointers are created inside **main( )** that specify that the data type of the list will be **char**. Pay special attention to this declaration:

```
list<char> start('a');
```

Notice how the desired data type is passed inside the angle brackets.

You should enter and execute this program. It builds a linked list that contains the characters of the alphabet and then displays them. However, by simply changing the type of data specified when **list** objects are created, you can change the type of data stored by the list. For example, you could create another object that stores integers by using this declaration:

```
list<int> int_start(1);
```

You can also use **list** to store data types that you create. For example, if you want to store address information, use this structure:

```
struct addr {
  char name[40];
  char street[40];
  char city[30];
  char state[3];
  char zip[12];
}
```

Then, to use **list** to generate objects that will store objects of type **addr**, use a declaration like this (assuming that **structvar** contains a valid **addr** structure):

```
list<addr> obj(structvar);
```

2. Here is another example of a generic class. It is a reworking of the **stack** class first introduced in Chapter 1. However, in this case, **stack** has been made into a template class. Thus, it can be used to store any type of objects. In the example shown here, a character stack and a floating point stack are created:

```
// This function demonstrates a generic stack.
#include <iostream.h>

#define SIZE 10

// Create a generic stack class
template <class StackType> class stack {
  StackType stck[SIZE]; // holds the stack
  int tos; // index of top-of-stack

public:
  void init() { tos = 0; } // initialize stack
  void push(StackType ch); // push object on stack
  StackType pop(); // pop object from stack
};

// Push an object.
template <class StackType> void stack<StackType>::push(StackType ob)
{
 if(tos==SIZE) {
    cout << "Stack is full";
    return;
  }
  stck[tos] = ob;
  tos++;
}
```

```
// Pop an object.
template <class StackType> StackType stack<StackType>::pop()
{
  if(tos==0) {
    cout << "Stack is empty";
    return 0; // return null on empty stack
  }
  tos--;
  return stck[tos];
}

main()
{
  // Demonstrate character stacks.
  stack<char> s1, s2;  // create two stacks
  int i;

  // initialize the stacks
  s1.init();
  s2.init();

  s1.push('a');
  s2.push('x');
  s1.push('b');
  s2.push('y');
  s1.push('c');
  s2.push('z');

  for(i=0; i<3; i++) cout << "Pop s1: " << s1.pop() << "\n";
  for(i=0; i<3; i++) cout << "Pop s2: " << s2.pop() << "\n";

  // demonstrate double stacks
  stack<double> ds1, ds2;  // create two stacks

  // initialize the stacks
  ds1.init();
  ds2.init();

  ds1.push(1.1);
  ds2.push(2.2);
  ds1.push(3.3);
  ds2.push(4.4);
  ds1.push(5.5);
  ds2.push(6.6);

  for(i=0; i<3; i++) cout << "Pop ds1: " << ds1.pop() << "\n";
  for(i=0; i<3; i++) cout << "Pop ds2: " << ds2.pop() << "\n";

  return 0;
}
```

As the **stack** class (and the preceding **list** class) illustrates, generic functions and classes provide a powerful tool that you can use to maximize your programming time because they allow you to define the general form of an algorithm that can be used with any type of data. You are saved from the tedium of creating separate implementations for each data type that you want the algorithm to work with.

3. A template class can have more than one generic data type. Simply declare all the data types required by the class in a comma-separated list within the **template** specification. For example, the following short example creates a class that uses two generic data types:

```
/* This example uses two generic data types in a
   class definition.
*/
#include <iostream.h>

template <class Type1, class Type2> class myclass
{
  Type1 i;
  Type2 j;
public:
  myclass(Type1 a, Type2 b) { i = a; j = b; }
  void show() { cout << i << ' ' << j << '\n'; }
};

main()
{
  myclass<int, double> ob1(10, 0.23);
  myclass<char, char *> ob2('X', "This is a test");

  ob1.show(); // show int, double
  ob2.show(); // show char, char *

  return 0;
}
```

This program produces the following output:

```
10 0.23
X This is a test
```

The program declares two types of objects. **ob1** uses integer and **double** data. **ob2** uses a character and a character pointer. For both cases, the compiler automatically generates the appropriate data and functions to accommodate the way the objects are created.

1. If you have not yet done so, compile and run the two generic class examples. Try declaring lists and/or stacks of different data types.

2. Create and demonstrate a generic queue class.

3. Create a generic class, called **input**, that does the following when its constructor is called:

   ▼ prompts the user for input,

   ▼ inputs the data entered by the user, and

   ▼ reprompts if the data is not within a predetermined range.

   Objects of type **input** should be declared like this:

   input ob("*prompt message*", *min-value*, *max-value*)

   Here, *prompt message* is the message that prompts for input. The minimum and maximum acceptable values are specified by *min-value* and *max-value*, respectively. (Note: the type of data entered by the user will be the same as the type of *min-value* and *max-value*.)

11.3 EXCEPTION HANDLING

C++ provides a built-in error handling mechanism that is called *exception handling*. Using exception handling, you can more easily manage and respond to run-time errors. C++ exception handling is built upon three keywords: **try**, **catch**, and **throw**. In the most general terms, program statements that you want to monitor for exceptions are contained in a **try** block. If an exception (i.e., an error) occurs within the **try** block, it is thrown (using **throw**). The exception is caught, using **catch**, and processed. The following elaborates upon this general description.

As stated, any statement that throws an exception must have been executed from within a **try** block. (Functions called from within a **try** block may also throw an exception.) Any exception must be caught by a **catch** statement that immediately follows the **try** statement that throws the exception. The general form of **try** and **catch** are shown here:

```
try {
  // try block
}
catch (type1 arg) {
  // catch block
}
catch (type2 arg) {
  // catch block
}
catch (type3 arg) {
  // catch block
}
    .
    .
    .
catch (typeN arg) {
  // catch block
}
```

The **try** block must contain that portion of your program that you want to monitor for errors. This can be as short as a few statements within one function or as all-encompassing as enclosing the **main( )** function code within a **try** block (which effectively causes the entire program to be monitored).

When an exception is thrown, it is caught by its corresponding **catch** statement which processes the exception. There can be more than one **catch** statement associated with a **try**. Which **catch** statement is used is determined by the type of the exception. That is, if the data type specified by a **catch** matches that of the exception, then that **catch** statement is executed. (And, all others are bypassed.) When an exception is caught, *arg* will receive its value. Any type of data may be caught, including classes that you create.

The general form of the **throw** statement is shown here:

throw *exception*;

throw must be executed either from within the **try** block, proper, or from any function that it calls (directly or indirectly). *exception* is the value thrown.

 NOTE *If you throw an exception for which there is no applicable* **catch** *statement, an abnormal program termination may occur. If your compiler complies with the proposed ANSI C++ standard, then throwing an unhandled exception causes the*

terminate( ) *function to be invoked. By default,* **terminate( )** *calls* **abort( )** *to stop your program, but you can specify your own termination handler, if you like. You will need to refer to your compiler's library reference for details.*

EXAMPLES

1. Here is a very simple example that shows the way C++ exception handling operates:

```
// A simple exception handling example.
#include <iostream.h>

main()
{
  cout << "start\n";

  try { // start a try block
    cout << "Inside try block\n";
    throw 10; // throw an error
    cout << "This will not execute";
  }
  catch (int i) { // catch an error
    cout << "Caught One! Number is: ";
    cout << i << "\n";
  }

  cout << "end";

  return 0;
}
```

This program displays the following output:

```
start
Inside try block
Caught One! Number is: 10
end
```

Look carefully at this program. As you can see, there is a **try** block containing three statements and a **catch(int i)** statement that processes an integer exception. Within the **try** block, only two of the three statements will execute: the first **cout** statement and the **throw**. Once an exception has been thrown, control passes to the **catch** expression and the **try** block is terminated. That is, **catch** is *not* called. Rather, program execution is transferred to it. (The stack is automatically reset as needed to accomplish this.) Thus, the **cout** statement following the **throw** will never execute.

After the **catch** statement executes, program control continues with the statements following the **catch**. However, commonly a **catch** block will end with a call to **exit( )**, **abort( )**, etc., because often exception handling is used to handle catastrophic errors.

2. As mentioned, the type of the exception must match the type specified in a **catch** statement. For example, in the preceding example, if you change the type in the **catch** statement to **double**, then the exception will not be caught and abnormal termination will occur. This change is shown here:

```
// This example will not work.
#include <iostream.h>

main()
{
  cout << "start\n";

  try { // start a try block
    cout << "Inside try block\n";
    throw 10; // throw an error
    cout << "This will not execute";
  }
  catch (double i) { // Won't work for an int exception
    cout << "Caught One! Number is: ";
    cout << i << "\n";
  }

  cout << "end";

  return 0;
}
```

This program produces the following output because the integer exception will not be caught by a **double catch** statement.

```
start
Inside try block
Abnormal program termination
```

3. An exception can be thrown from a statement that is outside the **try** block as long as it is within a function that is called from within the **try** block. For example, this is a valid program:

```
/* Throwing an exception from a function outside the
   try block.
*/
```

```
#include <iostream.h>

void Xtest(int test)
{
  cout << "Inside Xtest, test is: " << test << "\n";
  if(test) throw test;
}

main()
{
  cout << "start\n";

  try { // start a try block
    cout << "Inside try block\n";
    Xtest(0);
    Xtest(1);
    Xtest(2);
  }
  catch (int i) { // catch an error
    cout << "Caught One! Number is: ";
    cout << i << "\n";
  }

  cout << "end";

  return 0;
}
```

This program produces the following output:

```
start
Inside try block
Inside Xtest, test is: 0
Inside Xtest, test is: 1
Caught One! Number is: 1
end
```

4. A **try** block can be localized to a function. When this is the case, each time the function is entered, the exception handling relative to that function is reset. For example, examine this program:

```
#include <iostream.h>

// A try/catch can be inside a function other than main().
void Xhandler(int test)
{
```

```
      try{
        if(test) throw test;
      }
      catch(int i) {
        cout << "Caught One!  Ex. #: " << i << '\n';
      }
    }

main()
{
  cout << "start\n";

  Xhandler(1);
  Xhandler(2);
  Xhandler(0);
  Xhandler(3);

  cout << "end";

  return 0;
}
```

This program displays this output:

```
start
Caught One!  Ex. #: 1
Caught One!  Ex. #: 2
Caught One!  Ex. #: 3
end
```

As you can see, three exceptions are thrown. After each exception, the function returns. When the function is called again, the exception handling is reset.

5. As stated earlier, you can have more than one **catch** associated with a **try**. In fact, it is common to do so. However, each **catch** must catch a different type of exception. For example, the following program catches both integers and strings:

```
#include <iostream.h>

// Different types of exceptions can be caught.
void Xhandler(int test)
{
  try{
    if(test) throw test;
    else throw "Value is zero";
  }
  catch(int i) {
```

```
      cout << "Caught One!  Ex. #: " << i << '\n';
    }
    catch(char *str) {
      cout << "Caught a string: ";
      cout << str << '\n';
    }
  }

  main()
  {
    cout << "start\n";

    Xhandler(1);
    Xhandler(2);
    Xhandler(0);
    Xhandler(3);

    cout << "end";

    return 0;
  }
```

This program produces the following output:

```
start
Caught One!  Ex. #: 1
Caught One!  Ex. #: 2
Caught a string: Value is zero
Caught One!  Ex. #: 3
end
```

As you can see, each **catch** statement responds only to its own type.

In general, **catch** expressions are checked in the order in which they occur in a program. Only a matching statement is executed. All other **catch** blocks are ignored.

EXERCISES

1. By far, the best way to understand how C++ exception handling works is to play with it. Enter, compile, and run the preceding example programs. Then, experiment with them, altering pieces of them and observing the results.

2. What is wrong with this fragment?

```
main()
{
   throw 12.23;
```

3. What is wrong with this fragment?

```
try {
   // ...
   throw 'a';
   // ...
}
catch(char *) {
   // ...
}
```

4. What might happen if an exception is thrown for which there is no corresponding **catch** statement?

11.4   *M*ORE ABOUT EXCEPTION HANDLING

There are several additional features and nuances to C++ exception handling that make it easier and more convenient to use.

In some circumstances you will want an exception handler to catch all exceptions instead of just a certain type. This is easy to accomplish. Simply use this form of **catch**:

```
catch(...) {
   // process all exceptions
}
```

Here, the ellipsis matches any type of data.

When a function is called from within a **try** block, you can restrict what type of exceptions that function can throw. In fact, you can also prevent that function from throwing any exceptions whatsoever. To accomplish these restrictions, you must add a **throw** clause to a function definition. The general form of this is shown here:

```
ret-type func-name(arg-list) throw(type-list)
{
```

```
// ...
}
```

Here, only those data types contained in the comma-separated *type-list* may be thrown by the function. Throwing any other type of expression will cause abnormal program termination. If you don't want a function to be able to throw *any* exceptions, then use an empty list.

NOTE *If your compiler complies with the proposed ANSI C++ standard, then attempting to throw an exception that is not supported by a function will cause the* **unexpected( )** *function to be called. By default, this causes* **abort( )** *to be called, which causes abnormal program termination. However, you can specify your own termination handler, if you like. You will need to refer to your compiler's library reference for details.*

If you wish to rethrow an expression from within an exception handler, you may do so by simply calling **throw**, by itself, with no exception. This causes the current exception to be passed on to an outer **try/catch** sequence.

EXAMPLES

1. The following program illustrates **catch(...)**:

```
// This example catches all exceptions.
#include <iostream.h>

void Xhandler(int test)
{
  try{
    if(test==0) throw test; // throw int
    if(test==1) throw 'a'; // throw char
    if(test==2) throw 123.23; // throw double
  }
  catch(...) { // catch all exceptions
    cout << "Caught One!\n";
  }
}

main()
{
  cout << "start\n";
```

```
   Xhandler(0);
   Xhandler(1);
   Xhandler(2);

   cout << "end";

   return 0;
}
```

This program displays the following output:

```
start
Caught One!
Caught One!
Caught One!
end
```

As you can see, all three **throws** were caught using the one **catch** statement.

2. One very good use for **catch(...)** is as the last **catch** of a cluster of catches. In this capacity it provides a useful default or "catch all" statement. For example, this slightly different version of the preceding program explicitly catches integer exceptions but relies upon **catch(...)** to catch all others:

```
// This example uses catch(...) as a default.
#include <iostream.h>

void Xhandler(int test)
{
  try{
    if(test==0) throw test; // throw int
    if(test==1) throw 'a'; // throw char
    if(test==2) throw 123.23; // throw double
  }
  catch(int i) { // catch an int exception
    cout << "Caught " << i << '\n';
  }
  catch(...) { // catch all other exceptions
    cout << "Caught One!\n";
  }
}

main()
{
  cout << "start\n";

  Xhandler(0);
  Xhandler(1);
  Xhandler(2);
```

```
    cout << "end";

    return 0;
}
```

The output produced by this program is shown here:

```
start
Caught 0
Caught One!
Caught One!
end
```

As this example suggests, using **catch**(...) as a default is a good way to catch all exceptions that you don't want to handle explicitly. Also, by catching all exceptions, you prevent an unhandled exception from causing an abnormal program termination.

2. The following program shows how to restrict the types of exceptions that can be thrown from a function:

```
// Restricting function throw types.
#include <iostream.h>

// This function can only throw ints, chars, and doubles.
void Xhandler(int test) throw(int, char, double)
{
  if(test==0) throw test; // throw int
  if(test==1) throw 'a'; // throw char
  if(test==2) throw 123.23; // throw double
}

main()
{
  cout << "start\n";

  try{
    Xhandler(0); // also, try passing 1 and 2 to Xhandler()
  }
  catch(int i) {
    cout << "Caught int\n";
  }
  catch(char c) {
    cout << "Caught char\n";
  }
  catch(double d) {
    cout << "Caught double\n";
  }
```

```
   cout << "end";

   return 0;
}
```

In this program, the function **Xhandler( )** may only throw integer, character, and **double** exceptions. If it attempts to throw any other type of exception, then an abnormal program termination will occur. (That is, **unexpected( )** will be called.) To see an example of this, remove **int** from the list and retry the program.

It is important to understand that a function can only be restricted in what types of exceptions it throws back to the **try** block that called it. That is, a **try** block *within* a function may throw any type of exception so long as it is caught *within* that function. The restriction applies only when throwing an exception outside of the function.

3. The following change to **Xhandler( )** prevents it from throwing any exceptions:

```
// This function can throw NO exceptions!
void Xhandler(int test) throw()
{
  /* The following statements no longer work.  Instead,
     They will cause an abnormal program termination. */
  if(test==0) throw test;
  if(test==1) throw 'a';
  if(test==2) throw 123.23;
}
```

4. As you have learned, you can rethrow an exception. The most likely reason for doing so is to allow multiple handlers access to the exception. For example, perhaps one exception handler manages one aspect of an execption and a second handler copes with another. An exception can only be rethrown from within a **catch** block (or from any function called from within that block). When you rethrow an exception, it will not be recaught by the same **catch** statement. It will propagate to an outer **catch** statement. The following program illustrates rethrowing an exception. It rethrows a **char *** exception.

```
// Example of "rethrowing" an exception.
#include <iostream.h>

void Xhandler()
{
  try {
    throw "hello"; // throw a char *
  }
  catch(char *) { // catch a char *
```

```
              cout << "Caught char * inside Xhandler\n";
              throw ; // rethrow char * out of function
          }
      }

      main()
      {
        cout << "start\n";

        try{
          Xhandler();
        }
        catch(char *) {
          cout << "Caught char * inside main\n";
        }

        cout << "end";

        return 0;
      }
```

This program displays the following output:

```
start
Caught char * inside Xhandler
Caught char * inside main
end
```

1. Before continuing, compile and run all of the examples in this section. Be sure you understand why each program produces the output that it does.

2. What is wrong with this fragment?

```
try {
  // ...
  throw 10;
}
catch(int *p) {
  // ...
}
```

3. Show one way to fix the preceding fragment.

4. What **catch** expression catches all types of exceptions?

5. Here is a skeleton for a function called **divide( )**.

```
double divide(double a, double b)
{
  // add error handling
  return a/b;
}
```

This function returns the result of dividing **a** by **b**. Add error checking to this function using C++ exception handling. Specifically, prevent a divide by zero error. Demonstrate your solution in a program.

mastery

skills check

At this point you should be able to perform the following exercises and answer the questions.

1. Create a generic function that returns the mode of an array of values. (The *mode* of a set is the value that occurs most often.)

2. Create a generic function that returns the summation of an array of values.

3. Create a generic bubble sort (or use any other sorting algorithm you like).

4. Rework the **stack** class so that it can store pairs of different type objects on the stack. Demonstrate your solution.

5. Show the general forms of **try**, **catch**, and **throw**. In your own words, describe their operation.

6. Again, rework the **stack** class so that stack over- and underflows are handled as exceptions.

7. Check your compiler's user manual. See if it supports the **terminate( )** and **unexpected( )** functions. Generally, these functions can be configured to call any function you choose. If this is the case with your

compiler, try creating your own set of customized termination functions that handle otherwise unhandled exceptions.

This section checks how well you have integrated material in this chapter with that from preceding chapters.

1. In Chapter 4, a simple bounded array class was shown. On your own, convert it into a generic bounded array.

2. In Chapter 1, overloaded versions of the **abs( )** function were created. As a better solution, create a generic **abs( )** function on your own that will return the absolute value of any numeric object.

12

Miscellaneous Topics

chapter objectives

12.1 Static class members

12.2 Array-based I/O

12.3 Using linkage specifiers and the **asm** keyword

12.4 Creating a conversion function

12.5 Differences between C and C++

ONGRATULATIONS! You have come a long, long way since Chapter 1. By the time you finish this chapter you will be able to call yourself a C++ programmer. This chapter discusses a number of special topics and features. It also discusses some important differences between C and C++.

While this book provides a thorough introduction to C++, it is beyond its scope to cover every nuance and subtlety. If you wish to learn more about C++, including commonly supplied class libraries, more about C++ I/O, some special-purpose techniques, and several larger C++ examples, you will want to read my book *C++: The Complete Reference* (Berkeley: Osborne/McGraw-Hill, 1991).

review

skills check

Before proceeding, you should be able to correctly answer the following questions and do the exercises.

1. What is a generic function and what is its general form?

2. What is a generic class and what is its general form?

3. Write a generic function called **gexp( )** that returns the value of one of its arguments raised to the power of the other.

4. In Chapter 9, Section 7, Example 1 a **coord** class that held integer coordinates was created and demonstrated in a program. Create a generic version of the **coord** class so that it can hold coordinates of any type. Demonstrate your solution in a program.

5. Briefly, explain how **try**, **catch**, and **throw** work together to provide C++ exception handling.

6. Can **throw** be used if execution has not passed through a **try** block?

7. What purpose do **terminate( )** and **unexpected( )** serve?

8. What form of **catch** will handle all types of exceptions?

| 12.1 | S*TATIC CLASS MEMBERS*

It is possible for a class member variable to be declared as **static**. (It is also possible for a member function to be declared as **static**, but this usage is not common and is not examined here.) By using **static** member variables, a number of rather tricky problems can be bypassed.

In short, when you declare a member variable to be **static**, you cause only one copy of that variable to exist—no matter how many objects of that class are created. Each object simply shares that one variable. Remember, for normal member variables, each time an object is created, new copies of those variables are created and are accessible only by that object. (That is, for normal variables, each object possesses its own copies.) However, there is only one copy of a **static** member variable, and all objects of its class share it. Also, the same static variable will be used by any classes derived from the class that contains the **static** member.

Although it may seem odd when you first think about it, a **static** member variable exists *before* any object of its class is created. In essence, a **static** class member is a global variable that simply has its scope restricted to the class in which it is declared. In fact, as you will see in one of the following examples, it is actually possible to access a **static** member variable independent of any object.

When you declare a **static** data member within a class, you are not defining it. Instead, you must provide a definition for it elsewhere, outside the class. To do this, you redeclare the **static** variable, using the scope resolution operator to identify which class it belongs to.

All **static** member variables are initialized to zero by default. However, you can give a **static** class variable an initial value of your choosing, if you like.

Keep in mind that the principal reason **static** member variables are supported by C++ is to prevent the need to use global variables. As you can surmise, classes that rely upon global variables almost always violate the encapsulation principle that is so fundamental to OOP and C++.

EXAMPLES

1. Here is a simple example that uses a **static** member variable:

```
// A static member variable example.
#include <iostream.h>
class myclass {
  static int i;
public:
  void seti(int n) { i = n; }
```

```
    int geti() { return i; }
};

// Definition of myclass::i. i is still private to myclass.
int myclass::i;

main()
{
  myclass o1, o2;

  o1.seti(10);

  cout << "o1.i: " << o1.geti() << '\n'; // displays 10
  cout << "o2.i: " << o2.geti() << '\n'; // also displays 10

  return 0;
}
```

This program displays the following:

```
o1.i: 10
o2.i: 10
```

Looking at this program, you can see that only object **o1** actually sets the value of **static** member **i**. However, since **i** is shared by both **o1** and **o2** (and, indeed, by any object of type **myclass**), both calls to **geti( )** display the same result.

Notice how **i** is declared within **myclass** but defined outside of the class. This second step ensures that storage for **i** is defined. Technically, a class declaration is just that, only a declaration. No memory is actually set aside because of a declaration. Because a **static** data member *implies* that memory is allocated for that member, a separate definition is required that causes storage to be allocated.

 NOTE *For some C++ implementations, if you simply let the initial value of the **static** member variable default to zero, there is no need to define it outside the class. However, according to the proposed ANSI C++ standard, this is an anachronism. For this reason, you will probably want to include separate definitions for all your **static** member variables.*

2. Because a **static** member variable exists before any object of that class is created, it can be accessed within a program independent of any object. For example, the following variation of the preceding program sets the

value of **i** to 100 without any reference to a specific object. Notice the use of the scope resolution operator to access **i**.

```
// Reference a static independent of any object.
#include <iostream.h>

class myclass {
public:
  static int i;
  void seti(int n) { i = n; }
  int geti() { return i; }
};

int myclass::i;

main()
{
  myclass o1, o2;

  // set i directly
  myclass::i = 100; // no object is referenced.

  cout << "o1.i: " << o1.geti() << '\n'; // displays 100
  cout << "o2.i: " << o2.geti() << '\n'; // also displays 100

  return 0;
}
```

Because **i** is set to 100, the following output is displayed:

```
o1.i: 100
o2.i: 100
```

3. One very common use of a **static** class variable is to coordinate access to a shared resource, such as a disk file, printer, or network server. As you probably know from your previous programming experience, coordinating access to a shared resource requires some means of sequencing events. To get an idea of how **static** member variables can be used to control access to a shared resource, examine the following program. It creates a class called **output**, which maintains a common output buffer called **outbuf** that is, itself, a **static** character array. This buffer is used to receive output sent by the **outbuf( )** member function. This function sends the contents of **str** one character at a time. It does so by first acquiring access to the buffer and then sending all the characters in **str**. It locks out access to the buffer by other objects until it is done outputting. You should be able to follow its operation by studying the code and reading the comments.

```
// A shared resource example.
#include <iostream.h>
#include <string.h>

class output {
  static char outbuf[255]; // this is the shared resource
  static int inuse; // buffer available if 0; in use otherwise
  static int oindex; // index of outbuf
  char str[80];
  int i; // index of next char in str
  int who; // identifies the object, must be > 0
public:
  output(int w, char *s) { strcpy(str, s); i = 0; who = w; }

  /* This function returns -1 if waiting for buffer,
     it returns 0 if it is done outputting, and
     it returns who if it is still using the buffer.
  */
  int putbuf()
  {
    if(!str[i]) { // done outputting
      inuse = 0; // release buffer
      return 0; // signal termination
    }
    if(!inuse) inuse = who; // get buffer
    if(inuse != who) return -1; // in use by someone else
    if(str[i]) { // still chars to output
      outbuf[oindex] = str[i];
      i++; oindex++;
      outbuf[oindex] = '\0';  // always keep null-terminated
      return 1;
    }
  }
  void show() { cout << outbuf << '\n'; }
};

char output::outbuf[255]; // this is the shared resource
int output::inuse = 0; // buffer available if 0; in use otherwise
int output::oindex = 0; // index of outbuf

main()
{
  output o1(1, "This is a test"), o2(2, " of statics");

  while(o1.putbuf() | o2.putbuf()) ; // output chars

  o1.show();

  return 0;
}
```

---

1. Rework Example 3 so it displays which object is currently outputting characters and which one or ones are blocked from outputting a character because the buffer is already in use by another.

2. One interesting use of a **static** member variable is to keep track of the number of objects of a class that are in existence at any given point in time. The way to do this is to increment a **static** member variable each time the class's constructor is called and decrement it each time the class's destructor is called. Implement such a scheme and demonstrate that it works.

12.2   *A RRAY-BASED I/O*

In addition to console and file I/O, C++ supports a full set of functions that use character arrays as the input or output device. Although C++'s array-based I/O parallels, in concept, the array-based I/O found in C (specifically, C's **sscanf( )** and **sprintf( )** functions), C++'s array-based I/O is more flexible and useful because it allows user-defined types to be integrated into it. In some C++ literature, array-based I/O is referred to as *incore I/O* or *RAM-based I/O*. This book will continue to use the term "array-based" because it is the most descriptive. While it is not possible to cover every aspect of array-based I/O here, the most important and commonly used features are examined.

It is important to understand from the outset that array-based I/O still operates through streams. Everything you learned about C++ I/O in Chapters 8 and 9 is applicable to array-based I/O. In fact, you need to learn to use just a few new functions to take full advantage of array-based I/O. These functions link a stream to a region of memory. Once this has been accomplished, all I/O takes place through the I/O functions you have already learned about.

Before you can use array-based I/O, you must be sure to include the header file **strstream.h** in your file. In this header are defined the classes **istrstream**, **ostrstream**, and **strstream**. These classes create array-based input, output, and input/output streams, respectively. These classes have as a base **ios**, so all the functions and manipulators included in **istream**, **ostream**, and **iostream** are also available in **istrstream**, **ostrstream**, and **strstream**.

To use a character array for output, use this general form of the **ostrstream** constructor:

```
ostrstream ostr (char *buf, int size, int mode = ios::out);
```

Here, *ostr* will be the stream associated with the array *buf.* The size of the array is specified by *size.* Generally, *mode* is simply defaulted to output, but you can use any output mode flag defined by **ios** if you like.

Once an array has been opened for output, characters will be put into the array until it is full. The array will not be overrun. Any attempt to overfill the array will result in an I/O error. To find out how many characters have been written to the array, use the **pcount( )** member function, shown here:

```
int   pcount();
```

You must call this function in conjunction with a stream, and it will return the number of characters written to the array, including any null terminator.

To open an array for input, use this form of the **istrstream** constructor:

```
istrstream istr (const char *buf );
```

Here, *buf* is a pointer to the array that will be used for input. The input stream will be called *istr.* When reading input from an array, **eof( )** will return true when the end of the array has been reached.

To open an array for input/output operations, use this form of the **strstream** constructor:

```
strstream iostr (char *buf, int size, int mode);
```

Here, *iostr* will be an input/output stream that uses the array pointed to by *buf,* which is *size* characters long. For input/output operations, *mode* should be the value **ios::in | ios::out.**

It is important to remember that all I/O functions described earlier operate with array-based I/O, including the binary I/O functions and the random-access functions.

EXAMPLES

1. Here is a short example that shows how to open an array for output and write data to it:

```
// A short example using array-based output.
#include <iostream.h>
#include <strstream.h>
```

```
main()
{
  char buf[255]; // output buffer

  ostrstream ostr(buf, sizeof buf); // open output array

  ostr << "Array-based I/O uses streams just like ";
  ostr << "'normal' I/O\n" << 100;
  ostr << ' ' << 123.23 << '\n';

  // you can use manipulators, too
  ostr << hex << 100 << ' ';
  // or format flags
  ostr << ostr.setf(ios::scientific) << 123.23 << '\n';
  ostr << ends; // ensure that buffer is null-terminated

  // show resultant string
  cout << buf;

  return 0;
}
```

This program displays

```
Array-based I/O uses streams just like 'normal' I/O
100 123.23
64 01.2323e+02
```

As you can see, the overloaded I/O operators, built-in I/O manipulators, member functions, and format flags are fully functional when you use array-based I/O. (This is also true of any manipulators or overloaded I/O operators you create relative to your own classes.)

This program manually null terminates the output array by using the **ends** manipulator. Whether the array will be automatically null terminated or not is implementation dependent, so it is best to perform this manually if null termination is important to your application.

2. Here is an example of array-based input:

```
// An example using array-based input.
#include <iostream.h>
#include <strstream.h>

main()
{
  char buf[] = "Hello 100 123.125 a";

  istrstream istr(buf); // open input array
```

```
      int i;
      char str[80];
      float f;
      char c;

      istr >> str >> i >> f >> c;

      cout << str << ' ' << i << ' ' << f;
      cout << ' ' << c << '\n';
      return 0;
    }
```

This program reads and then redisplays the values contained in the input array **buf**.

3. Keep in mind that an input array, once linked to a stream, will appear the same as a file. For example, this program uses binary I/O and the **eof( )** function to read the contents of **buf**:

```
/* Demonstrate that eof() works with array-based I/O.
   Also, array-based I/O works with binary I/O functions.
*/
#include <iostream.h>
#include <strstream.h>

main()
{
  char buf[] = "Hello 100 123.125 a";

  istrstream istr(buf);
  char c;

  while(!istr.eof()) {
    istr.get(c);
    cout << c;
  }

  return 0;
}
```

4. This program performs input and output on an array:

```
// Demonstrate an input/output array.
#include <iostream.h>
#include <strstream.h>

main()
{
```

```
        char iobuf[255];

        strstream iostr(iobuf, sizeof iobuf, ios::in | ios::out);

        iostr << "This is a test\n";
        iostr << 100 << hex << 100 << ends;

        char str[80];
        int i;

        iostr.getline(str, 79); // read string up to \n
        iostr >> i; // read 100

        cout << str << ' ' << i << ' ';

        iostr >> i;
        cout << i;

        return 0;
}
```

The program first writes output to **iobuf**. It then reads it back. It first reads the entire line "This is a test" using the **getline( )** function. It then reads the decimal value 100 and the hexadecimal value 0x64.

EXERCISES

1. Modify Example 1 so it displays the number of characters written to **buf** prior to termination.

2. Write an application that uses array-based I/O to copy the contents of one array to another. (This is, of course, not the most efficient way to accomplish this task.)

3. Using array-based I/O, write a program that converts a string that contains a floating-point value into its internal representation.

12.3 USING LINKAGE SPECIFIERS AND THE asm KEYWORD

C++ provides two important mechanisms that make it easier to link C++ to other languages. One is the *linkage specifier,* which tells the compiler that one or more functions in your C++ program will be linked with another language that may have different parameter-passing conventions and the like. The second is the **asm** keyword, which allows you to embed assembly language instructions in your C++ source code. Both are examined here.

By default, all functions in a C++ program are compiled and linked as C++ functions. However, you can tell the C++ compiler to link a function so that it is compatible with another type of language. All C++ compilers allow functions to be linked as either C or C++ functions. Some also allow you to link functions with languages such as Pascal, Ada, or FORTRAN. To cause a function to be linked for a different language, use this general form of the linkage specification:

    extern "*language*" *function-prototype*;

Here, *language* is the name of the language you want the specified function to link to. If you want to specify linkage for more than one function, use this form of the linkage specification:

    extern "*language*" {
        function-prototypes
    }

All linkage specifications must be global; they cannot be used inside a function. Also, although not common, you can specify a linkage specification for objects, too.

The most common use of linkage specifications occurs when linking C++ programs to a third-party subroutine package that is compiled using some other language. It is entirely possible, however, that you will never need to use a linkage specification in your programming career.

Although it is generally possible to link assembly language routines with a C++ program, there is often an easier way to use assembly language. C++ supports the special keyword **asm**, which allows you to embed assembly language instructions within a C++ function. These instructions are then compiled as is. The advantage of using an in-line assembler is that your entire program is completely defined as a C++ program and there is no need to link separate assembly language files. The general form of the **asm** keyword is shown here:

    asm ("*op-code*");

where *op-code* is the assembly language instruction that will be embedded in your program.

It's important to note that Turbo C++ and Borland C++ accept these three slightly different forms of the **asm** statement:

asm *op-code*;

asm *op-code newline*

asm {
    instruction sequence
}

Here, *op-code* is not enclosed in double quotes. Because embedded assembly language instruction tends to be implementation dependent, you will want to read your compiler's user manual on this issue.

EXAMPLES

1. This program links **func( )** as a C, rather than a C++, function:

```
// Illustrate linkage specifier.
#include <iostream.h>

extern "C" int func(int x); // link as C function

// This function now links as a C function.
int func(int x)
{
   return x/3;
}
```

This function can now be linked with code compiled by using a C compiler.

2. The following fragment tells the compiler that **f1( )**, **f2( )**, and **f3( )** should be linked as C functions:

```
extern "C" {
  void f1();
  int f2(int x);
  double f3(double x, int *p);
}
```

3. This fragment embeds several assembly language instructions into **func( )**:

```
// Don't try this function!
void func()
{
  asm (mov bp, sp);
  asm (push ax);
  asm (mov cl, 4);
  // ...
}
```

 REMEMBER *You must be an accomplished assembly language programmer in order to successfully use in-line assembly language. Also, be sure to check your compiler's user manual for details regarding assembly language usage.*

EXERCISE

1. On your own, study the sections in your compiler's user manual that refer to linkage specifications and assembly language interfacing.

12.4 **C**REATING A CONVERSION FUNCTION

Sometimes it is useful to convert an object of one type into an object of another. While it is possible to use an overloaded operator function to accomplish such a conversion, there is often an easier (and better) way, called a conversion function. A *conversion function* converts an object into a value compatible with another type, which is often one of the built-in C++ types. In essence, a conversion function automatically converts an object into a value that is compatible with the type of the expression in which the object is used.

The general form of a conversion function is shown here:

operator *type*( ) { return *value*; }

Here, *type* is the target type you will be converting to and *value* is the value of the object after the conversion has been performed. Conversion functions return a value of type *type*. No parameters may be specified, and a conversion function must be a member of the class for which it performs the conversion.

As the examples will illustrate, a conversion function generally provides a cleaner approach to converting an object's value into another type than any other method available in C++ because it allows an object to be included directly in an expression involving the target type.

EXAMPLES

1. In the following program, the **coord** class contains a conversion function that converts to integer. In this case, the function returns the product of the two coordinates; however, any conversion appropriate to your specific application is allowed.

```
// A simple conversion function example.
#include <iostream.h>

class coord {
  int x, y;
public:
  coord(int i, int j) { x = i; y = j; }
  operator int() { return x*y; } // conversion function
};

main()
{
  coord o1(2, 3), o2(4, 3);
  int i;

  i = o1;  // automatically convert to integer
  cout << i << '\n';

  i = 100 + o2;  // convert o2 to integer
  cout << i << '\n';

  return 0;
}
```

This program displays 6 and 112.

In this example, notice that the conversion function is called when **o1** is assigned to an integer and when **o2** is used as part of a larger integer expression. As stated, by using a conversion function, you allow classes you create to be integrated into "normal" C++ expressions without having to create a series of complex overloaded operator functions.

2. Following is another example of a conversion function. This one converts a string of type **strtype** into a character pointer to **str**.

```cpp
#include <iostream.h>
#include <string.h>

class strtype {
  char str[80];
  int len;
public:
  strtype(char *s) { strcpy(str, s); len = strlen(s); }
  operator char *() { return str; } // convert to char*
};

main()
{
  strtype s("This is a test\n");
  char *p, s2[80];

  p = s; // convert to char *
  cout << "Here is string: " << p << '\n';

  // convert to char * in function call
  strcpy(s2, s);
  cout << "Here is copy of string: " << s2 << '\n';

  return 0;
}
```

This program displays the following:

```
Here is string: This is a test
Here is copy of string: This is a test
```

As you can see, not only is the conversion function invoked when object **s** is assigned to **p** (which is of type **char ***), but it is also used when **s** is used as a parameter to **strcpy( )**. Remember, **strcpy( )** has the following prototype:

char *strcpy(char **s1***, char ****s2***);**

Because the prototype specifies that *s2* is of type **char ***, the conversion function to **char *** is automatically called. This illustrates how a conversion function can also help you seamlessly integrate your classes into C++'s standard library functions.

1. Using the **strtype** class from Example 2, create a conversion that converts to type integer. In this conversion, return the length of the string held in **str**. Illustrate that your conversion function works.

2. Given this class:

```
class pwr {
  int base;
  int exp;
public:
  pwr(int b, int e) { base = b; exp = e; }
  // create conversion to integer here
};
```

create a conversion function that converts an object of type **pwr** to type integer. Have the function return the result of base^{exp}.

12.5 *D*IFFERENCES BETWEEN C AND C++

As you know, C is the foundation upon which C++ is built. This means that, in general, any C program is automatically a (non-object oriented) C++ program. However, because of C++'s support for object oriented programming, and certain implications caused by this support, there are some minor differences between C and C++. Some of these differences will prevent a C program from being compiled by a C++ compiler. In this section, these differences are enumerated. (Some have been mentioned earlier in this book, but are included here for completeness.)

 NOTE *Keep in mind that the non-OOP-related features of C and C++ differ in only a few minor points. For the most part, any C program is automatically a valid C++ program.*

One of the most important yet subtle differences between C and C++ is the fact that in C, a function declared like this,

```
int f();
```

says nothing about any parameters to that function. That is, when there is nothing specified between the parentheses following the function's name, in C this means that nothing is being stated, one way or the other, about any parameters to that function. It might have parameters; it might not have parameters. However, in

C++, a function declaration like this means that the function does not have parameters. That is, in C++, these two declarations are equivalent:

```
int f();
int f(void);
```

In C++, the **void** is optional. Many C++ programmers include the **void** as a means of making it completely clear to anyone reading the program that a function does not have any parameters. But this is technically unnecessary.

In C++, all functions must be prototyped. This is an option in C (although good programming practice suggests full prototyping be used in a C program).

A small but potentially important difference between C and C++ is that in C, a character constant is automatically elevated to an integer. In C++, it is not.

In C, it is not an error to declare a global variable several times, even though this is bad programming practice. In C++, this is an error.

In C, only the first 31 characters of an identifier are significant. In C++, at least the first 1,024 characters are significant. However, from a practical point of view, extremely long identifiers are unwieldy and are seldom needed.

In C, (while unusual), you can call **main( )** from within your program. This is not allowed by C++.

In C, you cannot take the address of a **register** variable. In C++, this is allowed. However, this is a feature you may not want to take advantage of because of portability restrictions.

EXERCISE

1. On your own, check your compiler's user manual to see if it lists any additional differences between C and its implementation of C++.

mastery
skills check

At this point you should be able to perform the following exercises and answer the questions.

1. What makes a **static** member variable different from other member variables?

2. What header file must be included in your program when you use array-based I/O?

3. Aside from the fact that array-based I/O uses memory as an input and/or output device, is there any difference between it and "normal" I/O in C++?

4. Given a function called **counter**( ), show the statement that causes the compiler to compile this function for C language linkage.

5. What does a conversion function do?

6. Are prototypes optional in C++?

7. How many characters are significant in a C++ identifier?

cumulative
skills check

This section checks how well you have integrated material in this chapter with that from the preceding chapters.

1. You have come a long way since Chapter 1. Take some time to skim through the book again. As you do so, think about ways you can improve the examples (especially those in the first six chapters) so that they take advantage of all the features of C++ you have learned.

2. Programming is learned best by doing. Write many C++ programs. Try to exercise those features of C++ that are unique to it.

3. Finally, remember: C++ gives you unprecedented power. It is important that you learn to use this power wisely. Because of this power, C++ lets you push the limits of your programming ability. However, if this power is misused, you can also create programs that are hard to understand, nearly impossible to follow, and extremely difficult to maintain. C++ is a powerful tool. But, like any other tool, it is only as good as the person using it.

A

C++ Keyword Extensions

A S mentioned in Chapter 1, there are several keywords that the ANSI C++ committee is considering for inclusion in the C++ standard. However, at the time of this writing there are no commonly available compilers that support these keywords or any guarantee that all (or any) of them will actually be included in the final C++ standard. None of these extended keywords were part of the original specification for C++, nor were they part of any common, preexisting implementation of C++, and they are not necessary to program in C++ or to fully take advantage of it. For these reasons, the extended keywords are not discussed in the book, proper. However, a list of these keywords along with a brief explanation is provided in this appendix. You will want to check your compiler's user manual to see if any of these keywords are supported.

bool
A type specifier. Values of type **bool** may only have the values **true** or **false**.

const_cast
Can be used to override **const** and/or **volatile** when performing a type conversion.

dynamic_cast
Performs a run-time cast for polymorphic class types.

false
See **bool**.

mutable
Allows a member of an object to override **const**ness. That is, a **mutable** member of a **const** object is not **const** and may be modified.

namespace
Declares a block in which other identifiers may be a declared. Thus, an identifier declared within a **namespace** becomes a "sub-identifier" linked to the surrounding **namespace** identifier. (In essence, **namespace** creates a named scope.)

reinterpret_cast
Casts one type of value into another. For example, it converts a pointer into an integer type.

static_cast

A non-polymorphic cast. For example, a base class pointer can be cast into a derived class pointer.

true

See **bool**.

typeid

Obtains the type of an expression.

using

Specifies a default scope resolution qualifier.

wchar_t

Supports wide characters (i.e., 16-bit characters). **wchar_t** allows C++ to accommodate the large character sets required by some languages.

B

Answers

1.2 EXERCISES

1.
```cpp
#include <iostream.h>

main()
{
  double hours, wage;

  cout << "Enter hours worked: ";
  cin >> hours;

  cout << "Enter wage per hour: ";
  cin >> wage;

  cout << "Pay is: $" << wage * hours;

  return 0;
}
```

2.
```cpp
#include <iostream.h>

main()
{
  double feet;

  do {
     cout << "Enter feet (0 to quit): ";
     cin >> feet;

     cout << feet * 12 << " inches\n";
  } while (feet != 0.0);

  return 0;
}
```

3.
```cpp
// This program computes the lowest common denominator.
#include <iostream.h>

main()
{
  int a, b, d, min;

  cout << "Enter two numbers: ";
  cin >> a >> b;
```

```
    min = a > b ? b : a;

    for(d = 2; d<min; d++)
      if(((a%d)==0) && ((b%d)==0)) break;
    if(d==min) {
      cout << "No common denominators\n";
      return 0;
    }
    cout << "The lowest common denominator is " << d << ".\n";

    return 0;
}
```

1.3   EXERCISES

1. The comment, although strange, is valid.

1.4   EXERCISES

2.
```
#include <iostream.h>
#include <string.h>

class card {
  char title[80]; // book title
  char author[40]; // author
  int number; // number in library
public:
  void store(char *t, char *name, int num);
  void show();
};

void card::store(char *t, char *name, int num)
{
  strcpy(title, t);
  strcpy(author, name);
  number = num;
}

void card::show()
{
  cout << "Title: " << title << "\n";
  cout << "Author: " << author << "\n";
```

```
    cout << "Number on hand: " << number << "\n";
}

main()
{
  card book1, book2, book3;

  book1.store("Dune", "Frank Herbert", 2);
  book2.store("The Foundation Trilogy", "Isaac Asimov", 2);
  book3.store("The Rainbow", "D. H. Lawrence", 1);

  book1.show();
  book2.show();
  book3.show();

  return 0;
}
```

3. ```
   #include <iostream.h>

   #define SIZE 100

   class q_type {
     int queue[SIZE]; // holds the queue
     int head, tail; // indices of head and tail
   public:
     void init(); // initialize
     void q(int num); // store
     int deq();  // retrieve
   };

   // Initialize
   void q_type::init()
   {
     head = tail = 0;
   }

   // Put value on a queue.
   void q_type::q(int num)
   {
     if(tail+1==head || (tail+1==SIZE && !head)) {
       cout << "Queue is full\n";
       return;
     }
   ```
   ```

```
    tail++;
    if(tail==SIZE) tail = 0; // cycle around
    queue[tail] = num;
}

// Remove a value from a queue.
int q_type::deq()
{
  if(head == tail) {
    cout << "Queue is empty\n";
    return 0;  // or some other error indicator
  }
  head++;
  if(head==SIZE) head = 0; // cycle around
  return queue[head];
}

main()
{
  q_type q1, q2;
  int i;

  q1.init();
  q2.init();

  for(i=1; i<=10; i++) {
    q1.q(i);
    q2.q(i*i);
  }

  for(i=1; i<=10; i++) {
    cout << "Dequeue 1: " << q1.deq() << "\n";
    cout << "Dequeue 2: " << q2.deq() << "\n";
  }

  return 0;
}
```

1.5 **EXERCISES**

1. The standard library function **strlen( )** is not prototyped. The program must include the standard header file **string.h** to fix the problem.

E*XERCISES*

```
1. #include <iostream.h>
   #include <math.h>

   // Overload sroot() for integers, longs, and doubles.

   int sroot(int i);
   long sroot(long i);
   double sroot(double i);

   main()
   {
     cout << "Square root of 90.34 is : " << sroot(90.34);
     cout << "\n";
     cout << "Square root of 90L is : " << sroot(90L);
     cout << "\n";
     cout << "Square root of 90 is : " << sroot(90);

     return 0;
   }

   // Return square root of integer.
   int sroot(int i)
   {
     cout << "computing integer root\n";
     return (int) sqrt((double) i);
   }

   // Return square root of long.
   long sroot(long i)
   {
     cout << "computing long root\n";
     return (long) sqrt((double) i);
   }

   // Return square root of double.
   double sroot(double i)
   {
     cout << "computing double root\n";
     return sqrt(i);
   }
```

2. The functions **atof( )**, **atoi( )**, and **atol( )** cannot be overloaded because they differ only in the type of data they return. Function overloading requires that either the type or the number of arguments differs.

3.
```
// Overload the min() function.

#include <iostream.h>
#include <ctype.h>

char min(char a, char b);
int min(int a, int b);
double min(double a, double b);

main()
{
  cout << "Min is: " << min('x', 'a') << "\n";
  cout << "Min is: " << min(10, 20) << "\n";
  cout << "Min is: " << min(0.2234, 99.2) << "\n";

  return 0;
}

// min() for chars
char min(char a, char b)
{
  return tolower(a)<tolower(b) ? a : b;
}

// min() for ints
int min(int a, int b)
{
  return a<b ? a : b;
}

// min() for doubles
double min(double a, double b)
{
  return a<b ? a : b;
}
```

4.
```
#include <iostream.h>
#include <stdlib.h>

// Overload sleep to accept integer or char * argument
void sleep(int n);
```

```
void sleep(char *n);

// Change this value to fit your processor speed.
#define DELAY 100000

main()
{
  cout << '.';
  sleep(3);
  cout << '.';
  sleep("2");
  cout << '.';

  return 0;
}

// Sleep() with integer argument.
void sleep(int n)
{
  long i;

  for( ; n; n--)
    for(i=0; i<DELAY; i++) ;
}

// Sleep() with char * argument.
void sleep(char *n)
{
  long i;
  int j;

  j = atoi(n);

  for( ; j; j—)
    for(i=0; i<F129AY; i++) ;
}
```

1 *M*ASTERY SKILLS CHECK

1. Polymorphism is the mechanism by which one general interface can be
   used to access many specific implementations. Encapsulation provides a
   protected linkage between code and its related data. Access to encapsulated
   routines may be tightly controlled, thus preventing unwanted tampering.

Inheritance is the process by which one object can acquire the traits of another. Inheritance is used to support a system of hierarchical classification.

2. Comments may be included in a C++ program by using either the normal C-like comment or the C++-specific single-line comment.

3.
```cpp
#include <iostream.h>

main()
{
  int b, e, r;
  cout << "Enter base: ";
  cin >> b;
  cout << "Enter exponent: ";
  cin >> e;

  r = 1;
  for( ; e; e--) r = r * b;

  cout << "Result: " << r;

  return 0;
}
```

4.
```cpp
#include <iostream.h>
#include <string.h>

// Overload string reversal function.
void rev_str(char *s); // reverse string in place
void rev_str(char *in, char *out); // put reversal into out

main()
{
  char s1[80], s2[80];

  strcpy(s1, "This is a test");

  rev_str(s1, s2);
  cout << s2 << "\n";

  rev_str(s1);
  cout << s1 << "\n";
```

```
  return 0;
}

// Reverse string, put result in s.
void rev_str(char *s)
{
  char temp[80];
  int i, j;

  for(i=strlen(s)-1, j=0; i>=0; i--, j++)
    temp[j] = s[i];

  temp[j] = '\0'; // null terminate result

  strcpy(s, temp);
}

// Reverse string, put result into out.
void rev_str(char *in, char *out)
{
  int i, j;

  for(i=strlen(in)-1, j=0; i>=0; i--, j++)
    out[j] = in[i];

  out[j] = '\0'; // null terminate result
}
```

2 *R*EVIEW SKILLS CHECK

```
1. #include <iostream.h>
   #include <string.h>

   main()
   {
     char s[80];

     cout << "Enter a string: ";
     cin >> s;

     cout << "Length: " << strlen(s) << "\n";

     return 0;
   }
```

2.
```cpp
#include <iostream.h>
#include <string.h>

class addr {
  char name[40];
  char street[40];
  char city[30];
  char state[3];
  char zip[10];
public:
  void store(char *n, char *s, char *c, char *t,
             char *z);
  void display();
};

void addr::store(char *n, char *s, char *c, char *t,
                 char *z)
{
  strcpy(name, n);
  strcpy(street, s);
  strcpy(city, c);
  strcpy(state, t);
  strcpy(zip, z);
}

void addr::display()
{
  cout << name << "\n";
  cout << street << "\n";
  cout << city << "\n";
  cout << state << "\n";
  cout << zip << "\n\n";
}

main()
{
  addr a;

  a.store("C. B. Turkle", "11 Pinetree Lane", "Wausau",
          "In", "46576");

  a.display();

  return 0;
}
```

3.
```cpp
#include <iostream.h>

int rotate(int i);
long rotate(long i);

main()
{
  int a;
  long b;

  a = 0x8000;
  b = 8;

  cout  << rotate(a);
  cout << "\n";
  cout << rotate(b);

  return 0;
}

int rotate(int i)
{
  int x;

  if(i & 0x8000) x = 1;
  else x = 0;

  i = i << 1;
  i += x;

  return i;
}

long rotate(long i)
{
  int x;

  if(i & 0x80000000) x = 1;
  else x = 0;

  i = i << 1;
  i += x;

  return i;
}
```

4. The integer **i** is private to **myclass** and cannot be accessed inside **main( )**.

2.1 EXERCISES

1.
```
#include <iostream.h>

#define SIZE 100

class q_type {
  int queue[SIZE]; // holds the queue
  int head, tail; // indices of head and tail
public:
  q_type(); // constructor
  void q(int num); // store
  int deq();   // retrieve
};

// Constructor
q_type::q_type()
{
  head = tail = 0;
}

// Put value on queue.
void q_type::q(int num)
{
  if(tail+1==head || (tail+1==SIZE && !head)) {
    cout << "Queue is full\n";
    return;
  }
  tail++;
  if(tail==SIZE) tail = 0; // cycle around
  queue[tail] = num;
}

// Remove value from queue.
int q_type::deq()
{
  if(head == tail) {
    cout << "Queue is empty\n";
    return 0;   // or some other error indicator
  }
  head++;
  if(head==SIZE) head = 0; // cycle around
```

```
      return queue[head];
  }

  main()
  {
    q_type q1, q2;
    int i;

    for(i=1; i<=10; i++) {
      q1.q(i);
      q2.q(i*i);
    }

    for(i=1; i<=10; i++) {
      cout << "Dequeue 1: " << q1.deq() << "\n";
      cout << "Dequeue 2: " << q2.deq() << "\n";
    }

    return 0;
  }
```

2.
```
  // Stopwatch emulator
  #include <iostream.h>
  #include <time.h>

  class stopwatch {
    double begin, end;
  public:
    stopwatch();
    ~stopwatch();
    void start();
    void stop();
    void show();
  };

  stopwatch::stopwatch()
  {
    begin = end = 0.0;
  }

  stopwatch::~stopwatch()
  {
    cout << "Stopwatch object being destroyed...";
    show();
  }
```

```
void stopwatch::start()
{
  begin = (double) clock() / CLK_TCK;
}

void stopwatch::stop()
{
  end = (double) clock() / CLK_TCK;
}

void stopwatch::show()
{
  cout << "Elapsed time: " << end - begin;
  cout << "\n";
}

main()
{
  stopwatch watch;
  long i;

  watch.start();
  for(i=0; i<320000; i++) ; // time a for loop
  watch.stop();

  watch.show();

  return 0;
}
```

3. A constructor cannot have a return type.

2.2   EXERCISES

```
1. // Dynamically allocated stack.
   #include <iostream.h>
   #include <stdlib.h>

   // Declare a stack class for characters
   class stack {
     char *stck; // holds the stack
     int tos; // index of top-of-stack
     int size; // size of stack
```

```
public:
  stack(int s); // constructor
  ~stack(); // destructor
  void push(char ch); // push character on stack
  char pop(); // pop character from stack
};

// Initialize the stack
stack::stack(int s)
{
  cout << "Constructing a stack\n";
  tos = 0;
  stck = (char *) malloc(s);
  if(!stck) {
    cout << "Allocation error...";
    exit(1);
  }
  size = s;
}

stack::~stack()
{
  free(stck);
}

// Push a character.
void stack::push(char ch)
{
  if(tos==size) {
    cout << "Stack is full\n";
    return;
  }
  stck[tos] = ch;
  tos++;
}

// Pop a character.
char stack::pop()
{
  if(tos==0) {
    cout << "Stack is empty\n";
    return 0; // return null on empty stack
  }
  tos--;
  return stck[tos];
```

```
}

main()
{
  // create two stacks that are automatically initialized.
  stack s1(10), s2(10);
  int i;

  s1.push('a');
  s2.push('x');
  s1.push('b');
  s2.push('y');
  s1.push('c');
  s2.push('z');

  for(i=0; i<3; i++) cout << "Pop s1: " << s1.pop() << "\n";
  for(i=0; i<3; i++) cout << "Pop s2: " << s2.pop() << "\n";

  return 0;
}
```

2.
```
#include <iostream.h>
#include <time.h>

class t_and_d {
  time_t systime;
public:
  t_and_d(time_t t); // constructor
  void show();
};

t_and_d::t_and_d(time_t t)
{
  systime = t;
}

void t_and_d::show()
{
  cout << ctime(&systime);
}

main()
```

```
{
  time_t x;

  x = time(NULL);

  t_and_d ob(x);

  ob.show();

  return 0;
}
```

3. ```
#include <iostream.h>

class box {
  double l, w, h;
  double volume;
public:
  box(double a, double b, double c);
  void vol();
};

box::box(double a, double b, double c)
{
  l = a;
  w = b;
  h = c;

  volume = l * w * h;
}

void box::vol()
{
  cout << "Volume is: " << volume << "\n";
}

main()
{
  box x(2.2, 3.97, 8.09), y(1.0, 2.0, 3.0);

  x.vol();
  y.vol();
  return 0;
}
```
```

1.
```cpp
#include <iostream.h>

class area_cl {
public:
  double height;
  double width;
};

class box : public area_cl {
public:
  box(double h, double w);
  double area();
};

class isosceles : public area_cl {
public:
  isosceles(double h, double w);
  double area();
};

box::box(double h, double w)
{
  height = h;
  width = w;
}

isosceles::isosceles(double h, double w)
{
  height = h;
  width = w;
}

double box::area()
{
  return width * height;
}

double isosceles::area()
{
  return 0.5 * width * height;
}
```

```
main()
{
  box b(10.0, 5.0);
  isosceles i(4.0, 6.0);

  cout << "Box: " << b.area() << "\n";
  cout << "Triangle: " << i.area() << "\n";

  return 0;
}
```

2.5 EXERCISES

1.
```cpp
// Stack class using a structure.
#include <iostream.h>

#define SIZE 10

// Declare a stack class for characters using a structure.
struct stack {
  stack(); // constructor
  void push(char ch); // push character on stack
  char pop(); // pop character from stack
private:
  char stck[SIZE]; // holds the stack
  int tos; // index of top-of-stack
};

// Initialize the stack.
stack::stack()
{
  cout << "Constructing a stack\n";
  tos = 0;
}

// Push a character.
void stack::push(char ch)
{
  if(tos==SIZE) {
    cout << "Stack is full";
    return;
  }
  stck[tos] = ch;
```

```
    tos++;
  }

  // Pop a character.
  char stack::pop()
  {
    if(tos==0) {
      cout << "Stack is empty";
      return 0; // return null on empty stack
    }
    tos--;
    return stck[tos];
  }

  main()
  {
    // create two stacks that are automatically initialized.
    stack s1, s2;
    int i;

    s1.push('a');
    s2.push('x');
    s1.push('b');
    s2.push('y');
    s1.push('c');
    s2.push('z');

    for(i=0; i<3; i++) cout << "Pop s1: " << s1.pop() << "\n";
    for(i=0; i<3; i++) cout << "Pop s2: " << s2.pop() << "\n";

    return 0;
  }
```

2. ```
   #include <iostream.h>

   union swap {
     unsigned char c[2];
     unsigned i;
     swap(unsigned x);
     void swp();
   };
   ```
   ```

```
swap::swap(unsigned x)
{
  i = x;
}

void swap::swp()
{
  unsigned char temp;

  temp = c[0];
  c[0] = c[1];
  c[1] = temp;
}

main()
{
  swap ob(1);

  ob.swp();
  cout << ob.i;

  return 0;
}
```

2.6 EXERCISES

1.
```
#include <iostream.h>

// Overload abs() three ways:

// abs() for ints
inline int abs(int n)
{
  cout << "In integer abs()\n";
  return n<0 ? -n : n;
}

// abs() for longs
inline long abs(long n)
{
  cout << "In long abs()\n";
  return n<0 ? -n : n;
}
```

```
// abs() for doubles
inline double abs(double n)
{
  cout << "In double abs()\n";
  return n<0 ? -n : n;
}

main()
{
  cout << "Absolute value of -10: " << abs(-10) << "\n";
  cout << "Absolute value of -10L: " << abs(-10L) << "\n";
  cout << "Absolute value of -10.01: " << abs(-10.01) << "\n";

  return 0;
}
```

2. The function might not be able to be inlined because the function contains a **for** loop. Many compilers will not inline functions containing loops.

2.7 *EXERCISES*

1.
```
#include <iostream.h>

#define SIZE 10

// Declare a stack class for characters.
class stack {
  char stck[SIZE]; // holds the stack
  int tos; // index of top-of-stack
public:
  stack() { tos = 0; }
  void push(char ch)
  {
    if(tos==SIZE) {
      cout << "Stack is full";
      return;
    }
    stck[tos] = ch;
    tos++;
  }

  char pop()
```

```
  {
    if(tos==0) {
      cout << "Stack is empty";
      return 0; // return null on empty stack
    }
    tos--;
    return stck[tos];
  }
};

main()
{
  // create two stacks that are automatically initialized.
  stack s1, s2;
  int i;

  s1.push('a');
  s2.push('x');
  s1.push('b');
  s2.push('y');
  s1.push('c');
  s2.push('z');

  for(i=0; i<3; i++) cout << "Pop s1: " << s1.pop() << "\n";
  for(i=0; i<3; i++) cout << "Pop s2: " << s2.pop() << "\n";

  return 0;
}
```

2.
```
#include <iostream.h>
#include <malloc.h>
#include <string.h>
#include <stdlib.h>

class strtype {
  char *p;
  int len;
public:
  strtype(char *ptr)
  {
    len = strlen(ptr);
    p = (char *) malloc(len+1);
```

```
      if(!p) {
        cout << "Allocation error\n";
        exit(1);
      }
      strcpy(p, ptr);
    }
    ~strtype() { cout << "Freeing p\n"; free(p); }

    void show()
    {
      cout << p << " - length: " << len;
      cout << "\n";
    }
};

main()
{
  strtype s1("This is a test"), s2("I like C++");

  s1.show();
  s2.show();

  return 0;
}
```

2   *M*ASTERY SKILLS CHECK

1. A constructor is the function that is called when an object is created. A destructor is the function that is called when an object is destroyed.

2. #include <iostream.h>

```
class line {
  int len;
public:
  line(int l);
};

line::line(int l)
{
  len = l;

  int i;
  for(i=0; i<len; i++) cout  << '*';
```

```
  }

  main()
  {
    line l(10);

    return 0;
  }
```

3. 10 1000000 −0.009

4. ```
   #include <iostream.h>

   class area_cl {
   public:
     double height;
     double width;
   };

   class box : public area_cl {
   public:
     box(double h, double w) { height = h; width = w; }
     double area() { return height * width; }
   };

   class isosceles : public area_cl {
   public:
     isosceles(double h, double w) { height = h; width = w; }
     double area() { return 0.5 * width * height; }};

   class cylinder : public area_cl {
   public:
     cylinder(double h, double w) { height = h; width = w; }
     double area()
     {
       return (2 * 3.1416 * (width/2) * (width/2)) +
               (3.1416 * width * height);
     }
   };

   main()
   {
   ```
   ```

```
   box b(10.0, 5.0);
   isosceles i(4.0, 6.0);
   cylinder c(3.0, 4.0);

   cout << "Box: " << b.area() << "\n";
   cout << "Triangle: " << i.area() << "\n";
   cout << "Cylinder: " << c.area() << "\n";

   return 0;
}
```

5. An in-line function's code is expanded in line. This means that the function is not actually called. This avoids the overhead associated with the function call and return mechanism. Its advantage is that it increases the execution speed. Its disadvantage is that it can increase the size of the program.

6.
```
#include <iostream.h>

class myclass {
   int i, j;
public:
   myclass(int x, int y) { i = x; j = y; }
   void show() { cout << i << " " << j; }
};

main()
{
   myclass count(2, 3);

   count.show();

   return 0;
}
```

7. In a class, members are private by default. In a structure, members are public by default.

2   *CUMULATIVE SKILLS CHECK*

1.
```
#include <iostream.h>

class prompt {
   int count;
```

```cpp
public:
  prompt(char *s) { cout << s; cin >> count; };
  ~prompt();
};

prompt::~prompt() {
  int i, j;

  for(i=0; i<count; i++) {
    cout << '\a';
    for(j=0; j<32000; j++) ; // delay
  }
}

main()
{
  prompt ob("Enter a number: ");

  return 0;
}
```

2. ```cpp
#include <iostream.h>

class ftoi {
  double feet;
  double inches;
public:
  ftoi(double f);
};

ftoi::ftoi(double f)
{
  feet = f;
  inches = feet * 12;
  cout << feet << " is " << inches << " inches.\n";
}

main()
{
  ftoi a(12.0), b(99.0);

  return 0;
}
```
```

```
3. #include <iostream.h>
   #include <stdlib.h>

   class dice {
     int val;
   public:
     void roll();
   };

   void dice::roll()
   {
     val = (rand() % 6) + 1; // generate 1 through 6
     cout << val << "\n";
   }

   main()
   {
     dice one, two;

     one.roll();
     two.roll();
     one.roll();
     two.roll();
     one.roll();
     two.roll();

     return 0;
   }
```

3 REVIEW SKILLS CHECK

1. The constructor is called **widgit( )** and the destructor is called **~widgit( )**.

2. The constructor function is called when an object is created (that is, comes into existence). The destructor is called when an object is destroyed.

3.
```
class Mars : public planet {
   // ...
   };
```

4. A function may be expanded in line either by preceding its definition with the **inline** specifier or by including its definition within a class declaration.

5. An in-line function must be defined before it is first used. Other common restrictions include the following: It may not contain any loops. It must

not be recursive. It may not contain a **goto** or a **switch** statement. Finally, it may not contain any **static** variables.

6. `sample ob(100, 'X');`

1. The assignment statement **x = y** is wrong because **cl1** and **cl2** are two different types of classes, and objects of differing class types may not be assigned.

2.
```cpp
#include <iostream.h>

#define SIZE 100

class q_type {
  int queue[SIZE]; // holds the queue
  int head, tail; // indices of head and tail
public:
  q_type(); // constructor
  void q(int num); // store
  int deq();  // retrieve
};

// Constructor
q_type::q_type()
{
  head = tail = 0;
}

// Put value on queue.
void q_type::q(int num)
{
  if(tail+1==head || (tail+1==SIZE && !head)) {
    cout << "Queue is full\n";
    return;
  }
  tail++;
  if(tail==SIZE) tail = 0; // cycle around
  queue[tail] = num;
}

// Remove value from queue.
int q_type::deq()
```

```
{
  if(head == tail) {
    cout << "Queue is empty\n";
    return 0;   // or some other error indicator
  }
  head++;
  if(head==SIZE) head = 0; // cycle around
  return queue[head];
}

main()
{
  q_type q1, q2;
  int i;

  for(i=1; i<=10; i++) {
    q1.q(i);
  }

  // assign one queue to another
  q2 = q1;

  // show that both have the same contents
  for(i=1; i<=10; i++)
    cout << "Dequeue 1: " << q1.deq() << "\n";

  for(i=1; i<=10; i++)
    cout << "Dequeue 2: " << q2.deq() << "\n";

  return 0;
}
```

3. If memory to hold a queue is dynamically allocated, then assigning one queue to another causes the dynamic memory allocated to the queue on the left side of the assignment statement to be lost and the memory allocated to the queue on the right side to be freed twice when the objects are destroyed. Either of these two conditions is an unacceptable error.

3.2   EXERCISES

1. ```
   #include <iostream.h>

   #define SIZE 10
   ```
   ```

```
// Declare a stack class for characters
class stack {
  char stck[SIZE]; // holds the stack
  int tos; // index of top-of-stack
public:
  stack(); // constructor
  void push(char ch); // push character on stack
  char pop(); // pop character from stack
};

// Initialize the stack
stack::stack()
{
  cout << "Constructing a stack\n";
  tos = 0;
}

// Push a character.
void stack::push(char ch)
{
  if(tos==SIZE) {
    cout << "Stack is full";
    return;
  }
  stck[tos] = ch;
  tos++;
}

// Pop a character.
char stack::pop()
{
  if(tos==0) {
    cout << "Stack is empty";
    return 0; // return null on empty stack
  }
  tos--;
  return stck[tos];
}

void showstack(stack o);

main()
{
  stack s1;
```

```
    int i;

    s1.push('a');
    s1.push('b');
    s1.push('c');

    showstack(s1);

    // s1 in main is still existent
    cout << "s1 stack still contains this: \n";
    for(i=0; i<3; i++) cout << s1.pop() << "\n";

    return 0;
}

// Display the contents of a stack.
void showstack(stack o)
{
    char c;

    // when this statement ends, the o stack is empty
    while(c=o.pop()) cout << c << "\n";
    cout << "\n";
}
```

This program displays the following:

```
Constructing a stack
c
b
a
Stack is empty
s1 stack still contains this:
c
b
a
```

2. The memory used to hold the integer pointed to by **p** in object **o** used to call **neg( )** is freed when the copy of **o** is destroyed when **neg( )** terminates even though this memory is still needed by **o** inside **main( )**.

EXERCISES

1.
```
#include <iostream.h>

class who {
  char name;
public:
  who(char c) {
      name = c;
      cout << "Constructing who #";
      cout << name << "\n";
  }
  ~who() { cout << "Destructing who #" << name << "\n"; }
};

who makewho()
{
  who temp('B');
  return temp;
}

main()
{
  who ob('A');

  makewho();

  return 0;
}
```

2. There are several situations in which it would be improper to return an object. Here is one: if an object opens a disk file when created and closes that file when it is destroyed, if that object is returned from a function, the file will be closed when the temporary object is destroyed.

EXERCISE

1.
```
#include <iostream.h>

class pr2;  // forward reference

class pr1 {
```

```
    int printing;
    // ...
  public:
    pr1() { printing = 0; }
    void set_print(int status) { printing = status; }
    // ...
    friend int inuse(pr1 o1, pr2 o2);
  };

  class pr2 {
    int printing;
    // ...
  public:
    pr2() { printing = 0; }
    void set_print(int status) { printing = status; }
    // ...
    friend int inuse(pr1 o1, pr2 o2);
  };

  // Return true if printer is in use.
  int inuse(pr1 o1, pr2 o2)
  {
    if(o1.printing || o2.printing) return 1;
    else return 0;
  }

  main()
  {
    pr1 p1;
    pr2 p2;

    if(!inuse(p1, p2)) cout << "Printer idle\n";

    cout << "Setting p1 to printing...\n";
    p1.set_print(1);
    if(inuse(p1, p2)) cout << "Now, printer in use.\n";

    cout << "Turn off p1...\n";
    p1.set_print(0);
    if(!inuse(p1, p2)) cout << "Printer idle\n";

    cout << "Turn on p2...\n";
    p2.set_print(1);
    if(inuse(p1, p2)) cout << "Now, printer in use.\n";
```

```
    return 0;
}
```

MASTERY SKILLS CHECK

1. For one object to be assigned to another, both must be of the same class type.

2. The trouble with the assignment of **ob1** to **ob2** is that the memory pointed to by **ob2**'s initial value of **p** is now lost because this value is overwritten by the assignment. This memory thus becomes impossible to free and the memory pointed to by **ob1**'s **p** is freed twice when it is destroyed—possibly causing damage to the dynamic allocation system.

3.
```
int light(planet p)
{
    return p.get_miles() / 186000;
}
```

4. Yes.

5.
```
// Load a stack with the alphabet.
#include <iostream.h>

#define SIZE 27

// Declare a stack class for characters
class stack {
    char stck[SIZE]; // holds the stack
    int tos; // index of top-of-stack
public:
    stack(); // constructor
    void push(char ch); // push character on stack
    char pop(); // pop character from stack
};

// Initialize the stack
stack::stack()
{
    cout << "Constructing a stack\n";
    tos = 0;
}

// Push a character.
void stack::push(char ch)
```

```
{
  if(tos==SIZE) {
    cout << "Stack is full";
    return;
  }
  stck[tos] = ch;
  tos++;
}

// Pop a character.
char stack::pop()
{
  if(tos==0) {
    cout << "Stack is empty";
    return 0; // return null on empty stack
  }
  tos--;
  return stck[tos];
}

void showstack(stack o);
stack loadstack();

main()
{
  stack s1;

  s1 = loadstack();
  showstack(s1);

  return 0;
}

// Display the contents of a stack.
void showstack(stack o)
{
  char c;

  // when this statement ends, the o stack is empty
  while(c=o.pop()) cout << c << "\n";
  cout << "\n";
}

// Load a stack with the letters of the alphabet.
stack loadstack()
```

```
{
  stack t;
  char c;
  for(c = 'a'; c<='z'; c++) t.push(c);
  return t;
}
```

6. When passing an object to a function or when returning an object from a function, temporaries are created that will be destroyed when the function terminates. When a temporary is destroyed, the destructor function may destroy something that is needed elsewhere in the program.

7. A friend is a nonmember function that is granted access to the private parts of the class for which it is a friend. That is, a friend function has access to the private parts of the class for which it is a friend but is not a member of that class.

▐ 3 ▌ *C*UMULATIVE SKILLS CHECK

1.
```
// Load a stack with the alphabet.
#include <iostream.h>
#include <ctype.h>

#define SIZE 27

// Declare a stack class for characters
class stack {
  char stck[SIZE]; // holds the stack
  int tos; // index of top-of-stack
public:
  stack(); // constructor
  void push(char ch); // push character on stack
  char pop(); // pop character from stack
};

// Initialize the stack
stack::stack()
{
  cout << "Constructing a stack\n";
  tos = 0;
}

// Push a character.
void stack::push(char ch)
```

```
{
  if(tos==SIZE) {
    cout << "Stack is full";
    return;
  }
  stck[tos] = ch;
  tos++;
}

// Pop a character.
char stack::pop()
{
  if(tos==0) {
    cout << "Stack is empty";
    return 0; // return null on empty stack
  }
  tos--;
  return stck[tos];
}

void showstack(stack o);
stack loadstack();
stack loadstack(int upper);

main()
{
  stack s1, s2, s3;

  s1 = loadstack();
  showstack(s1);

  // get uppercase letters
  s2 = loadstack(1);
  showstack(s2);

  // use lowercase letters
  s3 = loadstack(0);
  showstack(s3);

  return 0;
}

// Display the contents of a stack.
void showstack(stack o)
{
```

```
  char c;

  // when this statement ends, the o stack is empty
  while(c=o.pop()) cout << c << "\n";
  cout << "\n";
}

// Load a stack with the letters of the alphabet.
stack loadstack()
{
  stack t;
  char c;

  for(c = 'a'; c<='z'; c++) t.push(c);
  return t;
}

/* Load a stack with the letters of the alphabet. Uppercase
   letters if upper is 1; lowercase otherwise. */
stack loadstack(int upper)
{
  stack t;
  char c;

  if(upper) c = 'A';
  else c = 'a';

  for(; toupper(c)<='Z'; c++) t.push(c);
  return t;
}
```

2.
```
#include <iostream.h>
#include <malloc.h>
#include <string.h>
#include <stdlib.h>

class strtype {
  char *p;
  int len;
public:
  strtype(char *ptr);
  ~strtype();
  void show();
  friend char *get_string(strtype *ob);
```

```
};

strtype::strtype(char *ptr)
{
  len = strlen(ptr);
  p = (char *) malloc(len+1);
  if(!p) {
    cout << "Allocation error\n";
    exit(1);
  }
  strcpy(p, ptr);
}

strtype::~strtype()
{
  cout << "Freeing p\n";
  free(p);
}

void strtype::show()
{
  cout << p << " - length: " << len;
  cout << "\n";
}

char *get_string(strtype *ob)
{
  return ob->p;
}

main()
{
  strtype s1("This is a test");

  char *s;

  s1.show();

  // get pointer to string
  s = get_string(&s1);
  cout << "Here is string contained in s1: ";
  cout << s << "\n";

  return 0;
}
```

3. The outcome of the experiment is as follows: Yes, data from the base class is also copied when an object of a derived class is assigned to another. Here is a program that demonstrates this fact:

```cpp
#include <iostream.h>

class base {
  int a;
public:
  void load_a(int n) { a = n; }
  int get_a() { return a; }
};

class derived : public base {
  int b;
public:
  void load_b(int n) { b = n; }
  int get_b() { return b; }
};

main()
{
  derived ob1, ob2;

  ob1.load_a(5);
  ob1.load_b(10);

  // assign ob1 to ob2
  ob2 = ob1;

  cout << "Here is ob1's a and b: ";
  cout << ob1.get_a() << ' ' << ob1.get_b() << "\n";

  cout << "Here is ob2's a and b: ";
  cout << ob2.get_a() << ' ' << ob2.get_b() << "\n";

  /* As you can probably guess, the output is the same for
     each object. */

  return 0;
}
```

*R*EVIEW SKILLS CHECK

1. When one object is assigned to another of the same type, the current values of all data members of the object on the right are assigned to the corresponding data members on the left.

2. Trouble can occur when assigning one object to another when that assignment overwrites important data already existing in the object being assigned to. For example, a pointer to dynamic memory or to an open file can be overwritten and, therefore, lost.

3. When an object is passed to a function, a copy is made. However, the copy's constructor function is not called. The copy's destructor is called when the object is destroyed by the termination of the function.

4. The violation of the separation between an argument and its copy when passed to a parameter can be caused by several situations. For example, if dynamic memory is freed by a destructor, then that memory will also be lost to the argument. In general, if the destructor function destroys anything that the original argument requires, damage to the argument will occur.

5.
```cpp
#include <iostream.h>

class summation {
  int num;
  long sum; // summation of num
public:
  void set_sum(int n);
  void show_sum() {
    cout << num << " summed is " << sum << "\n";
  }
};

void summation::set_sum(int n)
{
  int i;

  num = n;

  sum = 0;
  for(i=1; i<=n; i++)
    sum += i;
}
```

```
summation make_sum()
{
  int i;
  summation temp;

  cout << "Enter number: ";
  cin >> i;

  temp.set_sum(i);

  return temp;
}

main()
{
  summation s;

  s = make_sum();

  s.show_sum();

  return 0;
}
```

6. For many compilers, in-line functions cannot contain loops.

7. ```
#include <iostream.h>

class myclass {
  int num;
public:
  myclass(int x) { num = x; }
  friend int isneg(myclass ob);
};

int isneg(myclass ob)
{
  return (ob.num < 0) ? 1 : 0;
}

main()
{
  myclass a(-1), b(2);

  cout << isneg(a) << ' ' << isneg(b);
```
```

```
   cout << "\n";

   return 0;
}
```

8. Yes, a friend function may be friends with more than one class.

4.1 EXERCISES

1. ```
   #include <iostream.h>

   class letters {
     char ch;
   public:
     letters(char c) { ch = c; }
     char get_ch() { return ch; }
   };

   main()
   {
     letters ob[10] = { 'a', 'b', 'c','d', 'e', 'f',
                        'g', 'h', 'i', 'j' };

     int i;

     for(i=0; i<10; i++)
       cout << ob[i].get_ch() << ' ';

     cout << "\n";

     return 0;
   }
   ```

2. ```
   #include <iostream.h>

   class squares {
     int num, sqr;
   public:
     squares(int a, int b) { num = a; sqr = b; }
     void show() {cout << num << ' ' << sqr << "\n"; }
   };

   main()
   {
   ```

```
        squares ob[10] = {
          squares(1, 1),
          squares(2, 4),
          squares(3, 9),
          squares(4, 16),
          squares(5, 25),
          squares(6, 36),
          squares(7, 49),
          squares(8, 64),
          squares(9, 81),
          squares(10, 100)
        };
        int i;

        for(i=0; i<10; i++) ob[i].show();

        return 0;
      }
```

3. ```
   #include <iostream.h>

   class letters {
     char ch;
   public:
     letters(char c) { ch = c; }
     char get_ch() { return ch; }
   };

   main()
   {
     letters ob[10] = {
       letters('a'),
       letters('b'),
       letters('c'),
       letters('d'),
       letters('e'),
       letters('f'),
       letters('g'),
       letters('h'),
       letters('i'),
       letters('j')
     };

     int i;
   ```
   ```

```
    for(i=0; i<10; i++)
      cout << ob[i].get_ch() << ' ';

    cout << "\n";

    return 0;
  }
```

4.2   *EXERCISES*

```
1. // Display in reverse order.
   #include <iostream.h>

   class samp {
     int a, b;
   public:
     samp(int n, int m) { a = n; b = m; }
     int get_a() { return a; }
     int get_b() { return b; }
   };

   main()
   {
     samp ob[4] = {
       samp(1, 2),
       samp(3, 4),
       samp(5, 6),
       samp(7, 8)
     };
     int i;

     samp *p;

     p = &ob[3]; // get address of last element

     for(i=0; i<4; i++) {
       cout << p->get_a() << ' ';
       cout << p->get_b() << "\n";
       p--;  // advance to previous object
     }

     cout << "\n";
```

```
    return 0;
}
```

2.
```
/* Create a two-dimensional array of objects.
   Access via a pointer. */
#include <iostream.h>

class samp {
  int a;
public:
  samp(int n) { a = n; }
  int get_a() { return a; }
};

main()
{
  samp ob[4][2] = {
    1, 2,
    3, 4,
    5, 6,
    7, 8
  };
  int i;

  samp *p;

  p = (samp *) ob;

   for(i=0; i<4; i++) {
     cout << p->get_a() << ' ';
     p++;
     cout << p->get_a() << "\n";
     p++;
   }

  cout << "\n";

  return 0;
}
```

4.3 EXERCISE

1.
```
// Use this pointer.
#include <iostream.h>
```

```
class myclass {
  int a, b;
public:
  myclass(int n, int m) { this->a = n; this->b = m; }
  int add() { return this->a + this->b; }
  void show();
};

void myclass::show()
{
  int t;

  t = this->add(); // call member function
  cout << t << "\n";
}

main()
{
  myclass ob(10, 14);

  ob.show();

  return 0;
}
```

4.4 ▉ *E*XERCISES

```
1. #include <iostream.h>

main()
{
  float *f;
  long *l;
  char *c;

  f = new float;
  l = new long;
  c = new char;

  if(!f || !l || !c) {
    cout << "Allocation error.";
    return 1;
  }
```

```
    *f = 10.102;
    *l = 100000;
    *c = 'A';

    cout << *f << ' ' << *l << ' ' << *c;
    cout << '\n';

    delete f; delete l; delete c;

    return 0;
}
```

2.
```
#include <iostream.h>
#include <string.h>

class phone {
  char name[40];
  char number[14];
public:
  void store(char *n, char *num);
  void show();
};

void phone::store(char *n, char *num)
{
  strcpy(name, n);
  strcpy(number, num);
}

void phone::show()
{
  cout << name << ": " << number;
  cout << "\n";
}

main()
{
  phone *p;

  p = new phone;

  if(!p) {
    cout << "Allocation error.";
    return 1;
```

```
      }

      p->store("Issac Newton", "111 555-2323");

      p->show();

      delete p;

      return 0;
   }
```

4.5 EXERCISES

1. ```
   char *p;

   p = new char [100];
   // ...
   strcpy(p, "This is a test");
   ```

2. ```
   #include <iostream.h>

   main()
   {
     double *p;

     p = new double (-123.0987);

     cout << *p << '\n';

     return 0;
   }
   ```

4.6 EXERCISES

1. ```
   #include <iostream.h>

   void rneg(int &i);
   void pneg(int *i);

   main()
   {
     int i = 10;
     int j = 20;
   ```
   ```

```
  rneg(i);
  pneg(&j);

  cout << i << ' ' << j << '\n';

  return 0;
}

void rneg(int &i)
{
  i = -i;
}

void pneg(int *i)
{
  *i = - *i;
}
```

2. When **triple( )** is called, the address of **d** is explicitly obtained by using the **&** operator. This is neither necessary nor legal. When a reference parameter is used, the argument is not preceded by the **&**.
3. The address of a reference parameter is automatically passed to the function. You need not obtain the address manually. Passing by reference is faster than passing by value. No copy of the argument is generated. Therefore, there is no chance of a side effect occurring because the copy's destructor is called.

4.7 EXERCISE

1. In the original program, the object is passed to **show( )** by value. Thus, a copy is made. When **show( )** returns, the copy is destroyed and its destructor is called. This causes **p** to be released, but the memory pointed to it is still needed by the arguments to **show( )**. Here is a corrected version that uses a reference parameter to prevent a copy from being made when the function is called:

```
// This program is now fixed.
#include <iostream.h>
#include <string.h>
#include <stdlib.h>
```

```
class strtype {
  char *p;
public:
  strtype(char *s);
  ~strtype() { delete p; }
  char *get() { return p; }
};

strtype::strtype(char *s)
{
  int l;

  l = strlen(s);

  p = new char [l];
  if(!p) {
    cout << "Allocation error\n";
    exit(1);
  }

  strcpy(p, s);
}

// Fix by using a reference parameter.
void show(strtype &x)
{
  char *s;

  s = x.get();
  cout << s << "\n";
}

main()
{
  strtype a("Hello"), b("There");

  show(a);
  show(b);

  return 0;
}
```

EXERCISES

1.
```cpp
// A bounded 2-d array example.
#include <iostream.h>
#include <stdlib.h>

class array {
  int isize, jsize;
  int *p;
public:
  array(int i, int j);
  &put(int i, int j);
  int get(int i, int j);
};

array::array(int i, int j)
{
  p = new int [i*j];
  if(!p) {
    cout << "Allocation error\n";
    exit(1);
  }
  isize = i;
  jsize = j;
}

// Put something into the array.
int &array::put(int i, int j)
{
  if(i<0 || i>=isize || j<0 || j>=jsize) {
    cout << "Bounds error!!!\n";
    exit(1);
  }
  return p[i*jsize + j];  // return reference to p[i]
}

// Get something from the array.
int array::get(int i, int j)
{
  if(i<0 || i>=isize || j<0 || j>=jsize) {
    cout << "Bounds error!!!\n";
    exit(1);
  }
  return p[i*jsize +j]; // return character
```

```
}

main()
{
  array a(2, 3);
  int i, j;

  for(i=0; i<2; i++)
    for(j=0; j<3; j++)
      a.put(i, j) = i+j;

  for(i=0; i<2; i++)
    for(j=0; j<3; j++)
      cout << a.get(i, j) << ' ';

  // generate out of bounds
  a.put(10, 10);

  return 0;
}
```

2. No. A reference returned by a function cannot be assigned to a pointer.

4 ***M*ASTERY SKILLS CHECK**

1. `#include <iostream.h>`

```
class a_type {
  double a, b;
public:
  a_type(double x, double y) {
    a = x;
    b = y;
  }
  void show() { cout << a << ' ' << b << '\n'; }
};

main()
{
  a_type ob[2][5] = {
    a_type(1, 1), a_type(2, 2),
    a_type(3, 3), a_type(4, 4),
    a_type(5, 5), a_type(6, 6),
    a_type(7, 7), a_type(8, 8),
```

```
    a_type(9, 9), a_type(10, 10)
  };

  int i, j;

  for(i=0; i<2; i++)
    for(j=0; j<5; j++)
      ob[i][j].show();

  cout << '\n';

  return 0;
}
```

2.
```
#include <iostream.h>

class a_type {
  double a, b;
public:
  a_type(double x, double y) {
    a = x;
    b = y;
  }
  void show() { cout << a << ' ' << b << '\n'; }
};

main()
{
  a_type ob[2][5] = {
    a_type(1, 1), a_type(2, 2),
    a_type(3, 3), a_type(4, 4),
    a_type(5, 5), a_type(6, 6),
    a_type(7, 7), a_type(8, 8),
    a_type(9, 9), a_type(10, 10)
  };

  a_type *p;

  p = (a_type *) ob;

  int i, j;

  for(i=0; i<2; i++)
    for(j=0; j<5; j++) {
      p->show();
```

```
        p++;
    }

    cout << '\n';

    return 0;
}
```

3. The **this** pointer is a pointer automatically passed to a member function that points to the object that generated the call.

4. The general forms of **new** and **delete** are

   p-var = new *type;*

   delete *p-var;*

   When using **new**, you don't need to use a type cast. The size of the object is automatically determined; you don't need to use **sizeof**. Also, you don't need to include **malloc.h** with your program.

5. A reference is essentially an implicit pointer constant that is effectively a different name for another variable or argument. One advantage of using a reference parameter is that no copy of the argument is made.

6.
```
#include <iostream.h>

void recip(double &d);

main()
{
  double x = 100.0;

  cout << "x is " << x << '\n';

  recip(x);

  cout << "Reciprocal is " << x << '\n';

  return 0;
}

void recip(double &d)
{
  d = 1/d;
}
```

████ **4** ████ $\mathcal{C}$**UMULATIVE SKILLS CHECK**

1. When accessing a member of an object by using a pointer, use the arrow (–>) operator.

2. ```cpp
   #include <iostream.h>
   #include <string.h>
   #include <stdlib.h>

   class strtype {
     char *p;
     int len;
   public:
     strtype(char *ptr);
     ~strtype();
     void show();
   };

   strtype::strtype(char *ptr)
   {
     len = strlen(ptr);
     p = new char [len+1];
     if(!p) {
       cout << "Allocation error\n";
       exit(1);
     }
     strcpy(p, ptr);
   }

   strtype::~strtype()
   {
     cout << "Freeing p\n";
     delete [] p;
   }

   void strtype::show()
   {
     cout << p << " - length: " << len;
     cout << "\n";
   }

   main()
   {
     strtype s1("This is a test"), s2("I like C++");
   ```
   ```

```
    s1.show();
    s2.show();

    return 0;
}
```

5

REVIEW SKILLS CHECK

1. A reference is a special type of pointer that is automatically dereferenced and that may be used interchangeably with the object it is pointing to. There are three types of references: parameter references, independent references, and references that are returned by functions.

2.
```
#include <iostream.h>

main()
{
  float *f;
  int *i;

  f = new float;
  i = new int;

  if(!f || !i) {
    cout << "Allocation error\n";
    return 1;
  }

  *f = 10.101;
  *i = 100;

  cout << *f << ' ' << *i << '\n';

  delete f;
  delete i;

  return 0;
}
```

3. The general form of **new** that includes an initializer is shown here:

   p-var = new *type* (*initializer*);

   For example, this allocates an integer and gives it the value 10:

```
int *p;

p = new int (10);
```

4.
```
#include <iostream.h>

class samp {
  int x;
public:
  samp(int n) { x = n; }
  int getx() { return x; }
};

main()
{
  samp A[10] = { 1, 2, 3, 4, 5, 6, 7, 8, 9, 10 };
  int i;

  for(i=0; i<10; i++) cout << A[i].getx() << ' ';

  cout << "\n";

  return 0;
}
```

5. Advantages: A reference parameter does not cause a copy of the object used in the call to be made. A reference is often faster to pass than a value. The reference parameter streamlines the call-by-reference syntax and procedure, reducing the chance for errors.

Disadvantages: Changes to a reference parameter alter the variable used in the call. A reference parameter opens the possiblilty of side effects in the calling routine.

6. No.

7.
```
#include <iostream.h>

void mag(long &num, long order);

main()
{
  long n = 4;
  long o = 2;

  cout << "4 raised to the 2nd magnitude is ";
```

```
      mag(n, o);
      cout << n << '\n';

      return 0;
    }

    void mag(long &num, long order)
    {
      for( ; order; order--) num = num * 10;
    }
```

5.1   EXERCISES

1.
```
   #include <iostream.h>
   #include <string.h>
   #include <stdlib.h>

   class strtype {
     char *p;
     int len;
   public:
     strtype();
     strtype(char *s, int l);
     char *getstring() { return p; }
     int getlength() { return len; }
   };

   strtype::strtype()
   {
     p = new char [255];
     if(!p) {
       cout << "Allocation error\n";
       exit(1);
     }
     *p = '\0'; // null string
     len = 255;
   }

   strtype::strtype(char *s, int l)
   {
     if(strlen(s) >= l) {
       cout << "Allocating too little memory!\n";
       exit(1);
     }
```

```
    p = new char [l];
    if(!p) {
      cout << "Allocation error\n";
      exit(1);
    }
    strcpy(p, s);
    len = l;
}


main()
{
  strtype s1;
  strtype s2("This is a test", 100);

  cout << "s1: " << s1.getstring() << " - Length: ";
  cout << s1.getlength() << '\n';

  cout << "s2: " << s2.getstring() << " - Length: ";
  cout << s2.getlength() << '\n';

  return 0;
}
```

2.
```
// Stopwatch emulator
#include <iostream.h>
#include <time.h>

class stopwatch {
  double begin, end;
public:
  stopwatch();
  stopwatch(clock_t t);
  ~stopwatch();
  void start();
  void stop();
  void show();
};

stopwatch::stopwatch()
{
  begin = end = 0.0;
}
```

```
stopwatch::stopwatch(clock_t t)
{
  begin = (double) t / CLK_TCK;
  end = 0.0;
}

stopwatch::~stopwatch()
{
  cout << "Stopwatch object being destroyed...";
  show();
}

void stopwatch::start()
{
  begin = (double) clock() / CLK_TCK;
}

void stopwatch::stop()
{
  end = (double) clock() / CLK_TCK;
}

void stopwatch::show()
{
  cout << "Elapsed time: " << end - begin;
  cout << "\n";
}

main()
{
  stopwatch watch;
  long i;

  watch.start();
  for(i=0; i<320000; i++) ; // time a for loop
  watch.stop();
  watch.show();

  // create object using initial value
  stopwatch s2(clock());
  for(i=0; i<250000; i++) ; // time a for loop
  s2.stop();
  s2.show();
```

```
    return 0;
}
```

5.2 EXERCISES

1. The **obj** and **temp** objects are constructed normally. However, when **temp** is returned by **f( )**, a temporary object is made and it is this temporary that generates the call to the copy constructor.

2. As the program is written, when an object is passed to **getval( )**, a bitwise copy is made. When **getval( )** returns and that copy is destroyed, the memory allocated to that object (which is pointed to by **p**) is released. However, this is the same memory still required by the object used in the call to **getval( )**. The correct version of the program is shown here. It uses a copy constructor to avoid this problem.

```
// This program is now fixed.
#include <iostream.h>
#include <stdlib.h>

class myclass {
  int *p;
public:
  myclass(int i);
  myclass(const myclass &o); // copy constructor
  ~myclass() { delete p; }
  friend int getval(myclass o);
};

myclass::myclass(int i)
{
  p = new int;

  if(!p) {
    cout << "Allocation error\n";
    exit(1);
  }
  *p = i;
}

// Copy constructor
myclass::myclass(const myclass &o)
{
  p = new int; // allocate copy's own memory
```

```
  if(!p) {
    cout << "Allocation error\n";
    exit(1);
  }
  *p = *o.p;
}

int getval(myclass o)
{
  return *o.p; // get value
}

main()
{
  myclass a(1), b(2);

  cout << getval(a) << " " << getval(b);
  cout << "\n";
  cout << getval(a) << " " << getval(b);

  return 0;
}
```

3. A copy constructor is invoked when one object is used to initialize another. A normal constructor is called when an object is created.

5.4 *EXERCISES*

```
1. #include <iostream.h>
   #include <stdlib.h>

   long mystrtol(const char *s, char **end, int base = 10)
   {
     return strtol(s, end, base);
   }

   main()
   {
     long x;
     char *s1 = "100234";
     char *p;
```

```
    x = mystrtol(s1, &p, 16);
    cout << "Base 16: " << x << '\n';

    x = mystrtol(s1, &p, 10);
    cout << "Base 10: " << x << '\n';

    x = mystrtol(s1, &p); // use default base of 10
    cout << "Base 10 by default: " << x << '\n';

    return 0;
}
```

2. All parameters taking default arguments must appear to the right of those that do not. That is, once you begin giving parameters defaults, all subsequent parameters must also have defaults. In the question, **q** is not given a default.

3.
```
// Note: This program is Turbo/Borland C++ specific.
#include <iostream.h>
#include <conio.h>

void myclreol(int len = -1);

main()
{
  int i;

  gotoxy(1, 1);
  for(i=0; i<24; i++)
    cout << "abcdefghijklmnopqrstuvwxyz1234567890\n";

  gotoxy(1, 2);
  myclreol();
  gotoxy(1, 4);
  myclreol(20);

  return 0;
}
// Clear to end-of-line unless len parameter is specified.
void myclreol(int len)
{
```

```
    int x, y;

    x = wherex();   // get x position
    y = wherey();   // get y position

    if(len == -1) len = 80-x;

    int i = x;

    for( ; i<=len; i++) cout << ' ';

    gotoxy(x, y); // reset the cursor
}
```

4. A default argument may not be another parameter or a local variable.

5.6   EXERCISE

1.
```
#include <iostream.h>

int dif(int a, int b)
{
    return a-b;
}

float dif(float a, float b)
{
    return a-b;
}

main()
{
    int (*p1)(int, int);
    float (*p2)(float, float);

    p1 = dif; // address of dif(int, int)
    p2 = dif; // address of dif(float, float);

    cout << p1(10, 5) << ' ';
    cout << p2(10.5, 8.9) << '\n';

    return 0;
}
```

1.
```
// Overload date() for time_t.
#include <iostream.h>
#include <stdio.h> // included for sscanf()
#include <time.h>

class date {
  int day, month, year;
public:
  date(char *str);
  date(int m, int d, int y) {
    day = d;
    month = m;
    year = y;
  }
  // overload for parameter of type time_t
  date(time_t t);
  void show() {
    cout << month << '/' << day << '/';
    cout << year << '\n';
  }
};

date::date(char *str)
{
  sscanf(str, "%d%*c%d%*c%d", &month, &day, &year);
}

date::date(time_t t)
{
  struct tm *p;

  p = localtime(&t); // convert to broken down time
  day = p->tm_mday;
  month = p->tm_mon;
  year = p->tm_year;
}

main()
{
  // construct date object using string
  date sdate("11/1/95");
```

```
// construct date object using integers
date idate(11, 1, 95);

/* construct date object using time_t - this
   creates an object using the system date */
date tdate(time(NULL));

sdate.show();
idate.show();
tdate.show();

return 0;
}
```

2. The class **samp** defines only one constructor, and this constructor requires an initializer. Therefore, it is improper to declare an object of type **samp** without one. (That is, **samp x** is an invalid declaration.)

3. One reason to overload a constructor is to provide flexibility, allowing you to choose the most appropriate constructor in the specific instance. Another is to allow both initialized and uninitialized objects to be declared. You may want to overload a constructor so that dynamic arrays can be allocated.

4. The general form of a copy constructor is shown here:

   classname (const *classname* &*obj*) {
     // body of constructor
   }

5. A copy constructor is called when an initialization takes place. Specifically, when one object is explicitly used to initialize another, when an object is passed as a parameter to a function, and when a temporary is created when an object is returned by a function.

6. The **overload** keyword tells the compiler that a function will be overloaded. It is anachronistic and no longer required when overloading functions.

7. A default argument is a value that is given to a function parameter when no corresponding argument appears when the function is called.

8. ```
   #include <iostream.h>
   #include <string.h>

   void reverse(char *str, int count = 0);
   ```
   ```

```
main()
{
   char *s1 = "This is a test";
   char *s2 = "I like C++";

   reverse(s1); // reverse entire string
   reverse(s2, 7);  // reverse 1st 7 chars

   cout << s1 << '\n';
   cout << s2 << '\n';

   return 0;
}

void reverse(char *str, int count)
{
   int i, j;
   char temp;

   if(!count) count = strlen(str)-1;

   for(i=0, j=count; i<j; i++, j--) {
      temp = str[i];
      str[i] = str[j];
      str[j] = temp;
   }
}
```

9. All parameters receiving default arguments must appear to the right of those that do not.

10. Ambiguity can be introduced by default type conversions, reference parameters, and default arguments.

11. It is ambiguous because the compiler cannot know which version of **compute( )** to call. Is it the first version, with **divisor** defaulting? Or is it the second version, which takes only one parameter?

12. When obtaining the address of an overloaded function, it is the type specification of the pointer that determines which function is used.

![5] **CUMULATIVE SKILLS CHECK**

1. ```cpp
   #include <iostream.h>

   void order(int &a, int &b)
   {
     int t;

     if(a<b) return;
     else { // swap a and b
       t = a;
       a = b;
       b = t;
     }
   }

   main()
   {
     int x=10, y=5;

     cout << "x: " << x << ", y: " << y << "\n";

     order(x, y);
     cout << "x: " << x << ", y: " << y << "\n";

     return 0;
   }
   ```

2. The syntax for calling a function that takes a reference parameter is identical to the syntax for calling a value parameter.

3. A default argument is essentially a shorthand approach to function overloading because the net result is the same. For example,

   ```cpp
   int f(int a, int b = 0);
   ```

   is functionally equivalent to these two overloaded functions:

   ```cpp
   int f(int a);
   ```

   ```cpp
   int f(int a, int b);
   ```

4. ```cpp
   #include <iostream.h>
   class samp {
     int a;
   ```

```
public:
  samp() { a= 0; }
  samp(int n) { a = n; }
  int get_a() { return a; }
};

main()
{
  samp ob(88);
  samp obarray[10];

  // ...
}
```

5. Copy constructors are needed when you, the programmer, must control precisely how a copy of an object is made. This is important only when the default bitwise copy creates undesired side effects.

REVIEW SKILLS CHECK 6

1. ```
   class myclass {
     int x, y;
   public:
     myclass(int i, int j) { x=i; y=j; }
     myclass() { x=0; y=0; }
   };
   ```

2. ```
   class myclass {
     int x, y;
   public:
     myclass(int i=0, int j=0) { x=i; y=j; }
   };
   ```

3. Once default arguments have begun, a nondefaulting parameter cannot occur.

4. A function cannot be overloaded when the only difference is that one takes a value parameter and the other takes a reference parameter. (The compiler cannot tell them apart.)

5. It is appropriate to use default arguments when there are one or more values that will occur frequently. It is inappropriate when there is no value or values that have a greater likelihood of occurring.

6. No, because there is no way to initialize a dynamic array. This class has only one constructor, and it requires initializers.

7. A copy constructor is a special constructor that is called when one object initializes another. This circumstance occurs the following three ways: When one object is explicitly used to initialize another, when an object is passed to a function, or when a temporary object is created as a function return value.

6.2 EXERCISES

```
1. // Overload the * and / relative to coord class.
   #include <iostream.h>

   class coord {
     int x, y; // coordinate values
   public:
     coord() { x=0; y=0; }
     coord(int i, int j) { x=i; y=j; }
     void get_xy(int &i, int &j) { i=x; j=y; }
     coord operator*(coord ob2);
     coord operator/(coord ob2);
   };

   // Overload * relative to coord class.
   coord coord::operator*(coord ob2)
   {
     coord temp;

     temp.x = x * ob2.x;
     temp.y = y * ob2.y;

     return temp;
   }

   // Overload / relative to coord class.
   coord coord::operator/(coord ob2)
   {
     coord temp;

     temp.x = x / ob2.x;
     temp.y = y / ob2.y;

     return temp;
```

```
}

main()
{
  coord o1(10, 10), o2(5, 3), o3;
  int x, y;

  o3 = o1 * o2;
  o3.get_xy(x, y);
  cout << "(o1*o2) X: " << x << ", Y: " << y << "\n";

  o3 = o1 / o2;
  o3.get_xy(x, y);
  cout << "(o1/o2) X: " << x << ", Y: " << y << "\n";

  return 0;
}
```

2. The overloading of the % operator is inappropriate because its operation is unrelated to the traditional use.

6.3	**EXERCISE**

1. ```
// Overload the < and > relative to coord class.
#include <iostream.h>

class coord {
  int x, y; // coordinate values
public:
  coord() { x=0; y=0; }
  coord(int i, int j) { x=i; y=j; }
  void get_xy(int &i, int &j) { i=x; j=y; }
  int operator<(coord ob2);
  int operator>(coord ob2);
};

// Overload the < operator for coord.
int coord::operator<(coord ob2)
{
  if(x<ob2.x && y<ob2.y) return 1;
  else return 0;
}

// Overload the > operator for coord.
```
```

```
int coord::operator>(coord ob2)
{
  return ((x > ob2.x) && (y > ob2.y));
}

main()
{
  coord o1(10, 10), o2(5, 3);

  if(o1>o2) cout << "o1 > o2\n";
  else cout << "o1 <= o2 \n";

  if(o1<o2) cout << "o1 < o2\n";
  else cout << "o1 >= o2\n";

  return 0;
}
```

6.4 EXERCISES

1.
```
// Overload the -- relative to coord class.
#include <iostream.h>

class coord {
  int x, y; // coordinate values
public:
  coord() { x=0; y=0; }
  coord(int i, int j) { x=i; y=j; }
  void get_xy(int &i, int &j) { i=x; j=y; }
  coord operator--(); // prefix
  coord operator--(int notused); // postfix
};

// Overload prefix -- for coord class.
coord coord::operator--()
{
  x--;
  y--;
  return *this;
}

// Overload postfix -- for coord class.
coord coord::operator--(int notused)
{
```

```
  x--;
  y--;
  return *this;
}

main()
{
  coord o1(10, 10);
  int x, y;

  o1--; // decrement an object
  o1.get_xy(x, y);
  cout << "(o1--) X: " << x << ", Y: " << y << "\n";

  --o1; // decrement an object
  o1.get_xy(x, y);
  cout << "(--o1) X: " << x << ", Y: " << y << "\n";
  return 0;
}
```

2.
```
// Overload the + relative to coord class.
#include <iostream.h>

class coord {
  int x, y; // coordinate values
public:
  coord() { x=0; y=0; }
  coord(int i, int j) { x=i; y=j; }
  void get_xy(int &i, int &j) { i=x; j=y; }
  coord operator+(coord ob2); // binary plus
  coord operator+(); // unary plus
};

// Overload + relative to coord class.
coord coord::operator+(coord ob2)
{
  coord temp;

  temp.x = x + ob2.x;
  temp.y = y + ob2.y;

  return temp;
}

// Overload unary + for coord class.
```

```
coord coord::operator+()
{
  if(x<0) x = -x;
  if(y<0) y = -y;

  return *this;
}

main()
{
  coord o1(10, 10), o2(-2, -2);
  int x, y;
  o1 = o1 + o2; // addition
  o1.get_xy(x, y);
  cout << "(o1+o2) X: " << x << ", Y: " << y << "\n";

  o2 = +o2; // absolute value
  o2.get_xy(x, y);
  cout << "(+o2) X: " << x << ", Y: " << y << "\n";

  return 0;
}
```

<hr>

6.5   *E XERCISES*

1. ```
/* Overload the - and / relative to coord class
       using friend functions. */
#include <iostream.h>

class coord {
  int x, y; // coordinate values
public:
  coord() { x=0; y=0; }
  coord(int i, int j) { x=i; y=j; }
  void get_xy(int &i, int &j) { i=x; j=y; }
  friend coord operator-(coord ob1, coord ob2);
  friend coord operator/(coord ob1, coord ob2);
};

// Overload - relative to coord class using friend.
coord operator-(coord ob1, coord ob2)
{
  coord temp;
```
```

```
    temp.x = ob1.x - ob2.x;
    temp.y = ob1.y - ob2.y;

    return temp;
}

// Overload / relative to coord class using friend
coord operator/(coord ob1, coord ob2)
{
    coord temp;

    temp.x = ob1.x / ob2.x;
    temp.y = ob1.y / ob2.y;

    return temp;
}

main()
{
    coord o1(10, 10), o2(5, 3), o3;
    int x, y;

    o3 = o1 - o2;
    o3.get_xy(x, y);
    cout << "(o1-o2) X: " << x << ", Y: " << y << "\n";

    o3 = o1 / o2;
    o3.get_xy(x, y);
    cout << "(o1/o2) X: " << x << ", Y: " << y << "\n";

    return 0;
}
```

2. ```
// Overload the * for ob*int and int*ob.
#include <iostream.h>

class coord {
    int x, y; // coordinate values
public:
    coord() { x=0; y=0; }
    coord(int i, int j) { x=i; y=j; }
    void get_xy(int &i, int &j) { i=x; j=y; }
    friend coord operator*(coord ob1, int i);
    friend coord operator*(int i, coord ob2);
};
```
```

```
// Overload * one way.
coord operator*(coord ob1, int i)
{
  coord temp;

  temp.x = ob1.x * i;
  temp.y = ob1.y * i;

  return temp;
}

// Overload * another way.
coord operator*(int i, coord ob2)
{
  coord temp;

  temp.x = ob2.x * i;
  temp.y = ob2.y * i;

  return temp;
}

main()
{
  coord o1(10, 10), o2;
  int x, y;

  o2 = o1 * 2;   // ob * int
  o2.get_xy(x, y);
  cout << "(o1*2) X: " << x << ", Y: " << y << "\n";

  o2 = 3 * o1; // int * ob
  o2.get_xy(x, y);
  cout << "(3*o1) X: " << x << ", Y: " << y << "\n";

  return 0;
}
```

3. By using friend functions, it is possible to have a built-in type as the left operand. When member functions are used, the left operand must be an object of the class for which the operator is defined.

4.
```
// Overload the -- relative to coord class using a friend.
#include <iostream.h>
```

```
class coord {
  int x, y; // coordinate values
public:
  coord() { x=0; y=0; }
  coord(int i, int j) { x=i; y=j; }
  void get_xy(int &i, int &j) { i=x; j=y; }
  friend coord operator--(coord &ob); // prefix
  friend coord operator--(coord &ob, int notused); // postfix
};

// Overload -- (prefix) for coord class using a friend.
coord operator--(coord &ob)
{
  ob.x--;
  ob.y--;
  return ob;
}

// Overload -- (postfix) for coord class using a friend.
coord operator--(coord &ob, int notused)
{
  ob.x--;
  ob.y--;
  return ob;
}

main()
{
  coord o1(10, 10);
  int x, y;

  --o1; // decrement o1 an object
  o1.get_xy(x, y);
  cout << "(--o1) X: " << x << ", Y: " << y << "\n";

  o1--; // decrement o1 an object
  o1.get_xy(x, y);
  cout << "(o1--) X: " << x << ", Y: " << y << "\n";

  return 0;
}
```

*E*XERCISE

1.
```cpp
#include <iostream.h>
#include <stdlib.h>

class dynarray {
  int *p;
  int size;
public:
  dynarray(int s);
  int &put(int i);
  int get(int i);
  dynarray &operator=(dynarray &ob);
};

// Constructor
dynarray::dynarray(int s)
{
  p = new int [s];
  if(!p) {
    cout << "Allocation error\n";
    exit(1);
  }

  size = s;
}

// Store an element.
int &dynarray::put(int i)
{
  if(i<0 || i>=size) {
    cout << "Bounds error!\n";
    exit(1);
  }

  return p[i];
}

// Get an element.
int dynarray::get(int i)
{
  if(i<0 || i>=size) {
    cout << "Bounds error!\n";
    exit(1);
```

```
  }

  return p[i];
}

// Overload = for dynarray.
dynarray &dynarray::operator=(dynarray &ob)
{
  int i;

  if(size!=ob.size) {
    cout << "Cannot copy arrays of differing sizes!\n";
    exit(1);
  }

  for(i = 0; i<size; i++) p[i] = ob.p[i];
  return *this;
}

main()
{
  int i;

  dynarray ob1(10), ob2(10), ob3(100);

  ob1.put(3) = 10;
  i = ob1.get(3);
  cout << i << "\n";

  ob2 = ob1;

  i = ob2.get(3);
  cout << i << "\n";

  // generates an error
  ob1 = ob3; //  !!!
  return 0;
}
```

6 MASTERY SKILLS CHECK

```
1. // Overload << and >>.
   #include <iostream.h>
```

```
class coord {
  int x, y; // coordinate values
public:
  coord() { x=0; y=0; }
  coord(int i, int j) { x=i; y=j; }
  void get_xy(int &i, int &j) { i=x; j=y; }
  coord operator<<(int i);
  coord operator>>(int i);
};

// Overload <<.
coord coord::operator<<(int i)
{
  coord temp;

  temp.x = x << i;
  temp.y = y << i;

  return temp;
}

// Overload >>.
coord coord::operator>>(int i)
{
  coord temp;
  temp.x = x >> i;
  temp.y = y >> i;

  return temp;
}

main()
{
  coord o1(4, 4), o2;
  int x, y;

  o2 = o1 << 2;  // ob << int
  o2.get_xy(x, y);
  cout << "(o1<<2) X: " << x << ", Y: " << y << "\n";

  o2 = o1 >> 2; // ob >> int
  o2.get_xy(x, y);
  cout << "(o1>>2) X: " << x << ", Y: " << y << "\n";
```

```
      return 0;
    }

2. #include <iostream.h>

    class three_d {
      int x, y, z;
    public:
      three_d(int i, int j, int k)
      {
        x = i; y = j; z = k;
      }
      three_d() { x=0; y=0; z=0; }
      void get(int &i, int &j, int &k)
      {
        i = x; j = y; k = z;
      }
      three_d operator+(three_d ob2);
      three_d operator-(three_d ob2);
      three_d operator++();
      three_d operator--();
    };

    three_d three_d::operator+(three_d ob2)
    {
      three_d temp;
      temp.x = x + ob2.x;
      temp.y = y + ob2.y;
      temp.z = z + ob2.z;

      return temp;
    }

    three_d three_d::operator-(three_d ob2)
    {
      three_d temp;

      temp.x = x - ob2.x;
      temp.y = y - ob2.y;
      temp.z = z - ob2.z;

      return temp;
    }

    three_d three_d::operator++()
```

```
{
  x++;
  y++;
  z++;

  return *this;
}

three_d three_d::operator--()
{
  x--;
  y--;
  z--;

  return *this;
}

main()
{
  three_d o1(10, 10, 10), o2(2, 3, 4), o3;
  int x, y, z;

  o3 = o1 + o2;
  o3.get(x, y, z);
  cout << "X: " << x << ", Y: " << y;
  cout << ", Z: " << z << "\n";

  o3 = o1 - o2;
  o3.get(x, y, z);
  cout << "X: " << x << ", Y: " << y;
  cout << ", Z: " << z << "\n";

  ++o1;
  o1.get(x, y, z);
  cout << "X: " << x << ", Y: " << y;
  cout << ", Z: " << z << "\n";

  --o1;
  o1.get(x, y, z);
  cout << "X: " << x << ", Y: " << y;
  cout << ", Z: " << z << "\n";

  return 0;
}
```

3.
```cpp
#include <iostream.h>

class three_d {
  int x, y, z;
public:
  three_d(int i, int j, int k)
  {
    x = i; y = j; z = k;
  }
  three_d() { x=0; y=0; z=0; }
  void get(int &i, int &j, int &k)
  {
    i = x; j = y; k = z;
  }
  three_d operator+(three_d &ob2);
  three_d operator-(three_d &ob2);
  friend three_d operator++(three_d &ob);
  friend three_d operator--(three_d &ob);
};

three_d three_d::operator+(three_d &ob2)
{
  three_d temp;

  temp.x = x + ob2.x;
  temp.y = y + ob2.y;
  temp.z = z + ob2.z;

  return temp;
}

three_d three_d::operator-(three_d &ob2)
{
  three_d temp;

  temp.x = x - ob2.x;
  temp.y = y - ob2.y;
  temp.z = z - ob2.z;

  return temp;
}

three_d operator++(three_d &ob)
{
  ob.x++;
```

```
    ob.y++;
    ob.z++;

    return ob;
}

three_d operator--(three_d &ob)
{
    ob.x--;
    ob.y--;
    ob.z--;

    return ob;
}

main()
{
    three_d o1(10, 10, 10), o2(2, 3, 4), o3;
    int x, y, z;

    o3 = o1 + o2;
    o3.get(x, y, z);
    cout << "X: " << x << ", Y: " << y;
    cout << ", Z: " << z << "\n";

    o3 = o1 - o2;
    o3.get(x, y, z);
    cout << "X: " << x << ", Y: " << y;
    cout << ", Z: " << z << "\n";

    ++o1;
    o1.get(x, y, z);
    cout << "X: " << x << ", Y: " << y;
    cout << ", Z: " << z << "\n";

    --o1;
    o1.get(x, y, z);
    cout << "X: " << x << ", Y: " << y;
    cout << ", Z: " << z << "\n";

    return 0;
}
```

4. For binary operators, a member operator function is passed the left operand implicitly by using **this**. A binary friend operator function is

passed both operands explicitly. Unary member operator functions have no explicit parameters. A friend unary operator function has one parameter.

5. You will need to overload the = operator when the default bit-wise copy is insufficient. For example, you may have objects in which you want only parts of the data in one object to be assigned to another.

6. No.

7.
```cpp
#include <iostream.h>

class three_d {
  int x, y, z;
public:
  three_d(int i, int j, int k)
  {
    x = i; y = j; z = k;
  }
  three_d() { x=0; y=0; z=0; }
  void get(int &i, int &j, int &k)
  {
    i = x; j = y; k = z;
  }
  friend three_d operator+(three_d ob, int i);
  friend three_d operator+(int i, three_d ob);
};

three_d operator+(three_d ob, int i)
{
  three_d temp;
  temp.x = ob.x + i;
  temp.y = ob.y + i;
  temp.z = ob.z + i;

  return temp;
}

three_d operator+(int i, three_d ob)
{
  three_d temp;

  temp.x = ob.x + i;
  temp.y = ob.y + i;
  temp.z = ob.z + i;

  return temp;
```

```
  }

main()
{
  three_d o1(10, 10, 10);
  int x, y, z;

  o1 = o1 + 10;
  o1.get(x, y, z);
  cout << "X: " << x << ", Y: " << y;
  cout << ", Z: " << z << "\n";

  o1 = -20 + o1;
  o1.get(x, y, z);
  cout << "X: " << x << ", Y: " << y;
  cout << ", Z: " << z << "\n";

  return 0;
}
```

8.
```
#include <iostream.h>

class three_d {
  int x, y, z;
public:
  three_d(int i, int j, int k)
  {
    x = i; y = j; z = k;
  }
  three_d() { x=0; y=0; z=0; }
  void get(int &i, int &j, int &k)
  {
    i = x; j = y; k = z;
  }
  int operator==(three_d ob2);
  int operator!=(three_d ob2);
  int operator||(three_d ob2);
};

int three_d::operator==(three_d ob2)
{
  return (x==ob2.x && y==ob2.y && z==ob2.z);
}

int three_d::operator!=(three_d ob2)
```

```
{
  return (x!=ob2.x && y!=ob2.y && z!=ob2.z);
}

int three_d::operator||(three_d ob2)
{
  return (x||ob2.x && y||ob2.y && z||ob2.z);
}

main()
{
  three_d o1(10, 10, 10), o2(2, 3, 4), o3(0, 0, 0);

  if(o1==o1) cout << "o1 == o1\n";

  if(o1!=o2) cout << "o1 != o2\n";

  if(o3 || o1) cout << "o1 or o3 is true\n";

  return 0;
}
```

▐ 6 ▐ **CUMULATIVE SKILLS CHECK**

```
1. /* For clarity, no error checking has been used. However
      you should add some if using this code for a real
      application.
   */
   #include <iostream.h>
   #include <string.h>

   class strtype {
     char s[80];
   public:
     strtype() { *s = '\0'; }
     strtype(char *p) { strcpy(s, p); }
     char *get() { return s; }
     strtype operator+(strtype s2);
     strtype operator=(strtype s2);
     int operator<(strtype s2);
     int operator>(strtype s2);
     int operator==(strtype s2);
   };
```

```
strtype strtype::operator+(strtype s2)
{
  strcat(s, s2.s);

  return *this;
}

strtype strtype::operator=(strtype s2)
{
  strcpy(s, s2.s);

  return *this;
}

int strtype::operator<(strtype s2)
{
  return strcmp(s, s2.s) < 0;
}

int strtype::operator>(strtype s2)
{
  return strcmp(s, s2.s) > 0;
}

int strtype::operator==(strtype s2)
{
  return strcmp(s, s2.s) == 0;
}

main()
{
  strtype o1("Hello"), o2(" There"), o3;

  o3 = o1 + o2;
  cout << o3.get() << "\n";

  o3 = o1;
  if(o1==o3) cout << "o1 equals o3\n";

  if(o1>o2) cout << "o1 > o2\n";

  if(o1<o2) cout << "o1 < o2\n";

  return 0;
}
```

1. No. Overloading an operator simply expands the data types upon which it can operate, but no preexisting operations are affected.

2. Yes. You cannot overload an operator relative to one of C++'s built-in types.

3. No, the precedence cannot be changed. No, the number of operands cannot be altered.

4.
```cpp
#include <iostream.h>

class array {
  int nums[10];
public:
  array();
  void set(int n[10]);
  void show();
  array operator+(array ob2);
  array operator-(array ob2);
  int operator==(array ob2);
};

array::array()
{
  int i;
  for(i=0; i<10; i++) nums[i] = 0;
}

void array::set(int *n)
{
  int i;

  for(i=0; i<10; i++) nums[i] = n[i];
}

void array::show()
{
  int i;

  for(i=0; i<10; i++)
    cout << nums[i] << ' ';

  cout << "\n";
}
```

```
array array::operator+(array ob2)
{
  int i;
  array temp;

  for(i=0; i<10; i++)
    temp.nums[i] = nums[i] + ob2.nums[i];

  return temp;
}

array array::operator-(array ob2)
{
  int i;
  array temp;

  for(i=0; i<10; i++)
    temp.nums[i] = nums[i] - ob2.nums[i];

  return temp;
}

int array::operator==(array ob2)
{
  int i;

  for(i=0; i<10; i++)
    if(nums[i]!=ob2.nums[i]) return 0;

  return 1;
}

main()
{
  array o1, o2, o3;

  int i[10] = {1, 2, 3, 4, 5, 6, 7, 8, 9, 10 };

  o1.set(i);
  o2.set(i);

  o3 = o1 + o2;
  o3.show();

  o3 = o1 - o3;
```

```
  o3.show();

  if(o1==o2) cout << "o1 equals o2\n";
  else cout << "o1 does not equal o2\n";

  if(o1==o3) cout << "o1 equals o3\n";
  else cout << "o1 does not equal o3\n";

  return 0;
}
```

5. `#include <iostream.h>`

```
class array {
  int nums[10];
public:
  array();
  void set(int n[10]);
  void show();
  friend array operator+(array ob1, array ob2);
  friend array operator-(array ob1, array ob2);
  friend int operator==(array ob1, array ob2);
};

array::array()
{
  int i;
  for(i=0; i<10; i++) nums[i] = 0;
}

void array::set(int *n)
{
  int i;

  for(i=0; i<10; i++) nums[i] = n[i];
}

void array::show()
{
  int i;

  for(i=0; i<10; i++)
    cout << nums[i] << ' ';

  cout << "\n";
```

```
}

array operator+(array ob1, array ob2)
{
  int i;
  array temp;

  for(i=0; i<10; i++)
    temp.nums[i] = ob1.nums[i] + ob2.nums[i];

  return temp;
}

array operator-(array ob1, array ob2)
{
  int i;
  array temp;

  for(i=0; i<10; i++)
    temp.nums[i] = ob1.nums[i] - ob2.nums[i];

  return temp;
}

int operator==(array ob1, array ob2)
{
  int i;

  for(i=0; i<10; i++)
    if(ob1.nums[i]!=ob2.nums[i]) return 0;

  return 1;
}

main()
{
  array o1, o2, o3;

  int i[10] = {1, 2, 3, 4, 5, 6, 7, 8, 9, 10 };

  o1.set(i);
  o2.set(i);

  o3 = o1 + o2;
  o3.show();
```

```
   o3 = o1 - o3;
   o3.show();

   if(o1==o2) cout << "o1 equals o2\n";
   else cout << "o1 does not equal o2\n";

   if(o1==o3) cout << "o1 equals o3\n";
   else cout << "o1 does not equal o3\n";

   return 0;
}
```

6. ```
#include <iostream.h>

class array {
  int nums[10];
public:
  array();
  void set(int n[10]);
  void show();
  array operator++();
  friend array operator--(array &ob);
};

array::array()
{
  int i;

  for(i=0; i<10; i++) nums[i] = 0;
}

void array::set(int *n)
{
  int i;

  for(i=0; i<10; i++) nums[i] = n[i];
}

void array::show()
{
  int i;

  for(i=0; i<10; i++)
    cout << nums[i] << ' ';
```
```

```
  cout << "\n";
}

// Overload unary op using member function.
array array::operator++()
{
  int i;

  for(i=0; i<10; i++)
    nums[i]++;

  return *this;
}

// Use a friend.
array operator--(array &ob)
{
  int i;

  for(i=0; i<10; i++)
    ob.nums[i]--;

  return ob;
}

main()
{
  array o1, o2, o3;

  int i[10] = {1, 2, 3, 4, 5, 6, 7, 8, 9, 10 };

  o1.set(i);
  o2.set(i);

  o3 = ++o1;
  o3.show();

  o3 = --o1;
  o3.show();

  return 0;
}
```

7. No. The assignment operator must be overloaded by using a member function.

EXERCISES

1. Legal statements are A and C.

2. A public member of a base becomes a public member of a derived class when inherited as public. When a public member of a base is inherited as private, it becomes a private member of the derived class.

EXERCISES

1. When a protected member of a base class is inherited as public, it becomes a protected member of the derived class. If it is inherited as private, it becomes a private member of the derived class. If it is inherited as protected, it becomes a protected member of the derived class.

2. The protected category is needed to allow a base class to keep certain members private while still allowing a derived class to have access to them.

3. No.

EXERCISES

1.
```cpp
#include <iostream.h>
#include <string.h>

class mybase {
  char str[80];
public:
  mybase(char *s) { strcpy(str, s); }
  char *get() { return str; }
};

class myderived : public mybase {
  int len;
public:
  myderived(char *s) : mybase(s) {
    len = strlen(s);
  }
  int getlen() { return len; }
```

```
    void show() { cout << get() << '\n'; }
};

main()
{
  myderived ob("hello");

  ob.show();
  cout << ob.getlen() << '\n';

  return 0;
}
```

2.
```
#include <iostream.h>

// A base class for various types of vehicles.
class vehicle {
  int num_wheels;
  int range;
public:
  vehicle(int w, int r)
  {
    num_wheels = w; range = r;
  }
  void showv()
  {
    cout << "Wheels: " << num_wheels << '\n';
    cout << "Range: " << range << '\n';
  }
};

class car : public vehicle {
  int passengers;
public:
  car(int p, int w, int r) : vehicle(w, r)
  {
    passengers = p;
  }
  void show()
  {
    showv();
    cout << "Passengers: " << passengers << '\n';
  }
};
```

```
class truck : public vehicle {
  int loadlimit;
public:
  truck(int l, int w, int r) : vehicle(w, r)
  {
    loadlimit = l;
  }
  void show()
  {
    showv();
    cout << "loadlimit " << loadlimit << '\n';
  }
};

main()
{
  car c(5, 4, 500);
  truck t(30000, 12, 1200);

  cout << "Car: \n";
  c.show();
  cout << "\nTruck:\n";
  t.show();

  return 0;
}
```

7.4 EXERCISES

1.
```
Constructing A
Constructing B
Constructing C
Destructing C
Destructing B
Destructing A
```

2.
```
#include <iostream.h>

class A {
  int i;
public:
  A(int a) { i = a; }
};
```

```
class B {
  int j;
public:
  B(int a) { j = a; }
};

class C : public A, public B {
  int k;
public:
  C(int c, int b, int a) : A(a), B(b) {
    k = c;
  }
};
```

7.5	**EXERCISES**

2. A virtual base class is needed when a derived class inherits two (or more) classes, each of which has inherited another base class. Without virtual base classes, two (or more) copies of the common base class would exist in the final derived class. However, by making the original base virtual, only one copy is present in the final derived class.

7	**MASTERY SKILLS CHECK**

```
1. #include <iostream.h>

class building {
protected:
  int floors;
  int rooms;
  double footage;
};

class house : public building {
  int bedrooms;
  int bathrooms;
public:
  house(int f, int r, double ft, int br, int bth) {
    floors = f;  rooms = r;  footage = ft;
    bedrooms = br; bathrooms = bth;
  }
  void show() {
```

```
      cout << "floors: " << floors << '\n';
      cout << "rooms: " << rooms << '\n';
      cout << "square footage: " << footage << '\n';
      cout << "bedrooms: " << bedrooms << '\n';
      cout << "bathrooms: " << bathrooms << '\n';
    }
};

class office : public building {
  int phones;
  int extinguishers;
public:
  office(int f, int r, double ft, int p, int ext) {
    floors = f;  rooms = r;  footage = ft;
    phones = p; extinguishers = ext;
  }
  void show() {
    cout << "floors: " << floors << '\n';
    cout << "rooms: " << rooms << '\n';
    cout << "square footage: " << footage << '\n';
    cout << "Telephones: " << phones << '\n';
    cout << "fire extinguishers: ";
    cout << extinguishers << '\n';
  }
};

main()
{
  house h_ob(2, 12, 5000, 6, 4);
  office o_ob(4, 25, 12000, 30, 8);

  cout << "House: \n";
  h_ob.show();

  cout << "\nOffice: \n";
  o_ob.show();

  return 0;
}
```

2. When a base class is inherited as public, the public members of the base become public members of the derived class, and the base's private members remain private to the base. If the base is inherited as private, all members of the base become private members of the derived class.

3. Members declared as protected are private to the base class but may be inherited (and accessed) by any derived class. When used as an inheritance access specifier, it causes all public and protected members of the base class to become protected members of the derived class.

4. Constructors are called in order of derivation. Destructors are called in reverse order.

5.
```cpp
#include <iostream.h>

class planet {
protected:
  double distance; // miles from the sun
  int revolve;  // in days
public:
  planet(double d, int r) { distance = d; revolve = r; }
};

class earth : public planet {
  double circumference; // circumference or orbit
public:
  earth(double d, int r) : planet(d, r) {
    circumference = 2*distance*3.1416;
  }
  void show() {
    cout << "Distance from sun: " << distance << '\n';
    cout << "Days in orbit: " << revolve << '\n';
    cout << "Circumference of orbit: ";
    cout << circumference << '\n';
  }
};

main()
{
  earth ob(93000000, 365);

  ob.show();

  return 0;
}
```

6. To fix the program, have **motorized** and **road_use** inherit **vehicle** as a virtual base class. Also, refer to Question 1 in the Cumulative Skills Check in this chapter.

---

7 **C**UMULATIVE SKILLS CHECK

1. For some compilers, a **switch** cannot be used in an in-line function. If this is the case with your compiler, then the functions were automatically made into "regular" functions.

2. The assignment operator is the only operator that is not inherited. The reason for this is easy to understand. Since a derived class will contain members not found in the base **class**, the overloaded = relative to the base has no knowledge of the members added by the derived class and, as such, cannot properly copy those new members.

---

8 **R**EVIEW SKILLS CHECK

1. ```cpp
#include <iostream.h>

class airship {
protected:
  int passengers;
  double cargo;
};

class airplane : public airship {
  char engine; // p for propeller, j for jet
  double range;
public:
  airplane(int p, double c, char e, double r)
  {
    passengers = p;
    cargo = c;
    engine = e;
    range = r;
  }
  void show();
};

class balloon : public airship {
  char gas; // h for hydrogen, e for helium
  double altitude;
public:
  balloon(int p, double c, char g, double a)
  {
    passengers = p;
```
```

```
        cargo = c;
        gas = g;
        altitude = a;
    }
    void show();
};

void airplane::show()
{
    cout << "Passengers: " << passengers << '\n';
    cout << "Cargo capacity: " << cargo << '\n';
    cout << "Engine: ";
    if(engine=='p') cout << "Propeller\n";
    else cout << "Jet\n";
    cout << "Range: " << range << '\n';
}

void balloon::show()
{
    cout << "Passengers: " << passengers << '\n';
    cout << "Cargo capacity: " << cargo << '\n';
    cout << "Gas: ";
    if(gas=='h') cout << "Hydrogen\n";
    else cout << "Helium\n";
    cout << "Altitude: " << altitude << '\n';
}

main()
{
    balloon b(2, 500.0, 'h', 12000.0);
    airplane b727(100, 40000.0, 'j', 40000.0);

    b.show();
    cout << '\n';
    b727.show();

    return 0;
}
```

2. The **protected** access specifier causes class members to be private to that class but still accessible by any derived class.

3. The program displays the following output, which indicates when the constructors and destructors are called.

```
Constructing A
Constructing B
Constructing C
Destructing C
Destructing B
Destructing A
```

4. Constructors are called in the order ABC, destructors in the order CBA.

5. ```cpp
#include <iostream.h>

class base {
  int i, j;
public:
  base(int x, int y) { i = x; j = y; }
  void showij() { cout << i << ' ' << j << '\n'; }
};

class derived : public base {
  int k;
public:
  derived(int a, int b, int c) : base(b, c) {
    k = a;
  }
  void show() { cout << k << ' '; showij(); }
};

main()
{
  derived ob(1, 2, 3);

  ob.show();

  return 0;
}
```

6. The missing words are "general" and "specific."

## 8.2 ▮ **E**XERCISES

1. ```cpp
#include <iostream.h>

main()
{
```

```
    cout.setf(ios::showpos);

    cout << -10 << ' ' << 10 << '\n';

    return 0;
}
```

2.
```
#include <iostream.h>

main()
{
    cout.setf(ios::showpoint | ios::uppercase | ios::scientific);

    cout << 100.0;

    return 0;
}
```

3. This statement, among others, resets the flags:

```
flags(0L);
```

4.
```
#include <iostream.h>

main()
{
  long f;

  f = cout.flags(); // store flags

  cout.setf(ios::showbase | ios::hex);
  cout << 100 << '\n';

  cout.flags(f); // reset flags

  return 0;
}
```

8.3 **E**XERCISES

1.
```
// Create a table of log10 and log from 2 through 100.
#include <iostream.h>
#include <math.h>
```

```
main()
{
  double x;

  cout.precision(5);
  cout << "          x        log x        ln e\n\n";

  for(x = 2.0; x <= 100.0; x++) {
    cout.width(10);
    cout << x << "   ";
    cout.width(10);
    cout << log10(x) << "   ";
    cout.width(10);
    cout << log(x) << '\n';
  }

  return 0;
}
```

2.
```
#include <iostream.h>
#include <string.h>

void center(char *s);

main()
{
  center("Hi there!");
  center("I like C++.");

  return 0;
}

void center(char *s)
{
  int len;

  len = 40+(strlen(s)/2);

  cout.width(len);
  cout << s << '\n';
}
```

8.4 **E**XERCISES

1a.
```cpp
// Create a table of log10 and log from 2 to 100.
#include <iostream.h>
#include <math.h>
#include <iomanip.h>

main()
{
  double x;

  cout << setprecision(5);
  cout << "          x         log x         ln e\n\n";

  for(x = 2.0; x <= 100.0; x++) {
    cout << setw(10) << x << "   ";
    cout << setw(10) << log10(x) << "   ";
    cout << setw(10) << log(x) << '\n';
  }

  return 0;
}
```

1b.
```cpp
#include <iostream.h>
#include <string.h>
#include <iomanip.h>

void center(char *s);

main()
{
  center("Hi there!");
  center("I like C++.");

  return 0;
}

void center(char *s)
{
  int len;

  len = 40+(strlen(s)/2);
```

```
          cout << setw(len) << s << '\n';
        }
```

2. `cout << setiosflags(ios::showbase | ios::hex) << 100;`

EXERCISES

1.
```
#include <iostream.h>
#include <string.h>
#include <stdlib.h>

class strtype {
  char *p;
  int len;
public:
  strtype(char *ptr);
   ~strtype();
  friend ostream &operator<<(ostream &stream, strtype &ob);
};

strtype::strtype(char *ptr)
{
  len = strlen(ptr);
  p = new char [len+1];
  if(!p) {
    cout << "Allocation error\n";
    exit(1);
  }
  strcpy(p, ptr);
}

strtype::~strtype()
{
  delete p;
}

ostream &operator<<(ostream &stream, strtype &ob)
{
  stream << ob.p;

  return stream;
}
```

```
   main()
   {
     strtype s1("This is a test"), s2("I like C++");

     cout << s1;
     cout << endl << s2 << endl;

     return 0;
   }
```

2.
```
   #include <iostream.h>

   class planet {
   protected:
     double distance; // miles from the sun
     int revolve;   // in days
   public:
     planet(double d, int r) { distance = d; revolve = r; }
   };

   class earth : public planet {
     double circumference; // circumference or orbit
   public:
     earth(double d, int r) : planet(d, r) {
       circumference = 2*distance*3.1416;
     }

     friend ostream &operator<<(ostream &stream, earth ob);
   };

   ostream &operator<<(ostream &stream, earth ob)
   {
     stream << "Distance from sun: " << ob.distance << '\n';
     stream << "Days in orbit: " << ob.revolve << '\n';
     stream << "Circumference of orbit: " << ob.circumference;
     stream << '\n';

     return stream;
   }

   main()
   {
     earth ob(93000000, 365);
```

```
    cout << ob;

    return 0;
}
```

3. An inserter cannot be a member function because the object that generates a call to the inserter is *not* an object of a user-defined class.

EXERCISES

1.
```
#include <iostream.h>
#include <string.h>
#include <stdlib.h>

class strtype {
  char *p;
  int len;
public:
  strtype(char *ptr);
   ~strtype();
  friend ostream &operator<<(ostream &stream, strtype &ob);
  friend istream &operator>>(istream &stream, strtype &ob);
};

strtype::strtype(char *ptr)
{
  len = strlen(ptr);
  p = new char [len+1];
  if(!p) {
    cout << "Allocation error\n";
    exit(1);
  }
  strcpy(p, ptr);
}

strtype::~strtype()
{
  delete p;
}

ostream &operator<<(ostream &stream, strtype &ob)
```

```
{
  stream << ob.p;

  return stream;
}

istream &operator>>(istream &stream, strtype &ob)
{
  char temp[255];

  stream >> temp;

  if(strlen(temp) >= ob.len) {
    delete ob.p;
    ob.p = new char [strlen(temp)+1];
    if(!ob.p) {
      cout << "Allocation error\n";
      exit(1);
    }
  }
  strcpy(ob.p, temp);

  return stream;
}

main()
{
  strtype s1("This is a test"), s2("I like C++");

  cout << s1;
  cout << '\n' << s2;

  cout << "\nEnter a string: ";
  cin >> s1;
  cout << s1;

  return 0;
}
```

2. ```
#include <iostream.h>

class factor {
  int num; // number
  int lfact; // lowest factor
```
```

```
public:
  factor(int i);
  friend ostream &operator<<(ostream &stream, factor ob);
  friend istream &operator>>(istream &stream, factor &ob);
};

factor::factor(int i)
{
  int n;

  num = i;

  for(n=2; n < (i/2); n++)
    if(!(i%n)) break;

  if(n<(i/2)) lfact = n;
  else lfact = 1;
}

istream &operator>>(istream &stream, factor &ob)
{
  stream >> ob.num;

  int n;

  for(n=2; n < (ob.num/2); n++)
    if(!(ob.num%n)) break;
  if(n<(ob.num/2)) ob.lfact = n;
  else ob.lfact = 1;

  return stream;
}

ostream &operator<<(ostream &stream, factor ob)
{
  stream << ob.lfact << " is lowest factor of ";
  stream << ob.num << '\n';

  return stream;
}

main()
{
```

```
    factor o(32);

    cout << o;

    cin >> o;
    cout << o;

    return 0;
}
```

8   MASTERY SKILLS CHECK

1. ```
#include <iostream.h>

main()
{
  cout << 100 << ' ';

  cout.setf(ios::hex);
  cout << 100 << ' ';

  cout.unsetf(ios::hex); // clear hex flag
  cout.setf(ios::oct);
  cout << 100 << '\n';

  return 0;
}
```

2. ```
#include <iostream.h>

main()
{
  cout.setf(ios::left);
  cout.precision(2);
  cout.fill('*');
  cout.width(20);

  cout << 1000.5364 << '\n';

  return 0;
}
```

3. `#include <iostream.h>`

```
main()
{
  cout << 100 << ' ';

  cout << hex << 100 << ' ';

  cout << oct << 100 << '\n';

  return 0;
}

#include <iostream.h>
#include <iomanip.h>

main()
{
  cout << setiosflags(ios::left);
  cout << setprecision(2);
  cout << setfill('*');
  cout << setw(20);

  cout << 1000.5364 << '\n';

  return 0;
}
```

4. ```
long f;

f = cout.flags(); // save

// ...

cout.flags(f); // restore
```

5. ```
#include <iostream.h>

class pwr {
  int base;
  int exponent;
  double result; // base to the exponent power
public:
  pwr(int b, int e);
  friend ostream &operator<<(ostream &stream, pwr ob);
  friend istream &operator>>(istream &stream, pwr &ob);
};
```

```
pwr::pwr(int b, int e)
{
  base = b;
  exponent = e;

  result = 1;
  for( ; e; e--) result = result * base;
}

ostream &operator<<(ostream &stream, pwr ob)
{
  stream << ob.base << "^" << ob.exponent;
  stream << " is " << ob.result << '\n';

  return stream;
}

istream &operator>>(istream &stream, pwr &ob)
{
  int b, e;

  cout << "Enter base and exponent: ";
  stream >> b >> e;

  pwr temp(b, e); // create temporary

  ob = temp;

  return stream;
}
main()
{
  pwr ob(10, 2);

  cout << ob;

  cin >> ob;
  cout << ob;

  return 0;
}
```

6. ```
   // This program draws boxes.
   #include <iostream.h>
   ```
   ```

```
class box {
  int len;
public:
  box(int l) { len = l; }
  friend ostream &operator<<(ostream &stream, box ob);
};

// Draw a box.
ostream &operator<<(ostream &stream, box ob)
{
  int i, j;

  for(i=0; i<ob.len; i++) stream << '*';
  stream << '\n';
  for(i=0; i<ob.len-2; i++) {
    stream << '*';
    for(j=0; j<ob.len-2; j++) stream << ' ';
    stream << "*\n";
  }
  for(i=0; i<ob.len; i++) stream << '*';
  stream << '\n';

  return stream;
}

main()
{
  box b1(4), b2(7);

  cout << b1 << endl << b2;

  return 0;
}
```

8 CUMULATIVE SKILLS CHECK

1. ```
   #include <iostream.h>

   #define SIZE 10

   // Declare a stack class for characters
   class stack {
     char stck[SIZE]; // holds the stack
   ```
   ```

```
  int tos; // index of top-of-stack
public:
  stack();
  void push(char ch); // push character on stack
  char pop(); // pop character from stack
  friend ostream &operator<<(ostream &stream, stack ob);
};

// Initialize the stack
stack::stack()
{
  tos = 0;
}

// Push a character.
void stack::push(char ch)
{
  if(tos==SIZE) {
    cout << "Stack is full";
    return;
  }
  stck[tos] = ch;
  tos++;
}

// Pop a character.
char stack::pop()
{
  if(tos==0) {
    cout << "Stack is empty";
    return 0; // return null on empty stack
  }
  tos--;
  return stck[tos];
}

ostream &operator<<(ostream &stream, stack ob)
{
  char ch;

  while(ch=ob.pop()) stream << ch;
  stream << endl;

  return stream;
}
```

```
main()
{
  stack s;

  s.push('a');
  s.push('b');
  s.push('c');

  cout << s;
  cout << s;

  return 0;
}
```

2.
```
#include <iostream.h>
#include <time.h>

class watch {
  time_t t;
public:
  watch() { t = time(NULL); }
  friend ostream &operator<<(ostream &stream, watch ob);
};

ostream &operator<<(ostream &stream, watch ob)
{
  struct tm *localt;

  localt = localtime(&ob.t);
  stream << asctime(localt) << endl;
  return stream;
}

main()
{
  watch w;

  cout << w;

  return 0;
}
```

3.
```
#include <iostream.h>
```

```
class ft_to_inches {
  double feet;
  double inches;
public:
  void set(double f) {
    feet = f;
    inches = f * 12;
  }
  friend istream &operator>>(istream &stream,
                             ft_to_inches &ob);
  friend ostream &operator<<(ostream &stream,
                             ft_to_inches ob);
};

istream &operator>>(istream &stream, ft_to_inches &ob)
{
  double f;

  cout << "Enter feet: ";
  stream >> f;
  ob.set(f);

  return stream;
}

ostream &operator<<(ostream &stream, ft_to_inches ob)
{
  stream << ob.feet << " feet is " << ob.inches;
  stream << " inches\n";

  return stream;
}
main()
{
  ft_to_inches x;

  cin >> x;
  cout << x;

  return 0;
}
```

*R*EVIEW SKILLS CHECK

1. ```cpp
#include <iostream.h>

main()
{
   cout.width(40);
   cout.fill(':');

   cout << "C++ is fun" << '\n';

   return 0;
}
```

2. ```cpp
#include <iostream.h>

main()
{
   cout.precision(4);
   cout << 10.0/3.0 << '\n';

   return 0;
}
```

3. ```cpp
#include <iostream.h>
#include <iomanip.h>

main()
{
   cout << setprecision(4) << 10.0/3.0 << '\n';

   return 0;
}
```

4. An inserter is an overloaded **operator<<( )** that outputs a class's data to an output stream. An extractor is an overloaded **operator>>( )** function that inputs a class's data from an input stream.

5. ```cpp
#include <iostream.h>

class date {
   char d[9]; // store date as string: mm/dd/yy
public:
   friend ostream &operator<<(ostream &stream, date ob);
   friend istream &operator>>(istream &stream, date &ob);
```

```
};

ostream &operator<<(ostream &stream, date ob)
{
  stream << ob.d << '\n';

  return stream;
}

istream &operator>>(istream &stream, date &ob)
{
  cout << "Enter date (mm/dd/yy): ";
  stream >> ob.d;

  return stream;
}

main()
{
  date ob;

  cin >> ob;
  cout << ob;

  return 0;
}
```

6. To use a parameterized manipulator, you must include **iomanip.h** in your program.

7. The predefined streams are

   cin
   cout
   cerr
   clog

9.1   *EXERCISES*

```
1. // Show time and date.
   #include <iostream.h>
   #include <time.h>

   // A time and date output manipulator.
```

```
ostream &td(ostream &stream)
{
  struct tm *localt;
  time_t t;

  t = time(NULL);
  localt = localtime(&t);
  stream << asctime(localt) << endl;

  return stream;
}

main()
{
  cout << td << '\n';

  return 0;
}
```

2. `#include <iostream.h>`

```
// Turn on hex output with uppercase X.
ostream &sethex(ostream &stream)
{
  stream.setf(ios::hex | ios::uppercase | ios::showbase);

  return stream;
}

// Reset flags.
ostream &reset(ostream &stream)
{
  stream.unsetf(ios::hex | ios::uppercase | ios::showbase);

  return stream;
}

main()
{
  cout << sethex << 100 << '\n';
  cout << reset << 100 << '\n';
```

```
    return 0;
  }
```

3.
```
#include <iostream.h>
#include <string.h>

// Skip 10 characters.
istream &skipchar(istream &stream)
{
  int i;
  char c;

  for(i=0; i<10; i++) stream >> c;

  return stream;
}

main()
{
  char str[80];

  cout << "Enter some characters: ";
  cin >> skipchar >> str;

  cout << str << '\n';

  return 0;
}
```

9.2 EXERCISES

1.
```
// Copy a file and display number of chars copied.
#include <iostream.h>
#include <fstream.h>

main(int argc, char *argv[])
{
  if(argc!=3) {
    cout << "Usage: CPY <input> <output>\n";
    return 1;
  }

  ifstream fin(argv[1]); // open input file
  ofstream fout(argv[2]);  // create output file
```

```
    if(!fin) {
      cout << "Cannot open input file\n";
      return 1;
    }

    if(!fout) {
      cout << "Cannot open output file\n";
      return 1;
    }

    char ch;
    unsigned count=0;

    fin.unsetf(ios::skipws);   // do not skip spaces
    while(!fin.eof()) {
      fin >> ch;
      fout << ch;
      count++;
    }

    cout << "Number of bytes copied: " << count << '\n';
    return 0;
}
```

The reason this program may display a result different from that shown when you list the directory is that some character translations may be taking place. Specifically, when a carriage-return/linefeed sequence is read, it is converted into a newline. When output, newlines are counted as one character but converted back into a carriage-return/linefeed sequence again.

2.
```
#include <iostream.h>
#include <fstream.h>

main()
{
  ofstream pout("phone");

  if(!pout) {
    cout << "Cannot open PHONE file\n";
    return 1;
  }

  pout << "Isaac Newton  415 555-3423\n";
  pout << "Robert Goddard 213 555-2312\n";
```

```
    pout << "Enrico Fermi  202 555-1111\n";

    pout.close();

    return 0;
}
```

3.
```
// Word count.
#include <iostream.h>
#include <fstream.h>
#include <ctype.h>

main(int argc, char *argv[])
{
  if(argc!=2) {
    cout << "Usage: COUNT <input>\n";
    return 1;
  }

  ifstream in(argv[1]);

  if(!in) {
    cout << "Cannot open input file\n";
    return 1;
  }

  int count=0;
  char ch;

  in >> ch; // find first non-space char

  // after first non-space found, do not skip spaces
  in.unsetf(ios::skipws); // do not skip spaces

  while(!in.eof()) {
    in >> ch;
    if(isspace(ch)) count++;
  }

  cout << "Word count: " << count << '\n';

  in.close();

  return 0;
}
```

EXERCISES

1.
```cpp
// Copy a file and display number of chars copied.
#include <iostream.h>
#include <fstream.h>

main(int argc, char *argv[])
{
  if(argc!=3) {
    cout << "Usage: CPY <input> <output>\n";
    return 1;
  }

  ifstream fin(argv[1]); // open input file
  ofstream fout(argv[2]);  // create output file

  if(!fin) {
    cout << "Cannot open input file\n";
    return 1;
  }

  if(!fout) {
    cout << "Cannot open output file\n";
    return 1;
  }

  char ch;
  unsigned count=0;

  while(!fin.eof()) {
    fin.get(ch);
    fout.put(ch);
    count++;
  }

  cout << "Number of bytes copied: " << count << '\n';
  return 0;
}

// Word count.
#include <iostream.h>
#include <fstream.h>
#include <ctype.h>
```

```
main(int argc, char *argv[])
{
  if(argc!=2) {
    cout << "Usage: COUNT <input>\n";
    return 1;
  }

  ifstream in(argv[1]);

  if(!in) {
    cout << "Cannot open input file\n";
    return 1;
  }

  int count=0;
  char ch;

  // find first non-space char
  do {
    in.get(ch);
  } while(isspace(ch));

  while(!in.eof()) {
    in.get(ch);
    if(isspace(ch)) count++;
  }

  cout << "Word count: " << count << '\n';

  in.close();

  return 0;
}
```

2.
```
// Output account info to a file using an inserter.
#include <iostream.h>
#include <fstream.h>
#include <string.h>

class account {
  int custnum;
  char name[80];
  double balance;
public:
  account(int c, char *n, double b)
```

```
    {
      custnum = c;
      strcpy(name, n);
      balance = b;
    }
    friend ostream &operator<<(ostream &stream, account ob);
};

ostream &operator<<(ostream &stream, account ob)
{
  stream << ob.custnum << ' ';
  stream << ob.name << ' ' << ob.balance;
  stream << '\n';

  return stream;
}

main()
{
  account  Rex(1011, "Ralph Rex", 12323.34);
  ofstream out("accounts");

  out << Rex;

  out.close();

  return 0;
}
```

9.4   EXERCISES

```
1. // Use get() to read a string that contains spaces.
   #include <iostream.h>
   #include <fstream.h>

   main()
   {
     char str[80];

     cout << "Enter your name: ";
     cin.get(str, 79);

     cout << str << '\n';
```

```
    return 0;
  }
```

The program functions the same using either **get( )** or **getline( )**.

```
2. // Use getline() to display a file.
   #include <iostream.h>
   #include <fstream.h>

   main(int argc, char *argv[])
   {
     if(argc!=2) {
       cout << "usage: PR <filename>\n";
       return 1;
     }

     ifstream in(argv[1]);
     if(!in) {
       cout << "Cannot open input file\n";
       return 1;
     }

     char str[255];

     while(!in.eof()) {
       in.getline(str, 254);
       cout << str << '\n';
     }

     in.close();

     return 0;
   }
```

9.5 EXERCISES

```
1. // Display a file backwards on the screen.
   #include <iostream.h>
   #include <fstream.h>

   main(int argc, char *argv[])
   {
     if(argc!=2) {
```

```
      cout << "usage: REVERSE <filename>\n";
      return 1;
    }

    ifstream in(argv[1]);
    if(!in) {
      cout << "Cannot open input file\n";
      return 1;
    }

    char ch;
    long i;

    // go to end of file (less eof char)
    in.seekg(0, ios::end);
    i = in.tellg()-2; // see how many bytes in file

    for( ;i>=0; i--) {
      in.seekg(i, ios::beg);
      in.get(ch);
      cout << ch;
    }

    in.close();

    return 0;
  }
```

2.
```
  // Swap characters in a file.
  #include <iostream.h>
  #include <fstream.h>

  main(int argc, char *argv[])
  {
    if(argc!=2) {
      cout << "usage: SWAP <filename>\n";
      return 1;
    }

    // open file for input/output
    fstream io(argv[1], ios::in | ios::out);
    if(!io) {
      cout << "Cannot open file\n";
      return 1;
    }
```

```
        char ch1, ch2;
        long i;

        for(i=0 ; !io.eof(); i+=2) {
          io.seekg(i, ios::beg);
          io.get(ch1);
          if(io.eof()) continue;
          io.get(ch2);
          if(io.eof()) continue;
          io.seekg(i, ios::beg);
          io.put(ch2);
          io.put(ch1);
        }

        io.close();

        return 0;
      }
```

9.6 **E**XERCISE

```
1. /* Display a file backwards on the screen,
      plus error checking. */
   #include <iostream.h>
   #include <fstream.h>

   main(int argc, char *argv[])
   {
     if(argc!=2) {
       cout << "usage: REVERSE <filename>\n";
       return 1;
     }

     ifstream in(argv[1]);
     if(!in) {
       cout << "Cannot open input file\n";
       return 1;
     }

     char ch;
     long i;

     // go to end of file (less eof char)
```

```
      in.seekg(0, ios::end);
      if(!in.good()) return 1;
      i = in.tellg()-2; // see how many bytes in file
      if(!in.good()) return 1;

    for( ;i>=0; i--) {
      in.seekg(i, ios::beg);
      if(!in.good()) return 1;
      in.get(ch);
      if(!in.good()) return 1;
      cout << ch;
    }

    in.close();
    if(!in.good()) return 1;

    return 0;
}

// Swap characters in a file with error checking.
#include <iostream.h>
#include <fstream.h>

main(int argc, char *argv[])
{
  if(argc!=2) {
    cout << "usage: SWAP <filename>\n";
    return 1;
  }

  // open file for input/output
  fstream io(argv[1], ios::in | ios::out);
  if(!io) {
    cout << "Cannot open file\n";
    return 1;
  }

  char ch1, ch2;
  long i;

  for(i=0 ;!io.eof(); i+=2) {
    io.seekg(i, ios::beg);
    if(!io.good()) return 1;
    io.get(ch1);
    if(io.eof()) continue;
```

```
      io.get(ch2);
      if(!io.good()) return 1;
      if(io.eof()) continue;
      io.seekg(i, ios::beg);
      if(!io.good()) return 1;
      io.put(ch2);
      if(!io.good()) return 1;
      io.put(ch1);
      if(!io.good()) return 1;
    }

    io.close();
    if(!io.good()) return 1;

    return 0;
  }
```

9 MASTERY SKILLS CHECK

1.
```
#include <iostream.h>

ostream &tabs(ostream &stream)
{
  stream << '\t' << '\t' << '\t' ;
  stream.width(20);

  return stream;
}

main()
{
  cout << tabs << "Testing\n";
  return 0;
}
```

2.
```
#include <iostream.h>
#include <ctype.h>

istream &findalpha(istream &stream)
{
  char ch;

  do {
    stream.get(ch);
```

```
      } while(!isalpha(ch));
      return stream;
   }

   main()
   {
      char str[80];

      cin >> findalpha >> str;
      cout << str << '\n';

      return 0;
   }
```

3.
```
   // Copy a file and reverse case of letters.
   #include <iostream.h>
   #include <fstream.h>
   #include <ctype.h>

   main(int argc, char *argv[])
   {
      char ch;

      if(argc!=3) {
        cout << "Usage: COPYREV <source> <target>\n";
        return 1;
      }

      ifstream in(argv[1]);
      if(!in) {
        cout << "Cannot open input file";
        return 1;
      }

      ofstream out(argv[2]);
      if(!out) {
        cout << "Cannot open output file";
        return 1;
      }

      while(!in.eof()) {
        ch = in.get();
        if(islower(ch)) ch = toupper(ch);
        else ch = tolower(ch);
        out.put(ch);
```

```
    };

    in.close();
    out.close();

    return 0;
  }
```

4.
```
// Count letters.
#include <iostream.h>
#include <fstream.h>
#include <ctype.h>

int alpha[26];

main(int argc, char *argv[])
{
  char ch;

  if(argc!=2) {
    cout << "Usage: COUNT <source>\n";
    return 1;
  }

  ifstream in(argv[1]);
  if(!in) {
    cout << "Cannot open input file";
    return 1;
  }

  // init alpha[]
  int i;
  for(i=0; i<26; i++) alpha[i] = 0;

  while(!in.eof()) {
    ch = in.get();
    if(isalpha(ch)) { // if letter found, count it
      ch = toupper(ch); // normalize
      alpha[ch-'A']++; // 'A'-'A' == 0, 'B'-'A' == 1, etc.
    }
  };

  // display count
  for(i=0; i<26; i++) {
```

```
      cout << (char) ('A'+ i) << ": " << alpha[i] << '\n';
    }

    in.close();

    return 0;
}

5. /* Copy a file and reverse case of letters
       with error checking. */
  #include <iostream.h>
  #include <fstream.h>
  #include <ctype.h>

  main(int argc, char *argv[])
  {
    char ch;

    if(argc!=3) {
      cout << "Usage: COPYREV <source> <target>\n";
      return 1;
    }

    ifstream in(argv[1]);
    if(!in) {
      cout << "Cannot open input file";
      return 1;
    }

    ofstream out(argv[2]);
    if(!out) {
      cout << "Cannot open output file";
      return 1;
    }

    while(!in.eof()) {
    ch = in.get();
      if(!in.good()) return 1;
      if(islower(ch)) ch = toupper(ch);
      else ch = tolower(ch);
      out.put(ch);
      if(!out.good()) return 1;
    };

    in.close();
```

```
    out.close();
    if(!in.good() && !out.good()) return 1;

    return 0;
}

// Count letters with error checking.
#include <iostream.h>
#include <fstream.h>
#include <ctype.h>

int alpha[26];

main(int argc, char *argv[])
{
  char ch;

  if(argc!=2) {
    cout << "Usage: COUNT <source>\n";
    return 1;
  }

  ifstream in(argv[1]);
  if(!in) {
    cout << "Cannot open input file";
    return 1;
  }

  // init alpha[]
  int i;
  for(i=0; i<26; i++) alpha[i] = 0;

  while(!in.eof()) {
    ch = in.get();
    if(!in.good() && !in.eof()) return 1;
    if(isalpha(ch)) { // if letter found, count it
      ch = toupper(ch); // normalize
      alpha[ch-'A']++; // 'A'-'A' == 0, 'B'-'A' == 1, etc.
    }
  };

  // display count
  for(i=0; i<26; i++) {
    cout << (char) ('A'+ i) << ": " << alpha[i] << '\n';
```

```
    }

    in.close();
    if(!in.good()) return 1;

    return 0;
}
```

6. To set the **get** pointer, use **seekg( )**. To set the **put** pointer, use **seekp( )**.

9 *C*UMULATIVE SKILLS CHECK

```
1. #include <fstream.h>
   #include <iostream.h>
   #include <string.h>

   #define SIZE 40

   class inventory {
     char item[SIZE]; // name of item
     int onhand; // number on hand
     double cost;  // cost of item
   public:
     inventory(char *i, int o, double c)
     {
       strcpy(item, i);
       onhand = o;
       cost = c;
     }
     void store(fstream &stream);
     void retrieve(fstream &stream);
     friend ostream &operator<<(ostream &stream, inventory ob);
     friend istream &operator>>(istream &stream, inventory &ob);
   };

   ostream &operator<<(ostream &stream, inventory ob)
   {
     stream << ob.item << ": " << ob.onhand;
     stream << " on hand at $" << ob.cost << '\n';

     return stream;
```

```
}

istream &operator>>(istream &stream, inventory &ob)
{
  cout << "Enter item name: ";
  stream >> ob.item;
  cout << "Enter number on hand: ";
  stream >> ob.onhand;
  cout << "Enter cost: ";
  stream >> ob.cost;

  return stream;
}

void inventory::store(fstream &stream)
{
  stream.write(item, SIZE);
  stream.write((char *) &onhand, sizeof(int));
  stream.write((char *) &cost, sizeof(double));
}

void inventory::retrieve(fstream &stream)
{
  stream.read(item, SIZE);
  stream.read((char *) &onhand, sizeof(int));
  stream.read((char *) &cost, sizeof(double));
}

main()
{
  fstream inv("inv", ios::in | ios::out); // input/output
  int i;

  inventory pliers("pliers", 12, 4.95);
  inventory hammers("hammers", 5, 9.45);
  inventory wrenches("wrenches", 22, 13.90);
  inventory temp("", 0, 0.0);

  // write to file
  pliers.store(inv);
  hammers.store(inv);
  wrenches.store(inv);

  do {
```

```
      cout << "Record # (-1 to quit): ";
      cin >> i;
      if(i == -1) break;
      inv.seekg(i*(SIZE+sizeof(int)+sizeof(double)), ios::beg);
      temp.retrieve(inv);
      cout << temp;
    } while(inv.good());

    inv.close();

    return 0;
  }
```

10 REVIEW SKILLS CHECK

1.
```
#include <iostream.h>

ostream &setsci(ostream &stream)
{
  stream.setf(ios::scientific | ios::uppercase);

  return stream;
}

main()
{
  double f = 123.23;

  cout << setsci << f;
  cout << '\n';

  return 0;
}
```

2.
```
// Copy and convert tabs to spaces.
#include <iostream.h>
#include <fstream.h>

main(int argc, char *argv[])
{
  if(argc!=3) {
    cout << "Usage: CPY <in> <out>\n";
    return 1;
```

```
      }

      ifstream in(argv[1]);
      if(!in) {
        cout << "Cannot open input file\n";
        return 1;
      }

      ofstream out(argv[2]);
      if(!out) {
        cout << "Cannot open output file\n";
        return 1;
      }

      char ch;
      int i = 8;

      while(!in.eof()) {
        in.get(ch);
        if(ch=='\t') for( ; i>=0; i--) out.put(' ');
        else out.put(ch);
        if(i == -1 || ch=='\n') i = 8;
        i--;
      }

      in.close();
      out.close();

      return 0;
    }

3. // Search file.
   #include <iostream.h>
   #include <fstream.h>
   #include <string.h>

   main(int argc, char *argv[])
   {
     if(argc!=3) {
       cout << "Usage: SEARCH <file> <word>\n";
       return 1;
     }

     ifstream in(argv[1]);
     if(!in) {
```

```
      cout << "Cannot open input file\n";
      return 1;
   }

   char str[255];
   int count=0;

   while(!in.eof()) {
     in >> str;
     if(!strcmp(str, argv[2])) count++;
   }

   cout << argv[2] << " found " << count;
   cout << " number of times.\n";

   in.close();

   return 0;
}
```

4. The statement is

```
out.seekp(234, ios::beg);
```

5. The functions are **rdstate( )**, **good( )**, **eof( )**, **fail( )**, and **bad( )**.

6. The C++ I/O can be customized to operate on classes that you create.

EXERCISES

1. ```
#include <iostream.h>

class num {
public:
  int i;
  num(int x) { i = x; }
  virtual void shownum() { cout << i << '\n'; }
};

class outhex : public num {
public:
  outhex(int n) : num(n) {}
  void shownum() { cout << hex << i << '\n'; }
};
```
```

```cpp
class outoct : public num {
public:
  outoct(int n) : num(n) {}
  void shownum() { cout << oct << i << '\n'; }
};

main()
{
  outoct o(10);
  outhex h(20);

  o.shownum();
  h.shownum();

  return 0;
}
```

2.
```cpp
#include <iostream.h>

class distance {
public:
  double d;
  distance(double f) { d = f; }
  virtual void trav_time()
  {
    cout << "Travel time at 60 mph: ";
    cout << d / 60 << '\n';
  }
};

class metric : public distance {
public:
  metric(double f) : distance(f) {}
  void trav_time()
  {
    cout << "Travel time at 100 kph: ";
    cout << d / 100 << '\n';
  }
};

main()
{
  distance *p, mph(88.0);
  metric kph(88);
```

```
   p = &mph;
   p->trav_time();

   p = &kph;
   p->trav_time();

   return 0;
}
```

EXERCISES

2. By definition, an abstract class contains at least one pure virtual function. This means that no body for that function exists relative to that class. Thus, there is no way that an object can be created because the class definition is not complete.

3. When **func( )** is called relative to **derived1**, it is the **func( )** inside **base** that is used. The reason this works is that virtual functions are hierarchical.

EXERCISE

1.
```
// Create a generic list class for integers.
#include <iostream.h>
#include <stdlib.h>

class list {
public:
  list *head;  // pointer to next item in list
  list *tail;
  list *next;
  int num; // value to be stored
public:
  list() { head = tail = next = NULL; }
  virtual void store(int i) = 0;
  virtual int retrieve() = 0;
};

// Create a queue type list.
class queue : public list {
public:
  void store(int i);
  int retrieve();
};
```

```
void queue::store(int i)
{
  list *item;

  item = new queue;
  if(!item) {
    cout << "Allocation error\n";
    exit(1);
  }
  item->num = i;

  // put on end of list
  if(tail) tail->next = item;
  tail = item;
  item->next = NULL;
  if(!head) head = tail;
}

int queue::retrieve()
{
  int i;
  list *p;

  if(!head) {
    cout << "List empty\n";
    return 0;
  }

  // remove from start of list
  i = head->num;
  p = head;
  head = head->next;
  delete p;

  return i;
}
// Create a stack type list.
class stack : public list {
public:
  void store(int i);
  int retrieve();
};

void stack::store(int i)
{
```

```
   list *item;

   item = new stack;
   if(!item) {
     cout << "Allocation error\n";
     exit(1);
   }
   item->num = i;

   // put on front of list for stack-like operation
   if(head) item->next = head;
   head = item;
   if(!tail) tail = head;
}

int stack::retrieve()
{
   int i;
   list *p;

   if(!head) {
     cout << "List empty\n";
     return 0;
   }

   // remove from start of list
   i = head->num;
   p = head;
   head = head->next;
   delete p;

   return i;
}

// Create a sorted list.
class sorted : public list {
public:
   void store(int i);
   int retrieve();
};

void sorted::store(int i)
{
   list *item;
   list *p, *p2;
```

```
      item = new sorted;
      if(!item) {
        cout << "Allocation error\n";
        exit(1);
      }
      item->num = i;

      // find where to put next item
      p = head;
      p2 = NULL;
      while(p) { // goes in middle
        if(p->num > i) {
          item->next = p;
          if(p2) p2->next = item;   // not 1st element
          if(p==head) head = item; // new 1st element
          break;
        }
        p2 = p;
        p = p->next;
      }
      if(!p) { // goes on end
        if(tail) tail->next = item;
        tail = item;
        item->next = NULL;
      }
      if(!head) // is first element
        head = item;
}

int sorted::retrieve()
{
  int i;
  list *p;

  if(!head) {
    cout << "List empty\n";
    return 0;
  }

  // remove from start of list
  i = head->num;
  p = head;
  head = head->next;
  delete p;
```

```
      return i;
}

main()
{
  list *p;

  // demonstrate queue
  queue q_ob;

  p = &q_ob; // point to queue

  p->store(1);
  p->store(2);
  p->store(3);

  cout << "Queue: ";
  cout << p->retrieve();
  cout << p->retrieve();
  cout << p->retrieve();

  cout << '\n';

  // demonstrate stack
  stack s_ob;

  p = &s_ob; // point to stack

  p->store(1);
  p->store(2);
  p->store(3);

  cout << "Stack: ";
  cout << p->retrieve();
  cout << p->retrieve();
  cout << p->retrieve();

  cout << '\n';

  // demonstrate sorted list
  sorted sorted_ob;

  p = &sorted_ob;
```

```
p->store(4);
p->store(1);
p->store(3);
p->store(9);
p->store(5);

cout << "Sorted: ";
cout << p->retrieve();
cout << p->retrieve();
cout << p->retrieve();
cout << p->retrieve();
cout << p->retrieve();

cout << '\n';


return 0;
}
```

10   **M**ASTERY SKILLS CHECK

1. A virtual function is essentially a placeholder function declared in a base class that is redefined by a class derived from that base. The process of redefinition is called overriding.

2. Nonmember functions and constructor functions may not be made virtual.

3. A virtual function supports run-time polymorphism through the use of base class pointers. When a base class pointer points to a derived class containing a virtual function, the specific function called is determined by the type of object being pointed to.

4. A pure virtual function is one that contains no definition relative to the base class.

5. An abstract class is a base class that contains at least one virtual function. A polymorphic class is one that contains at least one virtual function.

6. The fragment is incorrect because the redefinition of a virtual function must have the same return type and type and number of parameters as the original function. In this case, the redefinition of f( ) differs in the number of its parameters.

7. Yes.

1.
```cpp
// Create a generic list class for integers.
#include <iostream.h>
#include <stdlib.h>

class list {
public:
  list *head;  // pointer to next item in list
  list *tail;
  list *next;
  int num; // value to be stored
public:
  list() { head = tail = next = NULL; }
  virtual void store(int i) = 0;
  virtual int retrieve() = 0;
};

// Create a queue type list.
class queue : public list {
public:
  void store(int i);
  int retrieve();
  queue operator+(int i) { store(i); return *this; }
  int operator--(int unused) { return retrieve(); }
};

void queue::store(int i)
{
  list *item;

  item = new queue;
  if(!item) {
    cout << "Allocation error\n";
    exit(1);
  }
  item->num = i;

  // put on end of list
  if(tail) tail->next = item;
  tail = item;
  item->next = NULL;
  if(!head) head = tail;
}
```

```cpp
int queue::retrieve()
{
  int i;
  list *p;

  if(!head) {
    cout << "List empty\n";
    return 0;
  }

  // remove from start of list
  i = head->num;
  p = head;
  head = head->next;
  delete p;

  return i;
}

// Create a stack type list.
class stack : public list {
public:
  void store(int i);
  int retrieve();
  stack operator+(int i) { store(i); return *this; }
  int operator--(int unused) { return retrieve(); }
};

void stack::store(int i)
{
  list *item;

  item = new stack;
  if(!item) {
    cout << "Allocation error\n";
    exit(1);
  }
  item->num = i;

  // put on front of list for stack-like operation
  if(head) item->next = head;
  head = item;
  if(!tail) tail = head;
}
```

```
int stack::retrieve()
{
  int i;
  list *p;

  if(!head) {
    cout << "List empty\n";
    return 0;
  }

  // remove from start of list
  i = head->num;
  p = head;
  head = head->next;
  delete p;

  return i;
}

main()
{
  // demonstrate queue
  queue q_ob;

  q_ob + 1;
  q_ob + 2;
  q_ob + 3;

  cout << "Queue: ";
  cout << q_ob--;
  cout << q_ob--;
  cout << q_ob--;

  cout << '\n';

  // demonstrate stack
  stack s_ob;

  s_ob + 1;
  s_ob + 2;
  s_ob + 3;

  cout << "Stack: ";
  cout << s_ob--;
```

```
    cout << s_ob--;
    cout << s_ob--;

    cout << '\n';

    return 0;
}
```

2. Virtual functions differ from overloaded functions in that overloaded functions *must* differ in either the number of parameters or the type of parameters. An overridden virtual function must have exactly the same prototype (that is, the same return type and type and number of parameters) as the original function.

11 ▰ *R*EVIEW SKILLS CHECK

1. A virtual function is a function that is declared as **virtual** by a base class and then overridden by a derived class.

2. A pure virtual function is one that has no body defined within the base class. This means that the function must be overridden by a derived class. A base class that contains at least one pure virtual function is called abstract.

3. Run-time polymorphism is achieved through the use of virtual functions and base class pointers.

4. If a derived class does not override a non-pure virtual function, the derived class will use the base class's version of the virtual function.

5. The main advantage of run-time polymorphism is flexibility. The main disadvantage is loss of execution speed.

11.1 ▰ *E*XERCISES

2. ```
#include <iostream.h>

template <class X> X min(X a, X b)
{
  if(a<=b) return a;
  else return b;
}

main()
{
```
```

```
      cout << min(12.2, 2.0);
      cout << endl;
      cout << min(3, 4);
      cout << endl;
      cout << min('c', 'a');
      return 0;
    }
```

3.
```
#include <iostream.h>
#include <string.h>

template <class X> int find(X object, X *list, int size)
{
  int i;

  for(i=0; i<size; i++)
    if(object == list[i]) return i;
  return -1;
}

main()
{
  int a[] = {1, 2, 3, 4};
  char *c = "this is a test";
  double d[] = {1.1, 2.2, 3.3};

  cout << find(3, a, 4);
  cout << endl;
  cout << find('a', c, (int) strlen(c));
  cout << endl;
  cout << find(0.0, d, 3);

  return 0;
}
```

4. Generic functions are valuable because they allow you to define a general algorithm that can be applied to various types of data. (That is, specific versions of the algorithm need not be explicitly created by you.) Generic functions further help implement the concept of "one interface, multiple methods" which is a common theme in C++ programming.

2.
```
// Create a generic queue.
#include <iostream.h>

#define SIZE 100

template <class Qtype> class q_type {
  Qtype queue[SIZE]; // holds the queue
  int head, tail; // indices of head and tail
public:
  q_type() { head = tail = 0; }
  void q(Qtype num); // store
  Qtype deq();   // retrieve
};

// Put value on queue.
template <class Qtype> void q_type<Qtype>::q(Qtype num)
{
  if(tail+1==head || (tail+1==SIZE && !head)) {
    cout << "Queue is full\n";
    return;
  }
  tail++;
  if(tail==SIZE) tail = 0; // cycle around
  queue[tail] = num;
}

// Remove value from queue.
template <class Qtype> Qtype q_type<Qtype>::deq()
{
  if(head == tail) {
    cout << "Queue is empty\n";
    return 0;  // or some other error indicator
  }
  head++;
  if(head==SIZE) head = 0; // cycle around
  return queue[head];
}

main()
{
  q_type<int> q1;
  q_type<char> q2;
```

```
      int i;

      for(i=1; i<=10; i++) {
        q1.q(i);
        q2.q(i-1+'A');
      }

      for(i=1; i<=10; i++) {
        cout << "Dequeue 1: " << q1.deq() << "\n";
        cout << "Dequeue 2: " << q2.deq() << "\n";
      }

      return 0;
    }
```

3.
```
   #include <iostream.h>

   template <class X> class input {
     X data;
   public:
     input(char *s, X min, X max);
     // ...
   };

   template <class X>
   input<X>::input(char *s, X min, X max)
   {
     do {
       cout << s << ": ";
       cin >> data;
     } while( data < min || data > max);
   }

   main()
   {
     input<int> i("enter int", 0, 10);
     input<char> c("enter char", 'A', 'Z');

     return 0;
   }
```

11.3 EXERCISES

2. The **throw** is called before execution passes through a **try** block.

3. A character exception is thrown, but the **catch** statement will only handle a character pointer. (That is, there is not a corresponding **catch** statement to handle the character exception.)

4. If an exception is thrown for which there is no corresponding **catch**, **terminate( )** is called and abnormal program termination may occur.

11.4 EXERCISES

2. There is no corresponding **catch** statement for the **throw**. One way to fix the problem is to create a **catch(int)** handler. Another way to fix it is to catch all exceptions using a **catch(...)** handler.

3. See answer 2.

4. **catch(...)** catches all exceptions.

5.
```
#include <iostream.h>
#include <stdlib.h>

double divide(double a, double b)
{
  try {
    if(!b) throw(b);
  }
  catch(double) {
    cout << "Cannot divide by zero\n";
    exit(1);
  }
  return a/b;
}

main()
{
  cout << divide(10.0, 2.5) << endl;
  cout << divide(10.0, 0.0);

  return 0;
}
```

*M*ASTERY SKILLS CHECK

1.
```cpp
#include <iostream.h>
#include <string.h>

// A generic mode finding function.
template <class X> X mode(X *data, int size)
{
  register int t, w;
  X md, oldmd;
  int count, oldcount;

  oldmd = 0;
  oldcount = 0;
  for(t=0; t<size; t++) {
    md = data[t];
    count = 1;
    for(w = t+1; w < size; w++)
      if(md==data[w]) count++;
    if(count > oldcount) {
      oldmd = md;
      oldcount = count;
    }
  }
  return oldmd;
}

main()
{
  int i[] = { 1, 2, 3, 4, 2, 3, 2, 2, 1, 5};
  char *p = "this is a test";

  cout << "mode of i: " << mode(i, 10) << endl;
  cout << "mode of p: " << mode(p, (int) strlen(p));

  return 0;
}
```

2.
```cpp
#include <iostream.h>

template <class X> X sum(X *data, int size)
{
  int i;
  X result = 0;
```

```
    for(i=0; i<size; i++) result += data[i];

    return result;
}

main()
{
  int i[] = {1, 2, 3, 4};
  double d[] = {1.1, 2.2, 3.3, 4.4};

  cout << sum(i, 4) << endl;
  cout << sum(d, 4) << endl;

  return 0;
}
```

3.
```
#include <iostream.h>

// A generic bubble sort.
template <class X> void bubble(X *data, int size)
{
  register int a, b;
  X t;

  for(a=1; a < size; a++)
    for(b=size-1; b >= a; b--)
      if(data[b-1] > data[b]) {
        t = data[b-1];
        data[b-1] = data[b];
        data[b] = t;
      }
}

main()
{
  int i[] = {3, 2, 5, 6, 1, 8, 9, 3, 6, 9};
  double d[] = {1.2, 5.5, 2.2, 3.3};
  int j;

  bubble(i, 10); // sort ints
  bubble(d, 4);  // sort doubles


  for(j=0; j<10; j++) cout << i[j] << ' ';
```

```
  cout << endl;

  for(j=0; j<4; j++) cout << d[j] << ' ';
  cout << endl;

  return 0;
}
```

4. ```
/* This function demonstrates a generic stack that
   holds two values. */
#include <iostream.h>

#define SIZE 10

// Create a generic stack class
template <class StackType> class stack {
  StackType stck[SIZE][2]; // holds the stack
  int tos; // index of top-of-stack

public:
  void init() { tos = 0; }
  void push(StackType ob, StackType ob2);
  StackType pop(StackType &ob2);
};

// Push objects.
template <class StackType> void
stack<StackType::push(StackType ob, StackType ob2)
{
  if(tos==SIZE) {
    cout << "Stack is full";
    return;
  }
  stck[tos][0] = ob;
  stck[tos][1] = ob2;
  tos++;
}

// Pop objects.
template <class StackType>
StackType stack<StackType::pop(StackType &ob2)
{
  if(tos==0) {
    cout << "Stack is empty";
```
```

```
      return 0; // return null on empty stack
   }
   tos--;
   ob2 = stck[tos][1];
   return stck[tos][0];
}
main()
{
   // Demonstrate character stacks.
   stack<char> s1, s2;  // create two stacks
   int i;
   char ch;

   // initialize the stacks
   s1.init();
   s2.init();

   s1.push('a', 'b');
   s2.push('x', 'z');
   s1.push('b', 'd');
   s2.push('y', 'e');
   s1.push('c', 'a');
   s2.push('z', 'x');

   for(i=0; i<3; i++) {
      cout << "Pop s1: " << s1.pop(ch);
      cout << ' ' << ch << "\n";
   }
   for(i=0; i<3; i++) {
      cout << "Pop s2: " << s2.pop(ch);
      cout << ' ' << ch << "\n";
   }

   // demonstrate double stacks
   stack<double> ds1, ds2;  // create two stacks
   double d;

   // initialize the stacks
   ds1.init();
   ds2.init();

   ds1.push(1.1, 2.0);
   ds2.push(2.2, 3.0);
   ds1.push(3.3, 4.0);
   ds2.push(4.4, 5.0);
```

```
      ds1.push(5.5, 6.0);
      ds2.push(6.6, 7.0);

      for(i=0; i<3; i++) {
        cout << "Pop ds1: " << ds1.pop(d);
        cout << ' '<< d << "\n";
      }

      for(i=0; i<3; i++) {
        cout << "Pop ds2: " << ds2.pop(d);
        cout << ' '<< d << "\n";
      }

      return 0;
    }
```

5. The general forms of **try**, **catch**, and **throw** are shown here:

```
try {
 // try block
 throw exp;
}
catch(arg) {
 // ...
}
```

6.
```
/* This function demonstrates a generic stack
      that includes exception handling. */
#include <iostream.h>

#define SIZE 10

// Create a generic stack class
template <class StackType> class stack {
  StackType stck[SIZE]; // holds the stack
  int tos; // index of top-of-stack

public:
  void init() { tos = 0; } // initialize stack
  void push(StackType ch); // push object on stack
  StackType pop(); // pop object from stack
};
```

```cpp
// Push an object.
template <class StackType> void
stack<StackType::push(StackType ob)
{
  try {
    if(tos==SIZE) throw SIZE;
  }
  catch(int) {
    cout << "Stack is full";
    return;
  }
  stck[tos] = ob;
  tos++;
}

// Pop an object.
template <class StackType> StackType stack<StackType::pop()
{
  try {
    if(tos==0) throw 0;
  }
  catch(int) {
    cout << "Stack is empty";
    return 0; // return null on empty stack
  }
  tos--;
  return stck[tos];
}
main()
{
  // Demonstrate character stacks.
  stack<char> s1, s2;   // create two stacks
  int i;
  // initialize the stacks
  s1.init();
  s2.init();

  s1.push('a');
  s2.push('x');
  s1.push('b');
  s2.push('y');
  s1.push('c');
  s2.push('z');
```

```
for(i=0; i<3; i++) cout << "Pop s1: " << s1.pop() << "\n";
for(i=0; i<4; i++) cout << "Pop s2: " << s2.pop() << "\n";

// demonstrate double stacks
stack<double> ds1, ds2;  // create two stacks

// initialize the stacks
ds1.init();
ds2.init();

ds1.push(1.1);
ds2.push(2.2);
ds1.push(3.3);
ds2.push(4.4);
ds1.push(5.5);
ds2.push(6.6);

for(i=0; i<3; i++) cout << "Pop ds1: " << ds1.pop() << "\n";
for(i=0; i<4; i++) cout << "Pop ds2: " << ds2.pop() << "\n";

return 0;
}
```

12 ▎ *R*EVIEW SKILLS CHECK

1. In C++, a generic function defines a general set of operations that will be applied to various types of data. It is implemented using the keyword **template**. Its general form is shown here:

   ```
   template <class Ttype> ret-type func-name(param-list)
   {
     // ...
   }
   ```

2. In C++, a generic class defines all operations that relate to that class, but the actual data is specified as a parameter when an object of that class is created. Its general form is shown here:

```
template <class Ttype> class class-name
{
 // ...
}
```

3.
```
#include <iostream.h>

// Return a to the b.
template <class X> X gexp(X a, X b)
{
    X i, result=1;

  for(i=0; i<b; i++) result *= a;

  return result;
}

main()
{
  cout << gexp(2, 3) << endl;
  cout << gexp(10.0, 2.0);

  return 0;
}
```

4.
```
#include <iostream.h>
#include <fstream.h>

template <class CoordType> class coord {
  CoordType x, y;
public:
  coord(CoordType i, CoordType j) { x = i; y = j; }
  void show() { cout << x << ", " << y << endl; }
};

main()
{
  coord<int> o1(1, 2), o2(3, 4);

  o1.show();
  o2.show();
```

```
     coord<double> o3(0.0, 0.23), o4(10.19, 3.098);

     o3.show();
     o4.show();

     return 0;
   }
```

5. **try**, **catch**, and **throw** work together like this. Put all statements that you wish to monitor for exceptions within a **try** block. If an exception occurs, throw that exception using **throw** and handle it with a corresponding **catch** statement.

6. No.

7. **terminate( )** is called when an exception is thrown for which there is no corresponding **catch** statement. **unexpected( )** is called when an exception that is not supported by a function is thrown.

8. **catch(...)**

12.1   EXERCISES

1.
```
// A shared resource example that traces output.
#include <iostream.h>
#include <string.h>

class output {
  static char outbuf[255]; // this is the shared resource
  static int inuse; // buffer available if 0; in use otherwise
  static int oindex; // index of outbuf
  char str[80];
  int i; // index of next char in str
  int who; // identifies the object, must be > 0
public:
  output(int w, char *s) { strcpy(str, s); i = 0; who = w; }

  /* This function returns -1 if waiting for buffer,
     it returns 0 if it is done outputting, and
     it returns who if it is still using the buffer.
  */
  int putbuf()
```

```
    {
      if(!str[i]) { // done outputting
        inuse = 0; // release buffer
        return 0; // signal termination
      }
      if(!inuse) inuse = who; // get buffer
      if(inuse != who) {
        cout << "Process " << who << " Currently blocked\n";
        return -1; // in use by someone else
      }
      if(str[i]) { // still chars to output
        outbuf[oindex] = str[i];
        cout << "Process " << who << " sending char\n";
        i++; oindex++;
        outbuf[oindex] = '\0';  // always keep null-terminated
        return 1;
      }
    }
    void show() { cout << outbuf << '\n'; }
};

char output::outbuf[255]; // this is the shared resource
int output::inuse = 0; // buffer available if 0; in use otherwise
int output::oindex = 0; // index of outbuf

main()
{
  output o1(1, "This is a test"), o2(2, " of statics");

  while(o1.putbuf() | o2.putbuf()) ; // output chars

  o1.show();

  return 0;
}
```

2. ```
   #include <iostream.h>

   class test {
     static int count;
   public:
     test() { count++; }
   ```
   ```

```
     ~test() { count--; }
     int getcount() { return count; }
};

int test::count = 0;

main()
{
  test o1, o2, o3;

  cout << o1.getcount() << " objects in existence\n";

  test *p;

  p = new test; // allocate an object
  if(!p) {
    cout << "Allocation error\n";
    return 1;
  }

  cout << o1.getcount();
  cout << " objects in existence after allocation\n";

  // delete object
  delete p;

  cout << o1.getcount();
  cout << " objects in existence after deletion\n";

  return 0;
}
```

12.2 EXERCISES

```
1. /* This version displays the number of chars written
      to buf.
   */
   #include <iostream.h>
   #include <strstream.h>

   main()
   {
     char buf[255];
```

```
        ostrstream ostr(buf, sizeof buf);

        ostr << "Array-based I/O uses streams just like ";
        ostr << "'normal' I/O\n" << 100;
        ostr << ' ' << 123.23 << '\n';

        // you can use manipulators, too
        ostr << hex << 100 << ' ';
        // or format flags
        ostr << ostr.setf(ios::scientific) << 123.23 << '\n';
        ostr << ends; // ensure that buffer is null-terminated

        // show resultant string
        cout << buf;

        cout << ostr.pcount();

        return 0;
    }

2.  /* Use array-based I/O to copy contents of one array
        into another.
    */
    #include <iostream.h>
    #include <strstream.h>

    char inbuf[] = "This is a test of C++ array-based I/O";
    char outbuf[255];

    main()
    {
        istrstream istr(inbuf);
        ostrstream ostr(outbuf, sizeof outbuf);

        char ch;

        while(!istr.eof()) {
            istr.get(ch);
            ostr.put(ch);
        }
        ostr.put('\0'); // null terminate

        cout << "Input: " << inbuf << '\n';
        cout << "Output: " << outbuf << '\n';
```

```
      return 0;
    }
```

3.
```
   // Convert string to float.
   #include <iostream.h>
   #include <strstream.h>

   main()
   {
     float f;
     char s[] = "1234.564";   // float represented as string

     istrstream istr(s);

     // Convert to internal representation the easy way!
     istr >> f;

     cout << "Converted form: " << f << '\n';

     return 0;
   }
```

EXERCISES

1.
```
   // Convert string type to integer.
   #include <iostream.h>
   #include <string.h>

   class strtype {
     char str[80];
     int len;
   public:
     strtype(char *s) { strcpy(str, s); len = strlen(s); }
     operator char *() { return str; }
     operator int() { return len; }
   };

   main()
   {
     strtype s("Conversion functions are convenient");
     char *p;
     int l;
```

```
      l = s; // convert s to integer - which is length of string
      p = s; // convert s to char * - which is pointer to string

      cout << "The string:\n";
      cout << p << "\nis " << l << " chars long.\n";

      return 0;
    }
```

2.
```
   #include <iostream.h>
   #include <strstream.h>

   int p(int base, int exp);

   class pwr {
     int base;
     int exp;
   public:
     pwr(int b, int e) { base = b; exp = e; }
     operator int() { return p(base, exp); }
   };

   // Return base to the exp power.
   int p(int base, int exp)
   {
     int temp;

     for(temp=1; exp; exp--) temp = temp * base;

     return temp;
   }
    main()
   {
     pwr o1(2, 3), o2(3, 3);
     int result;

     result = o1;
     cout << result << '\n';

     result = o2;
     cout << result << '\n';

     // can use directly in a cout statement like this:
     cout << o1+100 << '\n';
```

```
    return 0;
}
```

MASTERY SKILLS CHECK

1. Unlike normal member variables, for which each object has its own copy, only one copy of a **static** member variable exists, and it is shared by all objects of that class.

2. To use array-based I/O, include **strstream.h**.

3. No.

4. `extern "C" int counter();`

5. A conversion function simply converts an object into a value compatible with another type. Conversion functions are typically used to convert objects into values compatible with the built-in data types.

6. No, prototypes are not optional in C++.

7. The proposed ANSI C++ standard states that at least the first 1,024 characters of an identifier are significant.

Index